A Garland Series

British Philosophers and Theologians of the 17th & 18th Centuries

---

A Collection of 101 Volumes

Edited by
René Wellek

Abraham Tucker

THE
LIGHT OF NATURE
PURSUED
1805

In seven volumes
Vol. II

Garland Publishing, Inc., New York & London

1977

BD
701
.T8
1976
v.2

Bibliographical note:

this facsimile has been made from a copy in the
Yale University Library
(K8.T79.d805)

Library of Congress Cataloging in Publication Data

Tucker, Abraham, 1705-1774.
   The light of nature pursued.

   (British philosophers and theologians of the
17th & 18th centuries ; no. 60)
   Reprint of the 1805 ed. printed by Bretell for
R. Faulder and T. Payne, London.
   1. Philosophy. I. Title. II. Series.
BD701.T8 1976   192   75-11262
ISBN 0-8240-1811-7 lib. bdg.

CANISIUS COLLEGE LIBRARY
BUFFALO, N.Y.

Printed in the United States of America

THE
LIGHT OF NATURE
PURSUED,

BY

ABRAHAM TUCKER, Esq.

Second Edition,
REVISED AND CORRECTED.

TOGETHER WITH

SOME ACCOUNT

OF THE

LIFE OF THE AUTHOR,

BY

SIR H. P. ST. JOHN MILDMAY, BART. M.P.

VOL. II.

LONDON:
PRINTED FOR R. FAULDER, NEW BOND-STREET; AND
T. PAYNE, MEWS-GATE, CHARING-CROSS.

Brettell, Printer, Marshall Street, Golden Square.

1805.

CONTENTS.

VOL. II.

	PAGE
CHAP. XII. *Imagination and Understanding*	1
——— XIII. *Conviction and Persuasion*	25
——— XIV. *Knowledge and Conception*	36
——— XV. *Composition of Motives*	48
——— XVI. *Species of Motives*	55
——— XVII. *Production of Motives*	61
——— XVIII. *Translation*	68
——— XIX. *Sympathy*	77
——— XX. *Introduction of Motives*	82
——— XXI. *Passions*	93
——— XXII. *Pleasure*	140
——— XXIII. *Use*	167
——— XXIV. *Honour*	178
——— XXV. *Necessity*	205
——— XXVI. *Reason*	212
——— XXVII. *Ultimate Good*	226
——— XXVIII. *Rectitude*	244
——— XXIX. *Virtue*	256
——— XXX. *Prudence*	285
——— XXXI. *Fortitude*	303
——— XXXII. *Temperance*	317
——— XXXIII. *Justice*	329
——— XXXIV. *Benevolence*	354
——— XXXV. *Moral Policy*	380
——— XXXVI. *Limitation of Virtue*	408

THE
LIGHT OF NATURE
PURSUED.

CHAP. XII.

IMAGINATION AND UNDERSTANDING.

WE have observed at our entrance upon these enquiries, that a compound may have properties resulting from the composition which do not belong to the parts singly whereof it consists. Therefore, though the mind, taken in the strict and philosophical sense, possesses only two faculties, the active and the perceptive, this does not hinder but that the mind, in the vulgar and grosser acceptation, may possess a greater variety of faculties, such as discerning, remembering, thinking, studying, contemplating, and a multitude of others: which are but different modes or species of perception, varying according or the state of the ideas there are to be perceived, and are all reducible under two general classes, Imagination and Understanding; neither of them born with us, but acquired by use and practice, and the latter growing out of the former. We come into the world a mere blank, void of all inscription whatsoever. Sensation first begins the writing, and our internal sense or reflection encreases the stock, which runs into various assortments, and produces other ideas different from the root whereout they spring; whence we quickly become provided with store of assemblages, associations, trains, and judgments.

These stores, together with the repository containing them, we may style the imagination, the very word implying so much; for being derived from image, which is the same as idea, it imports the receptacle of ideas. And whatever number of them is excited by external objects, or presented by the mechanical workings of our animal spirits, or other causes, I call an act of imagination or scene exhibited thereby. I know that imagination is applied in common discourse to ideas purely imaginary, having no existence in truth and nature, such as a Cyclops, a Chimera, the enchanted island of Circe, or whimsical Adventures of Pantagruel. But we find rhetoricians and critics extending the term to pictures of real originals drawn in the mind by descriptions of scenes actually existing,

existing, or occurrences actually happening. Mr. Addison, in his essay on the pleasures of imagination, treats of those conveyed by the works of art and nature. Therefore I shall not offend against propriety, by taking the word in the largest sense, as comprehending every representation to the mind, whether of things real or fantastical, either brought into view by some sensation, or starting up of their own accord.

Among these ideas, some being more engaging than the rest, attract the notice particularly to themselves: the mental eye singles them out from the whole scene exhibited before it, sees them in a stronger light, holds them longer in view, and thereby gives occasion to their introducing more of their own associates than they could have done in the rapidity of their natural course. This operation of the notice being frequently repeated, at length becomes itself an object of our observation, and thus we discover a power we have of heightening the colour of our ideas, of changing or directing their course by the application of our notice: and the exercise of this power I take to be what is commonly meant by an act of the Understanding.

2. Thus there are three ways in which ideas are made to affect us; by mechanical causes,

causes, when either sensible objects excite them, or the working of our animal spirits throws them up; by the notice being drawn to fix upon some appearing eminently inviting above their fellows; and by exerting this power of the notice purposely, in order to discern them more fully, or bring in others that do not occur of themselves. The two first belong to imagination, and the last to understanding.

To render my notion of this division the clearer, I shall endeavour to illustrate it by an example. Suppose a servant wench in London, after being fatigued with several hours hard labour, can get up stairs to repose herself awhile in indolence. She squats down upon a chair, shuts her eyes, and falls into a state between sleeping and waking; but her fancy roves upon the work she has been doing, the utensils employed therein, and the chit-chat of her fellow-servants. If the cat mews at the door, this changes the scene to puss's exploits in catching mice, or her fondling tricks while she lay purring in somebody's lap; until some other sensation or turn of fancy leads on a new train of ideas. Hitherto all proceeds mechanically: volition remains wholly inactive, there being nothing alluring enough to raise a desire of retaining it in view; but the images pass lightly and nimbly along, according

ing to the impulse received from the causes exciting them, without leaving any trace of themselves behind. Presently there arises a great noise and hubbub in the street. This rouses up the girl, and carries her in all haste to the window. She sees a crowd of people, and in the midst of them my Lord Mayor going by in procession. She minds nothing of the houses before her, nor the mob jostling one another below, for the prancing horses with their gorgeous trappings engage her whole attention, until drawn from them by the great coach all glorious with sculpture, gold, and paintings, which she follows with her eye as far as it can be discerned distinctly. Then the sheriffs, and whatever else appear remarkable in the train, have their share in her notice: which impresses the objects whereon it fixes so strongly, that the traces of them remain in her reflection after the objects themselves have been removed, and perhaps raise a curiosity of knowing what could be the occasion of this parade. Thus far imagination only is employed: but curiosity puts her upon searching for the means of gratifying it, which not occurring readily, she must use her understanding to discover and pursue them. So she examines the sheet almanack pasted up behind the door, to see what holiday it might be, but finding none, she casts about in her thoughts

thoughts for some other way of accounting for the coach of state being brought out; when at last it may be she recollects that somebody had told her there was to be an address presented to day to his majesty.

3. Although in the second article of the division above mentioned, our active power be employed as well as in the third, yet it is manifest we proceed in a different manner. In the former we act inadvertently, heedlessly, and without thinking, drawn only to pursue certain objects that happen to strike upon our fancy: in the other, we act knowingly and designedly with a view to introduce some other idea not already within our prospect, and with a consciousness and reflection upon what we are doing. For there is a reflex act whereby the mind turns inward upon herself to observe what ideas arise in her view, or what effect her activity has upon them, or the bodily members, distinct from that whereby she produces those effects. The one is commonly called reflecting, and the other acting, and both may be performed at the same time, or the latter singly without the former. The beginning of our lives I apprehend passes wholly without this reflection, which we acquire in time, and by degrees. When we have discovered our power of directing the notice, and attained some expertness

CHAP. 12.] *Understanding.* 7

ness in the management of that power, we may be said to have arrived at the use of our understanding.

The degrees of exertion in both faculties are very various, from the intensest study down to that common reflection we make in the ordinary transactions of life; and from the steady attention given to very engaging scenes to that transient notice we take of objects moderately alluring, when they pass swiftly in succession before us. All strong efforts of the understanding are laborious and fatiguing, visibly wasting the spirits, and affecting the head and stomach, if continued long; nor have the most abstracted reasonings less of that effect than others: which seems an undeniable evidence, that when the mind is thought to be most retired, and to converse solely with herself, she nevertheless uses some instrument or organ, and employs the bodily forces in carrying on her work.

It is common to style those actions mechanical that are performed without thought or forecast, especially if we cannot discover any inducement that led us into them, for we ascribe them to the force of habit or impulse, of passion or fancy: but how much soever habit or fancy may have thrown up the ideas, the motions ensuing thereupon could not have been produced without the agency of the mind.

mind. This was proper to be remarked, because, if we take the microscope and examine the minute constituent parts of action, we shall find that far the greater number of them, although certainly performed by our active power, are yet directed by sudden transient ideas starting up from time to time spontaneously. But those ideas skim so lightly as to leave no print of their foot in the memory; therefore, if we look for them the moment after, we cannot find them, and so persuade ourselves there were none. When a man walks he moves his legs himself, yet they seem to move habitually and involuntarily, without any care of his to make them step right and left, alternately, or to ascertain the length of their paces: nor is it an easy matter for him, with his utmost attention, to discern the ideas that occasion this regularity of their motions.

4. To this inadvertent action of the mind we owe that dexterity in the use of our powers, which is supposed to be an immediate gift of nature: for we are not born with the faculty of walking, or handling, or speaking. When little children go to put their coral into their mouths, they do not know how to get it thither, but hit it against their chin, or rub it about their cheek: when you would set them to walk, they jump with both legs at once,

once, or lift up their foot as if they were to step over a stile: and the first sounds they make are none other than those of grunting and crying. But the ideas formed daily in their imagination lead them on, step by step, to the management of their limbs, and first rudiments of speech, before they are capable of any thing that can be called learning or application. And afterwards we catch many little habits by accident or imitation, or fall into ways of acting by the force of example, or grow more perfect in our manner of proceeding merely by dint of practice. Nor does imagination stand idle even in those seasons wherein we most employ our understanding, but makes many bye motions of her own, or acts an under part, assisting to execute the plan laid by her partner.

For understanding endeavours to extend her prospect as far and wide as she can stretch; she aims at distant ends, considers remote consequences, joins the past and future with the present, and contemplates imperfect ideas, in order to strike out from thence something that may be a surer ground of our proceeding. Therefore she can direct only our larger actions, drawing the outlines of them, or giving the main turns to our courses of behaviour, but leaves the intermediate spaces to be filled up by habit, or

the

the transient ideas starting up in train to our notice. She moves too slowly to give constant employment to our active power, which while she is deliberating must take its directions elsewhere.

5. Thus it appears that imagination actuates most of our motions, and serves us perpetually in all the purposes of life, which understanding recommends, but the habitual and spontaneous rising of ideas prompts and directs us to complete. To this belongs all that expertness we have in any art or business or accomplishment whatsoever: nor can even science proceed to good effect without it, as containing something of art in the due management of our thoughts, and proper application of our enquiries. We have observed above, that many useful attainments are made in our infancy, and afterwards, without any thought or pains of ours: and even those we acquire by care and industry will stand in little stead until the trains we have hammered out by long labour have gotten a facility of springing up upon touch of a single link. Herein lies the difference between theory and practice: for there are many things we cannot do long after we know well enough how they are to be done, not because our active powers are insufficient for the work, but because the ideas, necessary for
conducting

conducting them along the minute parts of it, are not enured to rise currently and in their proper order.

The beginner in music must learn his notes one by one; then he must associate them with the keys or stops of his instrument, and these again with their correspondent sounds: next he must join the notes into bars, and by a proper composition of these form a tune. All this he must work out at first with painful application, and while such application is necessary, he proceeds slowly and awkwardly, making frequent mistakes, and taking up an hour to go through his tune, with much trouble to himself, and very little entertainment to the hearer. But when by long practice he has taught imagination to throw up her associations and trains spontaneously, he has no other use for thought than just to choose the tune, and give some slight directions now and then as they may be wanted: for his eye will run along the lines, and his fingers along the keys, mechanically; and it would require more attention to put them out of their course than to suffer them to proceed.

6. Hence we may judge of how great importance it is to have a well regulated and well exercised imagination; which, if we could possess compleatly, it would answer all our occasions better, with more ease and dispatch,

patch, than we could compass them in any other way. But as nature has not given us this faculty in perfection, nor will it grow up to full stature of its own accord, she has endued us with the privilege of understanding to form and improve it. Therefore it is our business to range our ideas into such assortments and trains as are best adapted to our purposes; to bring them under command, so as that they may be ready for any services to be required of them; and continually to keep a watchful eye over them while at work, to prevent their deviating into wrong channels.

Nor would understanding herself find so constant employment as she does, were it not for some principles and views laid up in store which start up occasionally to set her at work. For who would consider, or study, or contrive, unless to attain some purpose suggested to his reflection? Thus understanding often begins and terminates in imagination, which nevertheless does not derogate from its excellency, because very few of our most necessary and useful purposes could ever be attained without it. And indeed understanding may justly claim the merit of those very exploits performed by habit or expertness, when it was owing to her care and diligence that they were acquired, or to her command and contrivance that they had

their

their proper cues given, and proper tasks assigned them.

7. For the most part, both faculties go hand in hand co-operating in the same work, one sketching out the design, and the other executing the performance: but sometimes we find them acting at once in different employments. When two persons engage earnestly together in discourse as they walk, their thoughts are wholly intent upon the subject of their conversation: but the transient notices of their senses, and their habitual dexterity in the management of their limbs, guide them in the mean while through all the turnings of their path. And thus they may go currently on while the path lies smooth and open: but should any thing unusual happen in the way, and attention be so fully taken up as not to spare a glance away from the object that holds it, they may chance to run against a post or stumble over a stone. Your profound thinkers are sometimes absent in company, and commit strange mistakes for want of attending to the objects around them; or perhaps set out for one place and strike into the way leading to another. Which shows that the slightest and most common matters cannot be carried on safely, without some degree of thought and observation: not that habit and imagination cannot find employment

ployment for our active powers of themselves, but it is a great chance they wander from the plan assigned them, unless kept in order by frequent directions from understanding.

Thus the mind may be said to have two eyes, in their situation rather resembling those of a hare or a bird, than a human creature, as being placed on opposite sides, and pointed towards different sets of objects. Or may be more aptly compared to a man looking at a common field through a telescope, with one eye, still holding the other open: with the naked eye he sees the several lands, their length and shape, and the crops growing on each? with the glass he sees only one little spot, but in that he distinguishes the ears of corn, discerns butterflies fluttering about, and swallows shooting athwart him. Sometimes both eyes turn upon the same prospect, one tracing the larger, and the other the minuter parts: at other times they take different courses, one pursuing a train of little objects that have no relation to the scenes contemplated by the other.

8. Whatever knowledge we receive from sensation, or fall upon by experience, or grow into by habit and custom, may be counted the produce of imagination: and to this we may refer the evidence of the senses, the notices of appetite, our common notions
and

CHAP. 12.] *Understanding.* 15

and conceptions of things, and all that rises up spontaneously in our memory. Whatever has been infused into us by careful instruction or worked out by thought and industry, or gained by attentive observation, may be styled the attainments of understanding: among which may be reckoned what skill we have in any art or science, or in language, or in conducting the common affairs of life, or what we bring to our remembrance by recollection. Our tastes, sentiments, opinions, and moral senses, I apprehend, belong partly to one class and partly to the other: their seat lies in the imagination, but they are introduced there sometimes by an industrious use of the understanding, and sometimes by the mechanical influence of example and custom.

Understanding commonly draws imagination after it, but not always, nor immediately, Men seen from a great height look no bigger than pigmies, though we judge them to be of ordinary stature; but seen at the same distance upon a level, they appear as they should do, because we see them continually in the latter situation, and but rarely in the former. Then again, objects beheld over water, or other uniform surface, which deceives us in the distance, seem smaller than their real dimensions, because the scenes we
are

are commonly conversant with, contain a variety of distinguishable parts. For imagination gets her appearances by use, but use must come by time and degrees. A discovery that we have worked out by a consideration of various particulars, often loses its force as soon as the proofs whereon it depended have slipped out of our sight: the next time we employ our thoughts upon it we arrive at the conclusion sooner, and upon every repeated trial, our process grows shorter and shorter, until in time we learn to discern the thing so discovered to be true upon a very little reflection, without the suggestion of any proof: upon further acquaintance it takes the nature of a self-evident truth, the judgment arising instantaneously in the same assemblage with the terms, and then becomes a property of imagination. Thus these two faculties contribute to enlarge one another's stores: imagination suggests principles and inducements to set understanding in motion, or furnishes her with materials to work upon; and the judgments of the latter, either by the strong glare of their evidence, or more commonly by long familiarity, grow into appearances of the former.

9. From this last consideration it appears that understanding may transfer over some part of her treasures to imagination, that is,

by

CHAP. 12.] *Understanding.*

by making us so compleatly masters of them as that they shall always lie ready at hand, without requiring any time or trouble to rummage for them: the other part which she reserves to herself is such as will not occur without seeking, but must be drawn up into view by thought and voluntary reflection. For how perfect soever any person may be in architecture, sculpture, or painting, though upon the bare inspection of things belonging to those arts, he will discern more than the ignorant, yet by considering them attentively, he will strike out further observations that had escaped him at the first view. This then is the distinction I would make between the stores of knowledge contained in our mind. Those that have an aptness to rise up spontaneously, or be introduced instantly by sensation, whether originally deposited by custom, experience, or our own industry, I would assign to imagination; and their rising in such manner I should deem a movement of imagination. On the other hand, those which lie below the surface, and require some thought and reflection, be it ever so little, to fetch them up, I conceive belonging to the understanding: and that operation whereby they are so brought to light, I call an act of understanding.

Perhaps this allotment of the boundaries

between the two faculties may be thought arbitrary, and not warranted by any lawful authority, but I do not apprehend authority has yet interfered in the case: for though we often distinguish between understanding and imagination in our discourses, yet we as often use them promiscuously, and assign the same territories and operations to the one or the other, according to the humour we are in, or according to the light in which we happen to take things. Therefore in a matter so unsettled, every one is at liberty to do as he pleases, and I have chosen that partition which I think will be most convenient for the course I am following in bringing ourselves acquainted with the nature of the human mind.

10. It is customary with most persons in handling this subject to throw in some conjectures concerning the capacity of brute creatures: and indeed all we can say of them amounts to little more than conjecture, for we cannot penetrate into their sensories, nor receive information of any thing passing there from themselves, but can only guess at their ideas, by observing their motions. It seems generally agreed among learned and simple, to exclude them from all share of reason and understanding, which is esteemed the peculiar privilege of man, and thought

thought to constitute the essential difference between him and his fellow animals. But many judicious persons look upon this as a vulgar error, and hold that several other creatures possess a degree of understanding of the same kind with our own. Now the determination of this point seems to depend greatly upon what notion we entertain of understanding: if the description I have endeavoured to give of that faculty be admitted, I do not conceive the brutes have any portion of it belonging to them. For I cannot discover in them any thing of thinking, or observing, or meditating, or what is called labour of brain. Ideas of reflection cannot well be denied them, nor assemblages, associations, trains, and judgments, but such only as are impressed by external objects, or formed by accident, not by their own care and application. They remember, but do not recollect, nor seem capable of that reflex act whereby we turn inwards upon ourselves, to call up any thoughts we want, but are continually employed by such ideas as their senses, or their fancy suggest. They fix a strong attention upon things, but it is of the mechanical kind described before, where the notice is drawn by the glare of present objects, and not directed for the discovery of something unknown. They sometimes per-

severe a long while in pursuit of one design, as in hunting for their prey, which they prosecute by motions of their limbs and application of their senses, not their reflection, and retain no longer than while appetite continues to solicit: for though the hound when at fault, may take as much pains to recover the scent, as the huntsman to put him upon it, yet when returned home after the chace is over, he does not, like his master, ruminate upon the transactions of the day, endeavouring to find out his miscarriages, and draw rules from thence to conduct him better for the future. Their views seem confined to the present, without reflection upon yesterday, or regard for to-morrow: and though some of them lay in provision for a distant time, it will appear upon examination, that they are led into what they do by a present impulse. For the knowledge of future wants can arise only from experience of the past: but ants, bees, and squirrels, hatched in the spring, who never knew the scarcities of winter, do not fail to lay up their stores of corn, or honey, or nuts, the first summer of their lives. Or, if without any evidence you will suppose them instructed herein by their elders, what will you say to canary birds, taken young from their parents, and kept in a separate cage by themselves? who yet, if you supply them with
suitable

suitable materials, will build a nest as dexterously as the most experienced of their species.

11. This sagacity, in many instances surpassing the contrivance of man, and discerning things undiscoverable by human reason, is usually styled instinct: of which the world seems to have a very confused idea, esteeming it a kind of sixth sense, or a particular species of understanding different from our own. But I do not see why it may not be ascribed to the five senses, or to that internal feeling called appetite, which we find variously affected by objects in different creatures, and which may prompt them to take prudent measures unknowingly, and without foresight of the good effects resulting therefrom. Nor shall we be so much at a loss to know what instinct is, when we are shewn some footsteps of it, or at least something very like it in ourselves. If cattle, ants, and other animals, prognosticate the changes of weather, a shooting corn, or an old strain will enable a man to do the like: the same cause producing the same effect operates upon both, namely, the various degrees of moisture in the air exciting a particular feel in their flesh. What shall we say to the nauseas preceding fevers, or those longings one now and then hears of in sick persons, pointing out to them an effectual cure for their distempers,

pers, after having been given over by their physicians? I knew a person troubled with indigestion, for which he had three several remedies, each of which would give him relief at times, when the others would not: and he used always to know which of them to apply, only by the strong appetite and propensity he found in himself towards that particular thing. Now why may not this be called instinct, as well as that which every one has observed inclines a dog to gnaw the grass by way of medicine, when he finds himself out of order? Perhaps I should not aim much beside the mark if I were to define instinct those notices of sensation, or appetite, and those untaught arts of exercising the active powers which we do not usually experience in ourselves.

12. According to the division made in this chapter, sense, appetite, and instinct, fall under the class of imagination, as so many different species contained within that general term. Nor need we wonder that imagination in brutes, should have the advantage of ours in many respects, since there may be several causes assigned why it should be so. In the first place, nature makes greater haste in the perfecting their limbs, which are the instruments employed by the mind in the exercise of her active powers. The chicken breaks forth

CHAP. 12.] *Understanding.* 23

forth from the egg compleatly formed with beak, and legs, and other members, fitted for immediate use: but man comes into the world the most unfinished creature breathing, and arrives the latest to maturity, therefore cannot acquire expertness in the use of his limbs, while they continue imperfect and unsuited for action. In the next place, many animals have acuter senses, and more distinguishing appetites to direct them in their choice between things noxious and wholesome. Then as they have nothing beside imagination to employ them, they attend constantly to that; which of course therefore must strike out longer trains, and connect them stronger, and work them smoother than it can be expected to do in us, where it is perpetually disturbed and interrupted by being called off to assist in the services of reason. For the fewer ways we have to practise in, we shall grow the more perfect in them: thus persons deprived of any one sense, make a greater proficiency in improving the others, and he that should be obliged to walk in the dark, would do wisely to take a blind man for his guide. Besides this, we corrupt imagination by the perverse use of our understanding: for we contract depraved appetites, immoderate cravings, vitiated tastes, and pernicious fancies, which stifle many
salutary

salutary admonitions we might have received from sense and instinct, if preserved in their natural state.

But on the other hand, understanding, as we have already observed, makes over a part of her purchases to imagination, who thereby becomes seized of territories she could not have acquired herself. Among these I think may be reckoned principally the faculty of speech, which by constant practice we grow so current in, that we exercise it like Peter, when he proposed making the three tabernacles, while we wist not what we say. But the use of speech, although universal among mankind, is not to be found elsewhere, notwithstanding that the apprehensions of some men seem duller, and their stores of knowledge scantier upon the whole, than those of some animals; which one would think an evidence that the human faculties differ from all others in kind as well as in degree. And I apprehend the difference lies in this, that other creatures have fewer mental organs, being particularly void of those whereby we turn our attention inwards, or call up ideas to our reflection, so that we may be said to have two mental eyes, and they only one: by which means their circle of vision must necessarily be smaller than ours, although the objects within it may shine as clear or clearer than they do to us.

Upon

Upon the whole, the dispute concerning this matter seems to turn upon words more than upon things. For if any body shall look upon every deduction of consequences, how spontaneously soever occurring, to be reason; and every portion of knowledge, through what channel soever flowing in, that man could not attain without thought and application, to be understanding; I shall not refuse either of them to many birds, and beasts, and insects. And if he shall think them entitled still to further privileges, I will not contend with him; conceiving it enough just to offer my conjecture and pass on; for my business lies with the human mind, not the brutal.

CHAP. XIII.

CONVICTION AND PERSUASION.

These are commonly used as synonymous terms; or if any difference be made between them, it lies in this, that conviction denotes the beginning, and persuasion the continuance, of assent: for we are said to be convinced, when brought by fresh evidence to the belief of a proposition we did not hold for truth before, but remain persuaded of what
we

we have formerly seen sufficient grounds to gain our credit. I shall here take the liberty to employ them in a sense not exactly the same with that wherein they are ordinarily understood, using them as appellations of two things really distinct in themselves; one for those decisions made by our reason, and the other for those notions starting up in our fancy or reflection; wherein I shall not depart much from the distinction above mentioned: for as understanding requires some little consideration to bring up her judgments to the thought, this may be regarded in the nature of a new conviction which we had not the moment before; and imagination always follows the train that former custom has led her into.

Nor let it be thought I am only resuming the subjects already treated of in the two last chapters under the names of Judgment and Appearance: for we do not always fully confide even in the judgments of our understanding, but many times suspect some latent error where we cannot discern any, or opposite evidences occur which gain a momentary assent by turns, as each can catch the mental eye: but I do not call it conviction, until we fix upon some one determination of which we rest satisfied with a full assurance. So likewise appearance sometimes varies from persuasion,

for

CHAP. 13.] *Conviction and Persuasion.* 27

for when we see a stick thrust into water, we do not imagine it really bent because it seems to be so: nor does a man, who looks at his friend through an inverted telescope, fancy him even for an instant to be of that diminutive size to which he appears contracted: nor does he persuade himself he has two and twenty hands, when by holding up one of his own behind a multiplying glass he sees so many exhibited to his view.

There is sometimes a temporary persuasion we can lay aside at any time, as in reading a poem or a novel, where imagination enters fully into all the scenes of action described, and receives them as real facts recorded in some authentic history. Therefore fictions must be probable to give entertainment, for whatever carries a glaring absurdity, or is repugnant to our common notions of things, we cannot even fancy to be true. What are the changes of scene upon the stage, but contrivances to transport the audience in imagination into distant countries or companies? What are lively descriptions but representations to the mind, which make us ready to cry out that we actually see the things described, or hear the discourses related? In all these cases there is no conviction worked, for a very little reflection will make us sensible that all is pure invention: but understanding
purposely

purposely nods, that she may not by her unseasonable reflections interrupt the pleasure received from the soothing deception. Nay, she sometimes assists in the delusion; for a man by taking pains may work himself up into an imagination of being in places where he is not, and beholding objects nowhere existent. Tully, the great master of rhetoric, teaches that an orator cannot do justice effectually to his cause unless he makes the case his own, enters thoroughly into the interests of his client, and places himself in his situation. And Horace lays down the like rule: If, says he, you will draw tears from me, you must first be grieved yourself: which one cannot well be without imagining oneself interested in the misfortune. But these temporary persuasions may become permanent ones where the organs happen to be weak or disordered: and this I take to be the case of madness, which being a distemper often removable by medicines, seems another proof that the judgments of the mind depend upon the disposition of the bodily organs.

2. Conviction and persuasion influence one another reciprocally; the latter often following the former instantaneously, but more commonly in time and by degrees. Where we can have occular or other sensible demonstration of a mistake we are generally cured of

of it once for all, but where such evidence is not to be had it will not presently yield, and after being once driven out, will many times steal upon us again at unawares. Therefore if we see sufficient reasons to work a compleat conviction, but still find a reluctance in the mind to lay aside an inveterate error, we shall be more likely to succeed by frequently contemplating the proofs already suggested, than by accumulating new ones: for importunity and assiduity prevail more upon imagination than strength of argument, because our judgments as well as other ideas run in train, and require repeated efforts to turn them out of the course to which they have been habituated; like a distorted limb that must be brought to rights by continual application, not by violence. On the other hand, notions riveted in the fancy too often debauch the understanding, and even overpower the direct evidence of sense; and that among the greatest scholars as well as among the vulgar. For having found the Latin words Levis, light, and Lævis, smooth, Venit, he comes, and Venit, he came, marked with different quantities in their gradus, they adjudge them one short and the other long, and would be horribly shocked at the inharmoniousness of a verse wherein they should be introduced in each other's places: but as our modern Latinists

tinists pronounce those words it would puzzle the nicest ear to distinguish any difference in the sounds. On the contrary, they insist upon the first syllables in TENEO, LEVIA, having the same quantity with those in TENUI, LEVIBUS, though any body except themselves may discern they pronounce them quicker and shorter in the two latter than the former. And the like cause operates upon their judgment in our own language, where we place the particle A before a consonant, and AN before a vowel, for the better sounding of our words, not for their better appearance upon paper: but your very learned folks determine the sound by the spelling; for I suppose they would not for the world say An youthful sally, or A useful accomplishment, though both words begin exactly with the same initial sound. The same may be said with respect to the rule of H being no letter, which seems a notion peculiar to the schools, and not admitted elsewhere; for one may converse seven years among the politest companies, provided they be not deeply versed in Latin and Greek, without hearing any body talk of buying AN horse, or taking AN house.

3. Probably conviction would operate more effectually and constantly if we were capable of absolute certainty, for the force of that, one would think, must bear down all opposition at

a single

a single stroke: but there being always a possibility that our clearest reasonings may deceive us, this lessens the authority of reason, and leaves room for a lurking suspicion of its fallibility in particular instances.

But however this be, certain it is we cannot with our utmost endeavours always bend imagination to that ply which judgment would direct. If you desire your friend to take something out of your eye that troubles you, with a feather, how much soever you may be convinced of his tenderness and dexterity, yet when the feather approaches close to your eye, you cannot help winking, because you cannot exclude the sudden apprehension that he will hurt you. All the arguments in the world avail nothing in this case: yet I doubt not but by repeated trials a man might bring himself to stand such an operation without flinching. Why can bricklayers walk safely along the gutters of a high building, but because they have gained a confidence in their security? Any of us who has the perfect command of his limbs might do the same, if he could once totally throw aside the persuasion of danger. Low cielings, swagging beams appearing below the plaster, and walls standing out of the perpendicular, threaten a downfal: set twenty the most experienced workmen to examine the building, and though they unanimously assure you all is safe, this will not entirely remove your apprehensions, until, by constant habitation in the house, the persuasion dies away of itself. Fear cannot subsist without an apprehension of mischief; but it is well known that the strongest demonstration will not always dissipate our fears. Let a woman take a gun into her hand, examine the barrel and pan as long as she pleases, until she is fully convinced there is neither charge nor priming, yet if you present the muzzle against her head with threatening gestures and expressions, you will raise in her a sudden persuasion of danger. Some apprehensions, as of seeing spirits or apparitions, being grounded early in our childhood, can never be totally eradicated afterwards, neither by reason, nor example, nor ridicule, nor time, that cureth all things. Nor are the other passions void of their several persuasions, which they frequently retain against evidence. Hope and expectation will continue beyond all probability of success: and love sometimes flatters with an opinion of reciprocal kindness, notwithstanding the grossest repeated ill usage. The tenets of a sect or party, deeply inculcated betimes, keep their hold in spite of the strongest conviction: whence the saying applied

plied to persons obstinately attached to their notions, You shall not persuade them even though you do persuade them: or, as I would rather phrase the sentence, you shall not persuade them even though you convince them.

4. We have observed before, that imagination actuates most of our motions, and serves us perpetually in all the purposes of life: it often holds the reins of action alone, or at least guides them in those intermediate spaces while understanding looks forward towards the general plan. So that our behaviour depends for the most part upon what persuasions we have, and upon conviction little further than as that may draw the other after it. For how well soever we may be convinced of the reasonableness of our measures, we shall never pursue them heartily and currently while there remains a latent mistrust in their disfavour: nor can we be sure of accomplishing an enterprise so long as any cross apprehensions may rise to interrupt it. Besides, we cannot constantly keep a watchful eye upon our thoughts, but such notions as start up in the fancy will take direction of our active powers, while reflection is attentive to something else: and upon sudden emergencies, or in the hurry of business, we have not time to reflect, but must follow such per-

suasions as occur instantaneously. Add to this, that in our most careful deliberations understanding works upon materials supplied her from the storehouse of imagination: nor is it possible to examine the credit of every evidence giving testimony in the course of a long argumentation.

Hence appears the mighty import of habituating imagination to run in the track marked out by reason: for when we have made any useful discovery, and fully satisfied our judgment of its truth and expedience, the business is but half done; it as yet remains only a matter of speculation, and will not serve us as a principle either of our reasonings or behaviour: but when inculcated into a firm persuasion, so that it will arise upon every occasion in full vigour without waiting to be called up by consideration, then it becomes a practical rule, and will never fail to influence our conduct.

5. As much a paradox as it may seem, certain it is that people do not always know their own real sentiments, for they are apt to mistake conviction for persuasion. In time of deliberation they are mighty confident of their resolves, and think they will continue in full force beyond all possibility of change: but if imagination has not been brought under

CHAP. 13.] *Conviction and Persuasion.* 35

under due subjection to reason, they will find them fail, and give place to other notions at the time of execution. Hence proceeds an inconsistency in men's behaviour according as understanding or imagination gains the ascendant, which could never happen if the latter were inured to follow the former. Such deceits as these are taught us in our earliest youth: boys are made to say they love their book, or love to go to church, when in reality they cannot endure either; and after we grow up, it is no unprecedented thing for men to think they believe or disbelieve certain points in religion, philosophy, or morality, when in good truth they do not, because they esteem the contrary blameable or ridiculous. This deception may be sometimes practised upon other persons with good effect; for one may chance to bring a man into an useful persuasion, by persuading him he has it already, but it is very dangerous to be practised upon ourselves: for perhaps what we fancy blameable or ridiculous may be found otherwise upon a fair examination; or if we have any wrong turn in our mind, how shall we ever apply a proper remedy, or even attempt to rectify it unless we know what it is? It is a false and mischievous shame that would prompt us to conceal ourselves from ourselves: nor does any thing better show a true freedom and courage of thought than to search out the closest recesses of our heart impartially, and know all the persuasions, good or bad, that find harbour there.

CHAP. XIV.

KNOWLEDGE AND CONCEPTION.

Although our knowledge all arises from our conception of things, and generally is more full and compleat according as that is clearer, yet we know some things assuredly for true of which we cannot form any adequate conception. Different persons conceive variously of the same things, of which they all equally acknowledge the existence. Common people cannot easily conceive of opinions, tastes, sentiments, or inclinations, opposite to their own, though they see them exemplified in others: nor can they conceive the masterly performances of art or science, nor tricks of jugglers, nor any thing out of the usual course of their experience: but such as have severally applied themselves to

penetrate

penetrate into those matters, find nothing surprising in them. For it is the repugnancy of objects to what we have ordinarily seen or known that renders them inconceivable, and therefore familiarity may make them easy to our apprehension. The savage cannot comprehend how men convey their thoughts to one another by writing, and the communication of them by sounds would appear as wonderful, but that mankind fall into that method before they know what wonder is, that is, before they have gained any experience, to which new appearances may seem repugnant.

The studious familiarize themselves to trains of observation peculiar to themselves; therefore, as they can clearly apprehend what remains a mystery to others, so on the other hand they find difficulties that nobody else can discern. The plain man makes no boggle at the ideas of creation, annihilation, or vacuity: for he thinks he sees instances of them every day, in the production of plants from the ground, the consumption of fuel in the fire, and the emptiness of his pot every time he drinks out the liquor. But the naturalist considers that the materials composing the tree were existing either in the earth, the air or the vapours, before it grew up, that the

fire

fire only divides the billet into imperceptible particles, and that after the liquor is all poured out of the pot it may yet remain full of light, or air, or ether: therefore he conceives no powers in nature that can either give or destroy existence, and disputes incessantly concerning the reality of a vacuum.

2. There are perhaps few more inexplicable ideas than that of force, whereby bodies act upon one another, and which may be divided into two sorts, impulse and resistance. The wheelwright, the millwright, and the gunner, can reason about it accurately and effectually to serve the purposes of their several arts; but the philosopher knows not what to make of it. It is neither substance, nor form, nor quality: as impulse, it is something imparted by external agents; as resistance it is a property inherent in the body itself; yet resistance cannot subsist without an impulse received from some other body. It is the immediate cause of motion, nevertheless this cause may operate without producing its effect: for if you lay a dozen huge folios upon the table, they will press it strongly downwards with their weight, but the floor by its resistance presses it as strongly upwards; so the table, though receiving continual supplies of force, remains immoveable.

Some

CHAP. 14.] *Knowledge and Conception.* 39

Some things generally admitted for realities exceed the comprehensions of all men; as the velocity of light, travelling fifteen thousand miles in the swing of a clock pendulum, the greater velocity in the vibrations of ether, which we learn from Sir Isaac Newton overtake the rays of light, the minuteness of vessels carrying on circulation, and performing secretion in the bodies of scarce visible insects, the eternity of time, immensity of space, and all infinities in general.

As imagination takes her first impression from sensation, therefore I think we cannot form a clear conception of sensible objects whereof we have not had an idea conveyed by the senses. We have not any direct notion of very swift or very slow motions, because properly speaking we do not see either, but only gather them from the change of position in the objects moving, which in the former case seem at once to fill the whole space taken up in their passage, and in the latter appear stationary; nor can we frame an idea of very small or very great magnitudes, otherwise than by enlarging the one in our fancy to a discernible size, and supposing the other removed to a distance that will lessen them within the compass of our vision. Neither perhaps can we conceive

ideas

ideas of reflection whereof we have not experienced something similar passing in our own minds.

3. Things surpass our comprehension upon two accounts, either when they are so unmanageable in themselves as that we cannot form any likeness of them in our imagination, which is the case of all infinitudes; or when we cannot conceive the manner in which they should be effected. I can easily conceive Dedalus flying in the air, for I have seen a print of him in Garth's Metamorphosis: but when I consider the weight of a man's body, the unweildiness of wings sufficiently large to buoy him up, and the inability of his arms to flutter them fast enough, I cannot conceive the possibility of his ever practising that manner of travelling. Yet when we consider the small degree of force in rays of light, together with the solidity of glass, it seems as hard to conceive a possibility of their finding their way through so compact a body, as of Dedalus's flying; nevertheless constant experience convinces us of the fact.

When we have not an adequate conception of things themselves, nevertheless we may clearly affirm or deny something concerning them. Mr. Locke says we have a very confused

CHAP. 14.] *Knowledge and Conception.* 41

fused idea of substance. and perhaps not a much better of form considered in the abstract, yet we may rest assured that form is not substance, nor substance form, and pronounce many other things concerning them without hesitation. And as imperfect notions as we have of force and impulse, or the manner of propagating motion, still we may easily apprehend a difference between the manner of imparting it from body to body, and from mind to body: for bodies only transmit the force they have received from elsewhere, nor can communicate more than they have themselves, and their re-action is always equal and opposite to action; but the mind produces an impulse she has not herself, nor does she ever feel the limbs re-act against her when she moves them: on the other hand, she receives a perception from the organs of sensation which had it not themselves, and returns not their impulse by a re-action, whenever they act upon her. Both those productions, of perception by body, and of motion by mind, appear alike incomprehensible, when we attempt to penetrate into the manner how they are effected.

4. But in order to understand ourselves the better, when we would go about to explain the manner in which causes produce their effects,

effects, let us consider what we generally mean by explanation. He that would explain the contrivance of a clock being made to strike the hours, begins with showing how the weights pull round the main wheel, how that by its teeth catches hold of the next wheel, and so he points out all the movements successively till he comes to the hammer and the bell. Or if he would explain the manner of nutrition, he tells you of the digestion of the stomach, the secretion of chyle, its passage into the heart, the circulation of the blood, and thereby its dispersion throughout all parts of the flesh. Here we see that explaining is no more than enumerating the several parts of an operation, and tracing all the steps of its progress through intermediate causes and effects: therefore the manner of a remote effect being produced may be explained, but to call for an explanation of any cause operating immediately is absurd, because it is calling for an account of intermediate steps where there are none. In this case, we can only satisfy ourselves from experience, that such and such effects do constantly follow, upon the application of particular causes: all we can do further, is by remarking some difference in operations seemingly similar, as was attempted just now

with

CHAP. 14.] *Knowledge and Conception.* 43

with respect to the action of mind and body, to prevent our mistaking one thing for another, not with an intent to give that as an explanation of either. To endeavour extending our idea beyond the cause operating, and the effect produced, would be to aim at apprehending more than the object really contains.

The quality we find in subjects of producing immediate effects, we call a primary property, but we cannot trace every phenomenon to this first source: there are many properties observable in bodies, which we are well satisfied result from the action of other bodies upon them, though we cannot investigate their operations. Such as the four kinds of attraction, namely gravity, cohesion, magnetism, and electricity, the violence of fire, the sudden hardening of water by intense cold, the fusion of metals by intense heat, the vital circulation and secretion of humours in animals, and a multitude of the like sort, which a little reflection will easily suggest.

5. Number itself, whereon we can reason with the greatest accuracy and certainty of any subject, quickly exceeds our comprehension: it is a question with me whether we have a direct idea of any more than four, because beyond that little number we cannot
tell

tell how many objects lie before us upon inspection, without counting. Higher numbers we cannot ascertain, unless when by ranging them in order, which compounds the individuals into parcels, and thereby reduces them to fewer ideas, we can bring them within the compass of our apprehension: therefore we can presently reckon nine disposed into three equal rows, because then we need only consider them as three threes. The regular position of figures in numeration, and the contrivance of expressing the largest numbers by various combinations of a few numerals enables us to run those lengths we do in arithmetic. We talk currently of millions, and compute them with the utmost exactness, but our knowledge of two millions being double one million, is no more than the knowledge of two being the double of one: and we know the value of figures only by the number of places they stand removed to the left. When we cast up the largest accounts, we have only three or four names or characters in our view at a time: and by this compendious artifice of drawing multitudes into so narrow a compass, we find means easily to manage objects that would be too cumbersome and extensive for us to conccive of themselves.

Nature

CHAP. 14.] *Knowledge and Conception.* **45**

Nature abounds in mysteries, of which we may have a certain knowledge, but no clear conception : some are too large for imagination to grasp, some too minute for it to discern, others too obscure to be seen distinctly, and others though plainly discernible in themselves, yet remain inexplicable in the manner of production, or appear incompatible with one another. Therefore, though conception be the groundwork of knowledge, and the inconceivableness of a thing a good argument against its reality, yet is it not an irrefragable one; for it may be overpowered by other proofs drawn from premisses, whereof we have a clear conception and undoubted knowledge. I suppose it will be allowed that a man born blind can form no conception of light, nor how people can have sensations of objects at a vast distance, so as to determine thereby their magnitudes and situations: yet by conversing daily among mankind, he may find abundant reason to be satisfied of their possessing such a faculty. And as we proceed further in our investigation of nature, we shall find effects that cannot proceed from causes whereof we have had any experience, therefore must ascribe them to powers of which we can know nothing more than their being adequate to those effects;

fects; and what we know so imperfectly, we may justly pronounce inconceivable.

6. It is one of the most useful points of knowledge to distinguish, when the repugnancy of things to our common notions ought to make us reject them, and when not: for men have fallen into gross mistakes both ways. Some have been made to swallow the most palpable absurdities, under pretence that sense and reason are not to be trusted; others have denied facts verified by daily experience, because they could not conceive the manner wherein they were effected. There have been those who have disputed the reality of motion, of distance, of space, of bodies, of human action, upon account of some difficulties they could not reconcile to their ideas. I know of no other rule to go by in this point than that the strongest evidence ought always to prevail: wherefore nothing inconceivable in philosophy deserves credit, unless it necessarily follows from some premisses assuredly known and clearly conceived.

But though in some instances we may and must admit things our imagination cannot comprehend, yet it is well worth our care and study to render them as familiar to our comprehension as we can: for we shall find them gain easier persuasion with us, and become

CHAP. 14.] *Knowledge and Conception.* 47

come more serviceable both in our reasonings and practice. For there is a difficulty in the management of inconceivable ideas: wherefore we sometimes suffer conception to run contrary to knowledge, where it can be done without hazard. Every body now agrees that the Sun constantly keeps his station, and the earth circles round him as an attendant planet: yet we commonly think and speak of his diurnal and annual courses through the heavens, as being more convenient for our ordinary occasions. We may hereafter find it necessary to accommodate our language to the conceptions of mankind, though we should herein a little depart from our real sentiments: this necessity gave rise to the distinction between the esoteric and exoteric doctrine of the philosophers, the meat for men and milk for babes of Saint Paul, and the parabolical and plain, or direct and figurative styles. And we may meet with cases wherein it would be pernicious to entertain conceptions of things ourselves, of whose truth we have abundant reason to be satisfied; the rules of decency require this sometimes, and a regard to higher considerations at others.

CHAP.

CHAP. XV.

COMPOSITION OF MOTIVES.

If one were set to take an account of any of those vast woods in America, scarce ever trodden by human foot, he could not be expected to proceed with much regularity at first: he must follow wherever he should find an opening, and his observations upon the first trial would direct him to take another method of proceeding in making a second: when he had examined one quarter, he must return back to where he set out in order to examine another, and would often find occasion to take fresh notices of things that he thought he had sufficiently observed before. So in this my investigation of that wilderness, the human mind, I am forced to work my passage where I find it practicable; for I have no preconcerted plan, nor any favourite point, which I am determined to make good at all events: and though not without some general idea of the end to which my enquiries will lead me, yet have I not a full prospect of the track they will take. I am not to be considered as a professor instructing others in the science he is compleatly master of, but as a learner seeking after an improvement of my own knowledge: therefore strike into whatever turnings appear most likely to advance me forward on my way, and after having pursued them awhile, sometimes discover a necessity of returning back to take a fuller review of subjects I had considered before. This is at present my case with respect to Motives, and that vivifying ingredient which gives them their vigour and activity, Satisfaction, which I thought to have dismissed long ago, but now find myself unable to proceed further without taking them under examination afresh. If I do not perform my work with the regularity I wish, yet as charity covers a multitude of sins, so I hope an earnest desire of producing something that carries the appearance of benefit, will cover a multitude of defects in the performance. But because I would not neglect method where I can attain it, shall divide what I have next to offer under four general heads: the composition of motives, the several species of them, their production, and the causes introducing them to operate. We have observed before that motives, strictly such, are always something actually present in the thought, but they usually retain the name while remaining in the repository of our ideas, and not directly occurring to view; and I have distinguished them by the figurative expression of motives operating in the scale, or lying dormant in the box. Under the first head I shall consider them in their active state, under the two next in their quiescent, and the fourth will relate to their passage from the box into the scale.

2. By the composition of motives, I mean the matter whereof they are made, which consists of three principal parts: some action apprehended possible, some consequence, perception, or end, to be attained, which we have heretofore styled the Vehicle, and the satisfaction expected therein. Hence it appears that motives always contain a judgment of the action being possible, of its producing the effect, and of the satisfactoriness of that effect.

Were you privately to unlock the doors of a prison unknown to those within, they would never try to get out so long as they remained persuaded their endeavours would prove ineffectual. Indeed, a bare possibility of succeeding will often suffice to set us at work: you shall see men endeavouring to open doors that they believe to be made fast, but then it is with an apprehension of some chance that they may find means of opening them.

them. Sometimes impatience will raise a temporary persuasion, which the mind eagerly admits against evidence, because it sooths her uneasiness for a moment; while this lasts, it will make men strive to push through stone walls, but the instant it subsides, they give over their efforts. Nor can you instance any one action of our lives wherein there is not a momentary apprehension, either well or ill grounded, either suggested by understanding or fancy, of something we can do. This seems a strong argument against Hartley's vibratiuncles, since in every exertion of our activity, there must be a perception in the mind of its efficacy. Or if his doctrine were true, it would be of most pernicious consequence to prevail amongst mankind: for were it possible once totally to banish all opinion of power, nobody would ever stir a finger to help themselves. We see this now and then exemplified in persons deeply affected with hypochondriac disorders, who, while they fancy themselves under an utter inability of action, you can never bring them to move either hand or foot, until by some sudden alarm or pungent smart you can dissipate their ideas, and turn imagination into her ordinary channels.

3. But the practicability of an action alone will not incite us to undertake it, for we have many ways wherein we might exert our power continually occurring to our thoughts, which yet we forbear to pursue: and when we do act, it is not merely for the sake of acting, but for some end conceived attainable thereby, which our judgment or our fancy recommends. And this end I take to be always some perception the mind desires to have: if we put sugar into our mouths, it is for the sweetness of the taste; if we aim at things useful, it is for the thought of having them in our possession; if at things laudable, it is for the consciousness of having acted right. Even when we go abroad merely upon being tired of sitting, or while away the time in some trifling amusement, it is either to remove the uneasiness of indolence, or for the sensation our exercise will give us, or for some engagement we expect to find in what we do. Nor can one well conceive a man to make any movement, without a notion at the instant, of something to be effected thereby.

4. Neither will the idea of action and its event suffice, without an expectance of satisfaction in the attainment: for we pursue and reject the same things at times, according as we

CHAP. 15.] *Composition of Motives.* 53

we find ourselves in the humour. It is not barely the taste, nor the sight, nor the reflection of objects, but the satisfaction expected therein, that urges us to pursue them: those who have not a palate for sweet things, will never be tempted by the sweetness of sugar, nor will a man take pains to obtain things useful, if he have no concern for the future, nor things laudable, if he have no relish in the consciousness of having performed them. But as we cannot procure satisfaction without the application of something satisfactory, therefore other perceptions are regarded only as the vehicle necessary for conveyance, but that alone gives weight to the motive. If we search throughout all the actions of men, we shall find them always preferring that wherein they for the present apprehend the greatest satisfaction: even when they forego pleasures, or submit to pains, or undergo labours, they do it for the sake of something they conceive to be more satisfactory; and when they neglect the known greater good for some paltry appetite, it is because they find more satisfaction in present gratification than in the prospect of distant advantage. Nor if we consider the matter rightly, is this denied by those who ascribe the greatest power of self-moving to the mind: for though they

they contend for her having the privilege of annexing the idea of Best to whatever object she pleases, yet they admit that this idea so annexed, influences the active powers to pursue it.

5. For the most part we proceed upon some design more or less remote, and then our motive contains several ends of action one within another; understanding retaining the principal purpose in view, and imagination suggesting the means from time to time in their proper order. Thus a motive appears to be a very complicated idea, containing a variety of judgments, together with the subjects whereon they are passed. Besides this, we cannot go on currently without ideal causes to conduct us on our way, nor instruments to assist us, of which we must have a competent idea or we shall mistake in the use of them. But by long custom and familiarity, our compounds coalesce into one idea, and so, as I may say, take up no more room in the mind than if they were single and uniform: and by habituating ourselves to fix our notice upon a variety of objects in the scenes passing before us, such of them as may serve to prompt or shape our actions, occur at one glance, and as it were in one complex; which gives us

our

our readiness and dexterity in all those exercises of our powers to which we have been frequently accustomed.

CHAP. XVI.

SPECIES OF MOTIVES.

Satisfaction is always one and the same in kind how much soever it may vary in degree, for it is that state the mind is thrown into upon the application ot things agreeable; and whatever possesses that quality in equal degree, whether meats and drinks, or diversion, or gain, or acquisition of power, or reflection on past performances, fills it with the same content and complacence: wherefore the various species of motives must be distinguished by the variety of vehicles containing satisfaction.

Innumerable are the ways men find at different times to satisfy themselves; to enumerate them all would be endless and needless: therefore I shall endeavour, what is usually practised in such cases, to distinguish them into classes, and I think them reducible to
these

these four, Pleasure, Use, Honour, and Necessity. For I cannot recollect any thing we undertake unless it be either for some amusement we hope to find in it, or for some service we expect it will do us, or for the credit that will redound from it in the estimation of others or ourselves, or because compelled thereto by the urgency of our situation. Sometimes two or more of these join forces to move us, and sometimes we have them all four in view at once: a man on bespeaking a suit of cloaths, may do it because his old ones are worn out, and he must have something to put upon his back; he may choose his piece of cloth for the closeness and strength that will render it most serviceable, he directs the cut and make so as to appear fashionable, and perhaps orders a dab of gold or silver lace to please his own fancy.

2. There is another division running through all the classes above mentioned, which distinguishes them into motives of reason and motives of fancy: the one giving birth to our considerate, and the other to our inadvertent actions; and both of these for the most part find room to operate without interrupting each other: when two persons walk together to some place on business, they may swing their arms, or whistle, or discourse, or practise

some

some other little amusement, which neither retards nor forwards them on their way. Nor are we scarce ever so totally engaged in the prosecution of any design as not to make many motions that do not directly tend to the furtherance of it. Or fancy may alter the shape of our actions without turning them aside from their purpose: a man may go on tiptoe for a whim, and make as much speed that way for a while as he desires, but when he finds it grow tiresome, he will return to his ordinary gait.

Our larger undertakings contain many ends, subordinate to one another, and all conducive to the principal; each of which in turn wholly occupies the thought, but the principal all along lies dormant in the mind, ready to operate as occasion shall offer. Thus a traveller, going on a long journey, has the next baiting place for the object of his pursuit during every particular stage: but if anything happens suggesting an alteration or addition to his plan, then the main purpose of his journey presently occurs and weighs with him in his deliberations. Most of us have a few leading aims that shape the general course of our lives, such as the attainment of some art or science, advancement of our fortune, engagement to a profession or favourite diversion: and these branch out into divisions
which

which again contain inferior views; like the governors of provinces or generals of armies, who have their subaltern officers commanding the private men. In some persons there is one predominant purpose, usually styled the ruling passion, as wealth, power, or fame, that like Aaron's serpent, swallows up all the rest, and will suffer nothing to weigh that does not coincide with its interests.

3. We observed a little while ago how understanding and imagination influence each other: there are few of our purposes to be attained at a single stroke, but judgment recommends the thing to be done, and the trains of imagination, or that habitual expertness we have acquired in works of the like nature, successively suggests the means of performing it; which must be looked upon as ideal causes, having no satisfaction of their own, but taking a tincture of that belonging to the design they tend to promote.

On the other hand, imagination often sets understanding at work. How many people employ all their sagacity and contrivance to compass some sudden whim they take into their heads without ever considering whether it be worth the while! And indeed in our most prudent proceedings we generally set out on some motive arising involuntarily to our view: for when sense, appetite, or a train of reflection

CHAP. 16.] *Species of Motives.* 59

reflection instigates to an undertaking, and nothing occurs to render the expedience of it doubtful, what has understanding to do but concert proper measures for complicating it?

4. Wherefore as the motives deposited in our imagination bear so great a sway in our proceedings, it is well worth the pains to examine what kinds of them we are capable of, in order to store up such as may serve us best and most effectually: but this is no easy matter, as well by reason of their smallness as of their obscurity. The satisfactions urging to our by-motions, while attention fixes on something else, are of the evanescent kind, as Hartley calls them, by an epithet taken from the mathematicians, who term those angles evanescent that lie between a perpendicular and the foot of an hyperbola: yet these little angles are sufficient to begin an opening between the two lines, and so are the little satisfactions sufficient to produce sudden and short actions, and afford us that complacence we feel in the common transactions of life. But there are other satisfactions, which, though strong enough of themselves to strike the eye, yet are covered from our sight whenever we endeavour to look upon them by other objects intervening. When we attempt to recollect the inducements of our conduct, there commonly occurs, instead of them, specious

cious reasons serving to justify it to ourselves or the world. How many people ascribe their actions to disinterestedness, or benevolence, or virtue, when they were prompted by fear, or resentment, or profit, or reputation? They fancy themselves possessed of those motives, but really have no such thing in their composition, or have them so feeble as never to weigh against any thing else lying in counterbalance. For it must be noted, that when we reflect on our past behaviour, we have not in view before us that state of mind we were actually in at the time of acting, which is gone and over, but its representative idea; and our ideas being perpetually upon the float, leave room for another representation to slip in such aims as bear an unfavourable aspect, hiding themselves, or taking shelter under others more reputable, which renders it extremely difficult to discover what real motives we have belonging to us, without continually keeping a watchful eye and fixing our attention upon them at the very instant of their operating.

5. The want of knowing what motives lie in the storehouse of imagination, has probably given rise to the notion of an arbitrary power which some attribute to the Will: for being acquainted only with the motives of understanding, and those strong instigations of passion

sion which can escape nobody's observation, and yet finding that those incitements do not operate with equal effect upon all occasions, but sometimes one prevails, and sometimes the other, they can assign no cause of the difference besides an inherent authority in the Will to determine its own motions. But if one could discern all the various turns imagination is apt to take, it might not be difficult from thence to account for the turns of volition: and whenever the dictates of reason appear to act with more or less weight than was expected, one might always discover some secret inclination, or wilfulness, or persuasion, or moral sense at bottom that casts the balance. Therefore I shall endeavour, as far as I am able, to trace out the minute and obscure motives, as well as the more observable, when I come to consider each of my four classes particularly.

CHAP. XVII.

PRODUCTION OF MOTIVES.

For reasons before given, it seems probable there is some particular organ or fibre, which I have called the spring, that affects us with satisfaction and uneasiness.

Whether

Whether there be a several spring for either, or that one affects us differently according to its different motions, I shall not pretend to determine: but this spring never plays, unless touched by some of those organs which excite our other perceptions. Hence proceeds the necessity of a vehicle, because we cannot obtain satisfaction without the ministry of some idea that shall prove satisfactory, nor fall under uneasiness without the feeling or thought of something that shall render us uneasy.

But in what manner soever our ideas operate either way, certain it is that nature, in the formation of our bodies, first gives them their respective qualities; for many sensations from our birth give us pain, and others afford us pleasure, and those sensations are not of our own procuring, but excited in us by external objects wherewith volition has no concern: therefore nature does not furnish us with motives, which must be worked out by experience of what hurts or delights us; for we can have no inducement for action before we know what to choose or reject. Our senses each of them respectively convey pleasure from certain objects, and pain from others; but those sensations do not discover the means of procuring them, therefore they cannot generate a motive; which must arise from

CHAP. 17.] *Production of Motives.* 63

from the remembrance of what exercises of our power have used to bring the objects to our organs, or to remove them. Even appetite, as given by nature, is no more than a pleasing or irksome feel, according to the several degrees of its intenseness; nor does it grow into desire until we have learned what will satisfy it. One may observe that little children, when uneasy through hunger or sleepiness, do not know what is the matter with them, and are so far from being moved by appetite towards the gratification of it, that they fight against their victuals and other methods of relief when applied to them.

We have observed before, that every motive contains a judgment, and that the first judgment we ever passed must precede the first act we ever performed. How we attain this first judgment, whether by participation of the mother's ideas, or by the mental organs being thrown mechanically into a modification that shall excite a perception of judgment, I am not able to explain: but thus much we may conclude for certain, that little children come into the world with a general notion of action, though they know very little how to apply their powers for particular purposes. When any thing affects them with pleasure or pain, they put themselves

selves into violent agitations, throwing about their arms and legs, and working with every muscle of their body: and at other times you see them very full of motion continually while awake. By thus perpetually exerting their powers, they light upon such motions as happen to relieve them in their wants or please them with the sensation they feel in the exercise: the idea of those motions and their effect in time sinking into their reflection, urges them to repeat the like upon other occasions, and thus instructed by accident they gradually rise to the more perfect management of their limbs and organs.

2. As motives have their foundation in the knowledge of things satisfactory, or the contrary, of course they will follow the quality found in certain sensations of affecting us either way, and consequently will depend upon that which gives them their respective qualities: therefore many of our propensities and aversions, and our appetites, may be termed natural, although not innate; because unavoidably fallen into by experience of those properties of affecting us, which nature has given to several sensations. But the matter of our composition, whereon our sensations depend, being extremely soft and pliable, is susceptible of change from alterations in the grosser parts of our frame: therefore nature
does

does not entirely preserve the texture she had given us originally, but in the growth of our bodies brings other wheels of the machine to catch the spring of satisfaction. Children, boys, young men and old, have their different sources of enjoyment; and it has been observed of our tastes, that they vary every seven years. Custom likewise, commonly styled a second nature, varies the position of our mechanism, so as to produce an affection from the same touches different from that they produced originally. What parts of our flesh are tenderer at first than the soles of our feet? yet continual use brings them to be callous, and enables them to bear our weight without trouble. Bitters or tobacco offend the taste or smell of those who never tried them before; but use reconciles men to them, then renders them pleasant, and afterwards indifferent again. Nor have particular accidents, or the dispositions of our body less effect to change the quality of objects: a surfeit will give an antipathy to things we were fond of before; a fever makes us nauseate our ordinary food; fulness, emptiness, or drowsiness, renders those motions of our limbs irksome that used to delight us. Nature has so constructed our muscles, that they remove from one spring to the other in the course of their play: after long sitting we find our legs stiff, a few steps
make

make their movement pleasant, a long walk renders it laborious, and a longer fatigues us. The same is notorious with respect to the other senses, wherein weariness takes the name of satiety: uncouth motions or sensations we find troublesome, familiar ones generally agreeable, but continued too long they become tiresome; whence comes the observation, that variety makes the pleasure of life. As the sources of our enjoyment vary we quickly perceive it, and our motives vary accordingly; for those objects we conceive in our present circumstances agreeable, move us to pursue them.

3. It may be presumed, that nature gives our mental organs an aptness to affect us agreeably with their motion, though this quality cannot operate till there have been a competent number of trains worked in the imagination to give them play: for I think we may perceive an amusement in every easy motion of our thoughts, though upon matters indifferent, when they are not strained by intense application, nor stopped by difficulties, nor run upon melancholy subjects; and so we may in every motion of our limbs and exercise of our senses, unless prevented by some such hindrances as those above mentioned, or by the notice being drawn off upon something else.

But

But imagination derives most of her affecting quality from sensation; for the first ideas of reflection being only sensations repeated though in a fainter degree, they return with some portion of the satisfaction accompanying them at their first entrance. For the remembrance of past enjoyments generally fills us with delight, if it be not destroyed by another reflection of their being to be had no more; and this delight encreases upon the prospect of their being repeated, for whatever we apprehend will please us when attained, gives actual pleasure in the approach towards it. Which adds strength to our motives, or rather gives them their whole vigour, for present satisfaction being our constant pursuit, nothing remote could ever move us if it did not afford an immediate enjoyment in the expectation, or there were no uneasiness in the thought of missing it.

4. Thus far our motives may be styled natural, for though nature does not directly infuse them, she supplies us with sensations that cannot fail to attract our notice, and thereby informs us what to choose, and what to refuse. But we receive a considerable accession to our stock of motives from other sources. Our situation and circumstances in life, and variety of accidents falling out, furnish

nish us with many; our intercourse among mankind with many more, some of them thrown upon us designedly by education and instruction, and others formed insensibly by custom and example; some we fall into by habit without intending it, and others we work out for ourselves by our own care and industry. But the principal supply of our stores comes from Translation: upon which, though perhaps I may not have a great deal to say, yet because we shall find frequent occasion to mention it hereafter, therefore I shall make a chapter of it by itself.

CHAP. XVIII.

TRANSLATION.

We have taken notice in the chapter on judgment (§ 38) of the transferable nature of assent, and how it passes from the premisses to the conclusion; I do not mean while we retain the whole process of argumentation in view, for then assent does not adhere directly to the point concluded on, but only connects with it remotely, by the intervening evidence. But daily experience testifies that conviction will often remain after the grounds of it have slipped out of our thought:

CHAP. 18.] *Translation.* 69

thought: whenever we reflect on the thing proved, there occurs a judgment of its being true, united in the same assemblage without aid of any proof to support it; and this many times after the proofs are so far gone out of our memory that we cannot possibly recal them. By this channel we are supplied with many truths, commonly reputed self-evident, because though we know them assuredly for truths, we cannot discover how we came by that knowledge. In like manner we have store of propensities, generally esteemed natural, because we cannot readily trace them to any other origin than that quality of affecting us, assigned by nature to certain ideas. But having shown how translation prevails in satisfaction, as well as assent, there will appear reason to conclude, that we derive our inclinations and moral senses through the same channel as our knowledge, without having them interwoven originally into our constitution.

As every motive contains an opinion of the object moving us being satisfactory, whatever appears conducive to procure it we must necessarily judge expedient: but this does not compleat the translation, for there requires something more to transfer satisfaction than assent. If a man wishes to see some fine house and gardens, but the way lies along very dirty roads,

roads, the circumstance of slouching through mire does not immediately become a motive of action with him: but if he had frequent occasion to ride along bad roads upon very desirable errands, though he might never come to like the exercise, they would grow much more tolerable to him than he found them at first. For the perpetual tendency of measures to what will please us greatly, alters their quality of affecting us, and in many cases renders them pleasant of themselves: and when this happens they become motives, the translation being perfectly made.

2. Imagination is not so scanty but that it can exhibit several objects to our notice at once, and this I may say in longitude as well as latitude presenting a chain of causes and effects lying beyond one another. As few of our desires can be accomplished by a single effort, there occurs together with the object of our wishes, several means tending successively to compass it; which means have no satisfaction of their own, but take a tincture from that whereto they conduce: under this prospect, the object lying at the end of the line only is our motive; but as whatever we apprehend will please gives actual pleasure in the approach, therefore we pursue the intermediate steps for the satisfaction of that approach.

But

But the line of our pursuit frequently runs to a greater length than imagination has room to contain, and some of the means necessary to attain our end, require our whole attention to compass them; in this case, so much of the line as lies beyond those means, drops out of our thought for a time, but leaves that tincture of satisfaction it had given them behind: the means then become motives for the present, for our motive upon every occasion, is always that furthest point we have in view at the instant of acting; whatever inducements we might have had to fix upon that point, are not motives while absent from our thought. Thus, if a man, being to ride a long journey, wants to buy a horse, which he does not know readily where to procure, the enquiries necessary to be made, and steps to be taken for that purpose, occupy him entirely, until he has gotten one to his liking: all this while the acquisition of a horse actuates his motions, and he will assign that for his motive to anybody who shall ask why he bestirs himself, unless they recal another idea into his head, by asking further what he wants the horse for. But these are only temporary motives, which borrow satisfaction for a time from another hand, and have it not of their own property,

there-

therefore are not to be reckoned among our stock of motives reposited in the storehouse.

But many times it happens that we find the same means conducive to our enjoyments of various kinds, and upon repeated occasions, which gives them the tincture so often, that at last it becomes their natural colour: they then move us of themselves, without needing any further inducement to recommend them; and then the translation is perfectly compleated. Sometimes they receive their quality by one strong impression: a burnt child dreads the fire, and some persons having received hurt by a sword can never endure the sight of one afterwards. But oftner the quality comes gradually by use: boys are driven by fear to their lessons until they take a liking to them; and many find amusement in professions they first entered into much against the grain. Nor is it uncommon for this quality to adhere so strongly, that no change of circumstances can disengage it: old people retain a fondness for their youthful sports after they have lost all sensation of pleasure in the exercise; and your hard students continue to plod on without prospect of any good to come of it, and after it appears manifestly prejudicial to their health.

3. Translation takes place solely in the mental organs, yet seems to bear some resemblance

blance in the manner of it with those changes made in our bodies by custom. Sailors bring their hands to a hardness by continually handling the ropes, so that they lose a great deal of the sensibility belonging to them. Nature perhaps at first designed us for quadrupeds, but the continual cares of our nurses enure us to an erect posture, so that we should now find it extremely troublesome to go upon all four. In these cases there is an alteration made in the texture of our flesh, or disposition of our muscles, whereby the same motions and objects give us different sensations from what they formerly did. In like manner when inclination passes from the end to the means, though there be no change in the grosser parts, nor difference of sensation effected, yet we may suppose some variation in the posture of our internal organs, those which did not affect us at all before, being brought to fasten on the spring of satisfaction by frequent application thereto.

But in what manner soever translation be effected, nobody can deny that we often acquire a liking to things from their having frequently promoted our other desires, where no alteration in our muscles or animal œconomy can be suspected. I need instance only in one very common propensity, whose derivation from prior inclinations will not be controverted.

verted. Every body will acknowledge that the value of money arises solely from the use of it: if we had not found it commanding the pleasures and conveniences of life, we should never have thought it worth our regard. Nature gave us no such desire, but we are forced to take pains in teaching children to be careful, and those with whom such pains have proved unsuccessful, cannot rest till they get rid of their money, or, as we say, it burns in their pockets. Nevertheless, the continual experience we find of money supplying our wants and fancies, gives it a general estimation among mankind, so that the desire of gain becomes a powerful motive of action. Few of us being suggested an acquisition of fortune by some honest, creditable, and easy method, but would feel an immediate pleasure in the pursuit, without looking forward to the many pretty things he could purchase: nor would he be thought a prudent man who should hesitate to receive a sum until he could find out some particular uses whereto he might apply it. And in some persons the love of riches rises to such an exorbitant pitch, as to overwhelm all those desires which first made them valuable: a covetous man will deny himself the pleasures, the conveniences, even the necessaries of life, for the sake of hoarding up his pelf, and seems to retain no other

motive

motive in his storehouse than that of dying worth a plumb. What shall we say then? is there a different structure of parts between the miser, the generous œconomist, and the spendthrift? Their organs of sensation continue the same, there is no hardness of flesh, no stiffness or flexibility of muscles, in the one more than the other: but their imagination has received a different cast, and the mental organs, exhibiting their ideas of reflection, been made to communicate differently with the spring of satisfaction. For though the niggard may possibly be prevailed on to do a generous deed once in his life, yet even then he feels a secret reluctance in parting with his cash: which reluctance is involuntary, therefore forced upon him by the act of some other agent distinct from himself, for we may suppose he would give cheerfully if he could; but this agent can be none other than the internal and finer parts of his mechanism, which, being differently connected, affect him in a different manner from what they would another person.

One might produce many other instances to show that our motives generate one another; that the children survive after their parents are dead and forgotten; and sometimes, like the viper's brood, destroy those that gave them birth. Many of these descendant motives

motives gain the credit of being coeval with ourselves, and that even among the considerate and studious: they are currently reputed to have been, like Melchizedech, without father or mother, because we find no mention in our records of any they had. But upon a strict and impartial scrutiny it may be not impossible to trace out their origin, and perhaps make it appear that all the motives actuating us in our riper years, except sensations of pleasure and pain, or our natural and acquired appetites, are of the translated kind. Through this channel we derive most of our tastes, inclinations, sentiments, moral senses, checks of conscience, obligations, impulses of fancy, attachments to professions, fondness for diversions, regard to reputation, views of prudence, virtues and vices, and in general all those pursuits, whether of distant or present aims, that render the occupations of men different from the amusements of children.

CHAP. XIX.

SYMPATHY.

This title may perhaps give occasion to expect a dissertation upon those sympathetic cures spoken of by Sir Kenelm Digby, who tells you that wounds have been healed by applying salves and plaisters to the instrument that made them. Or of that similitude supposed to be in the constitution of two persons, so that any good or evil befalling one of them shall instantly affect the other at a great distance, by means of certain cognate effluvia passing to and fro between them. But I deal in no such wonders; common experience is my guide, and that must have informed every body how much we continually sympathize with the sentiments and affections of the company among whom we converse. As this quality contributes greatly to introduce our motives into act, and by frequently introducing them to produce new ones, it seems properly to claim a place between those two subjects.

2. We are not long in the world from our first entrance before we perceive that our

pleasures

pleasures and pains depend much upon the actions of those about us : on a little further progress, we discover that their actions follow their disposition of mind, and afterwards learn to distinguish those dispositions by certain marks of them in their looks and gestures. This makes children perpetually attentive to the motions and countenance of persons into whose hands they fall : nor does there want another cause to render them more so, for having but few stores in their own imagination, they catch the ideas of other people to supply themselves with employment. And in our advanced years we cannot well carry on any business or argument, or enjoy the pleasures of conversation, without entering into the thoughts and notions of one another. When we arrive at the use of understanding, the judgment of others weighs with us as a just and natural evidence, inducing us to judge accordingly; but we have seen how the judgment of expedience, frequently reiterated, transfers satisfaction upon the measures so conceived expedient: and we purposely imitate the ways and manners of our teachers, or other persons whom we esteem more expert and knowing in any matter than ourselves. Thus we acquire much of our sympathy by inadvertent notice, and add more by design and industry; until custom in both ways has
worked

worked out trains wherein imagination learns to run involuntarily and mechanically. This appears most evident in compassion, for we cannot help sympathizing with distress, though we feel it painful to ourselves, and know it can afford no relief to the party suffering.

3. But we catch our other affections, too, from the prospect of them exhibited before us: a sprightly countenance makes us cheerful, and a face of melancholy damps our spirits; we pursue other people's hopes, and take alarm at their terrors; we grow to love things we perceive them fond of, and contract aversions from their dislike. Nor is immediate sensation the only thing that can work this effect upon us; for we find the same produced by stories of accidents befalling persons at a distance; we receive impression from facts recorded in history, and feel ourselves affected with the affections of those who have been dead a thousand years ago. Nay, we find ourselves interested in imaginary scenes, partaking the pleasures and pains of fictitious characters in a play or a novel: and as we take a tincture of the affections, so we imbibe the opinions, and insensibly adopt the views of those with whom we have continual intercourse, which gives example the prevalence over precept, and enables evil communications to corrupt good manners. Even sensations

sations may undergo a change by the effect we see them have upon others: we may get a relish to a dish upon observing the company eat eagerly of it, and nauseate a joint of meat because somebody at table fancies it to have an unsavoury smell. How many people take their taste of music from the applauses of connoisseurs? How hideous does a once admired pattern of silk become in the ladies' eyes upon being grown out of fashion? What change do imbibed notions make in the ears of great scholars, as we have remarked in Chap. XIII. § 2, so that they cannot distinguish between a long sound and a short, a vowel and a consonant? None can have avoided observing how apt we are to mimic the gestures, fall into the habits, and copy the imperfections we see continually before us: and it has been observed a thousand times, that laughing and yawning generally go round the company. We participate in some measure the ideas of all men, but more with those of whom we have a good opinion or frequent converse, than with strangers; for the judgment of the former carries greater weight upon us for our estimation of their persons, and that of the latter makes up by repetition for what it wanted in strength.

4. But were we to give a full latitude to sympathy, we should whiffle about with every wind,

wind, nor could ever keep steady to one tenor of conduct, because we should perpetually meet with somebody or other leading us by their example to swerve from it. This teaches us a reserve and caution against taking impressions too hastily, and confines our propensity to imitation within due bounds. Yet where there are not urgent reasons to the contrary, I do not see why we may not let sympathy take its course, as it gives an easier flow to our thoughts, renders us more sociable, and assists us in making many improvements.

There are some who carry this reserve to extremities, so far as to throw their mind into a disposition contrary to that they see exhibited: this temper whoever pleases may call Antipathy, as being the opposite to Sympathy. It generally takes its rise or terminates in ill nature, rendering the possessors morose, contemptuous, and intractable: they repine at others' successes, and rejoice at the sight of disappointment; if you talk seriously to them, they fall to joking; and if you would make them merry, they put on a more than ordinary solemnity of countenance. There are those who affect this contrariety of humour towards mankind in general, but it is more usually practised with respect only to such against whom we have conceived some great prejudice. And, indeed, if ever allowable, it is so when we fall under a necessity f consorting with persons of whose errors or evil principles we have just cause for suspicion, to prevent our taking contagion from them. Yet some situations render us all so unapt for imitation, that we rather take disgust at the expression of affections not tallying with our own: in our seasons of jollity we cannot endure a melancholy aspect, and when under affliction, any levity disturbs us: but this proceeds rather from the force of sympthathy, than otherwise; for that perpetually urges the mind to assimilate her trains to patterns she cannot follow under her present circumstances.

CHAP. XX.

INTRODUCTION OF MOTIVES.

Sensation first moves us to action, in order to continue it if pleasant, or remove it if painful: thus the taste of victuals urges children to take more of them into their mouths, and the smart of a pin to catch away their hands from it. When they have gotten

competent

CHAP. 20.] *Introduction of Motives.* 83

competent stores of reflection, these too affect them in like manner with sensation, and sometimes overpower it; for you may draw off a child's notice from any little pain or craving of appetite, by diverting it with playthings. As imagination becomes worked into trains, the notice, being put into one by some particular object, will run on to other ideas very different from those the object exhibited. Nor does imagination fail to suggest fancies of her own motion without any object to introduce them: of what kind they shall be, depends greatly upon constitution, the present state of our animal spirits or disposition of mind, inclining us either to seriousness or gaiety, business or diversion. Habits, too, attract the notice to follow them inadvertently by that ease there is in giving way to the little transient desires they present rather than restraining them. And when experience has brought us acquainted with the properties of things external, and the command we have over the ideas of our mind, which knowledge gives us the use of our understanding, we can then procure motives for ourselves; either by application of such objects as will raise any particular desire, or by putting reflection upon the hunt for something that will please us, or suggesting inducements to strengthen us in our purpose, or by resolution to banish some intruding ideas, and fix our whole attention upon others.

2. Thus there are three causes contributing to introduce motives into the scale: the action of the mind, impulse of external objects, and mechanical play of our organs; and these three mutually influence one another. The mind operates two ways, either by design or inadvertently; for when she turns her notice upon an idea, though with no other view than for the present amusement it affords, this occasions it to lead in a train of its associates, and often awakens a desire that would have lain dormant without such attention. Therefore, if we have any hurtful inclination belonging to us, it is very dangerous to let our thoughts run upon objects relative thereto; for we may raise a disturber we did not expect, nor can quiet again whenever we please: and perhaps desire scarce ever rises to any high pitch, unless assisted by some action of the mind tending to foment it. But when the mind acts with design, nevertheless she has that design suggested by something happening to her from without, or by the spontaneous working of imagination; to which sources she must have recourse in search for motives of her conduct, or gathering encouragements to support her in an undertaking. Even in the most arbitrary exercises of her power,

power, as when she endeavours to attain her purpose by dint of resolution, she uses some instrument to do her work. A man that holds his hand near a roasting fire, must have some reason for so doing, either to cure a burn, under the notion of fire driving out fire, or to try how long he can hold it there, or for some other purpose which appears satisfactory at the time, or else it would never have put him upon the attempt: this satisfactory purpose, then, he strives to retain in full vigour, without suffering it to fluctuate or fade, and withdraws his notice from that uneasiness the smart of the fire would throw upon him. Herein he acts upon the mental eye much in the same manner as we do upon the bodily, when we wink against a glaring light, or stretch our nerves to observe some obscure object that cannot be discerned without straining: or as we do upon the organs of hearing, when of two persons talking to us at once, we disregard the one, and attend wholly to the other. And in all cases of resolution, we may perceive the like method practised: we do not annex the idea of Best to what had it not before, but among opposite subjects, whereto that idea is already annexed, we hold one under contemplation, and exclude the rest, or strengthen it with other considerations, from whence that idea may be transferred.

Things

Things external are made to operate upon us either by natural causes, or the situation we stand in, or the company we consort with: but what effect they shall produce in us depends greatly upon the cast of our imagination. For we have observed before, that the same objects affect people variously, exciting different judgments, and suggesting different motives in one from what they do in another: nor does the mind want a power many times of applying or removing objects, and of encreasing or diminishing in some measure the impression of those before her by an operation upon her organs.

In like manner the spontaneous courses of our ideas, although depending chiefly upon habit, and running into those trains of thought to which we have been accustomed, yet may be diverted by objects occurring, or drawn aside by the force of sympathy, or controlled by the power of the mind, so as to take another track than they would have followed of their own accord;

3. If we examine our proceedings carefully, we shall find in all of them a mixture of volition and machinery, and perhaps the latter bearing a greater share than the former. We never enter upon an undertaking without some purpose starting up in our thoughts, or recommended by the present occasion as expedient

pedient or agreeable: we choose the measures for accomplishing it from among the stores presented by our understanding; and though we perform the work by our own activity, yet our manner of proceeding is such as former practice has made ready to us, and the minute steps necessary for compleating it, rise mechanically in our imagination. Our latent motives, which bear so great a sway in the behaviour of most men, cannot owe their appearance to the mind, because they escape her observation when she would discover them: and our minute motives prompting us to inadvertent actions, which are far more numerous than commonly supposed, must take rise from some other spring, because the mind perceives them not the moment before they operate, nor remembers them the moment after. Nor are the grosser parts of our machine without their influence upon our actions: the natural temperament of our constitution, the accidental condition of our humours, the brisk or slow circulation of our animal spirits, the circumstances of health or sickness, freshness or weariness, fulness or emptiness, render the mind alert or unapt for exercise, turn imagination into different trains, excite desires of various kinds, and in great measure model the shape of our behaviour.

4. What

4. What is the particular structure of our machine, how the several parts of it communicate, or in what manner they operate upon one another, we cannot pretend to describe, and therefore must express ourselves by figures. Sometimes we talk of characters imprinted, or traces engraven in the memory, sometimes of roads and tracks worn in the imagination, of weights hanging in the balance, springs impelling to action, wheels resembling those of clock-work, images striking upon the mental eye, or streams and currents running in various channels. Those expressions, if intended for a physical account of our interior frame, could not all be admitted, as being inconsistent with one another: but when we speak figuratively of a matter we cannot describe directly, we may vary our images without inconsistency, for the same will not answer in every case, therefore it is allowable to take any that shall afford the greatest resemblance according to the present occasion for which we want to apply it.

But if we may guess at the internal texture of our machine by the grosser parts of it discoverable upon dissection, they will lead us to imagine that our ideas are conveyed by a multitude of little tubes affecting us variously according to the motions excited in them, or according

cording to the courses of some subtile fluid they contain; or should we, with Doctor Hartley, suppose the nerves to be solid capilaments, and the business performed by an ether surrounding them on the outside, this will amount to the same thing; because a number of these small strings placed close together will form tubes of the interstices between them, which may serve as channels for the foresaid ether to pass along. Therefore if I were to compare the human machine to any of our contrivances of art, I should choose for my foundation a large Organ; wherein the bellows answer to the animal circulation, the pipes to the organs of sensation and reflection, and the organist to the mind. But the organist here does not make all the music: for the pipes are so contrived as to sound with the striking of things external upon them, or by the mere working of the bellows, which plays as it were by clock-work without a blower. Yet is this but an imperfect representation of the natural machine: to make our comparison more compleat, we must suppose other sets of pipes for conveying objects of the other senses; besides innumerable smaller ones returning an echo to the larger, and new modulating the sounds or lights received from them, which supplies us with our ideas of reflection. These little vessels

are

are so soft and flexible, that they will change their form and run into various contextures with one another, whereon depend our inclinations and stores of knowledge: for as a pipe will give a different sound according to the length or other dimensions it consists of, so objects affect us differently according to the disposition of the channels through which they pass. Nor must we omit the many conveyances necessary for distributing the alimentary juices, which serve like oil to moisten and supple the works or to repair the waste made by continual use. Add to this a multitude of other pipes which dilate and shorten upon inflation, and thereby draw certain strings fastened to their extremities; from whence proceeds muscular motion, and the power of acting upon the several parts of our machine, as well the grosser as the finer. And all this infinite variety of works, so complicated with one another, and yet so exactly disposed as not to interfere with each other in their play, Nature has stowed within the narrow compass of a human body: which if an artist were to endeavour to imitate by constructing an engine that should perform those few of the human movements that art can imitate, it would require an immense fabric to contain every thing necessary for executing his purpose. But the most wonderful circumstance

stance of all is, that our organist sits in utter darkness with respect to the nearest parts of his instrument, which are to be the immediate subjects of his action, having no notice of any thing but what comes to him through his pipes: he knows not the situation of his keys, on which hand lies the base or the treble, nevertheless, after a competent practice in his trade, he acquires such an unaccountable expertness, that he never touches the wrong key, but takes his measures exactly, without perceiving what they are, and upon an idea only of some remote consequence they will produce.

5. Since there is so close a connection between the parts of our machine acted upon by the mind and those moved by the animal circulation, it follows that each must have an influence upon the other. Our vital spirits, according as they stand disposed, force a particular kind of ideas upon the mind, and the latter in every exertion of her power causes an alteration in the courses of the former: sometimes designedly, but oftner as a natural consequence of something else she intends. He that runs means only to arrive the sooner at the place whither he would go, but besides this he quickens his pulse, heats his flesh, and puts himself out of breath, effects which

which he did not think of, nor perhaps should have ensued had it been at his option to have helped them. The like happens on other exercises of our activity, which propagate a motion to the several parts of our body corresponding respectively with the organs employed in those exercises; and these parts, by frequently receiving such motions, become disposed to fall into them again mechanically, or upon the slightest touch, and thereby excite the same ideas that generated them. From hence arise our habits, which though learned at first by single, but perhaps inadvertant acts of the mind, yet recur upon us afterwards involuntarily. Hence likewise spring the passions, which I take to be only a stronger sort of habits acquired early in our childhood, when the matter of our composition being tender and pliable, may be worked easily into new channels wherein the animal spirits may flow more copiously. For I do not imagine that nature gave us passions, she may indeed have made each man more susceptible of one sort than another, but they are brought into form by the action of the mind bending her notice continually to particular sets of objects. Just as nature may have prepared one man for a dancer by giving him strength and suppleness in his joints, or

another

another for a singer by giving him a clear and sonorous voice; but it is art and practice that invest them with the respective faculties of dancing or singing.

CHAP. XXI.

PASSIONS.

We have taken notice that children, on their first entrance into the world, have a general notion of action, though they know not in what manner to apply it: therefore when any thing affects them strongly, they strain every nerve, and exert all their little powers of motion. But as they grow acquainted with the uses of those powers, they confine their efforts to some particular quarter: yet their knowledge for a long while being very imperfect, they still employ more exertion than necessary, striving to attain that by vehemence which they want skill to accomplish by management. These efforts made upon the organs of reflection, as well as those of motion, being frequently repeated upon the same parts, widen the passages communicating with the vital circulation, which thereby more readily admit the animal

mal spirits, and take in a larger flow than they were capable of in their natural state. Whence proceeds the violence and obstinacy of passion, which will scarce allow any ideas to enter the mind besides those of its own cast, nor can be put out of its course until the ferment subsides of itself: wherein there is no room to doubt of the animal spirits being concerned, when we consider the effects generally visible upon the pulse, the nerves, and the countenance. Thus it appears we work out the passions by our own activity, not indeed with a deliberate design which the infant mind is scarce capable of at the time when she lays the foundation of them, but by that inadvertent notice she is led to fix upon striking objects.

The passions seem to have their particular provinces in the several parts of our machine: what alterations they produce in the body it belongs to the painter, the sculptor, and the anatomist to ascertain, and what play they give the mental organs belongs to no professor whatever, as lying beyond the reach of any science yet attained by human sagacity. So there remains only for me to examine what ideas give rise to each of them, and hang upon the mind during their influence: nor shall I attempt a compleat dissertation upon

upon them all, but offer such few observations as may occur concerning the principal.

2. Immediate satisfaction being the point that constantly attracts our notice, and gives influence to all our other ideas, we must look there as the most likely place to find the source of our passions. Whatever present action in our power promises satisfaction prompts the mind to pursue it, and this state of mind we call desire; for I take desire to be nothing else but the prospect of some agreable perception, together with some present act apprehended productive thereof: this therefore is the spring that begins to set us in motion, and actuates us incessantly in every exercise of our powers, for we never stir a fibre but for the sake of something we desire to have produced thereby; and Mr. Locke declares himself of the same opinion, where he says desire is always the thing that determines the Will. But this common desire is not a passion, being too gentle to deserve that name: otherwise we could never possess our minds in tranquillity, because there is scarce a moment in our waking hours wherein we are not urged to something either momentous or trifling. But when the purpose we aim at does not ensue upon our first endeavours, the mind redoubles her efforts under an apprehension that a stronger exertion may succeed

succeed where a weaker did not: for it has been commonly remarked that difficulties lying in the way of desire, like water thrown upon coals, if not enough to extinguish it make it burn with a fiercer flame. After having frequently practised exertions of this sort, the spirits get a habit of rising in a ferment, which will let no other idea intrude besides that of the engaging object; and then desire takes the form of a passion. I know that strong sensations, and cravings of appetite, will raise violent commotions in the earliest times of life, before any habit can be acquired: but sense and appetite have always been distinguished from passion, wherein the organs of reflection bear a principal share, and ideas hang longer, and make deeper impression upon the mind than sensation could have enabled them to do, which additional force they must have derived from habit.

But an objection may be started against my making the prospect of means tending towards an attainable satisfaction to constitute desire, because it is very well known, that men too often set their hearts upon things they see no possibility of obtaining. This I acknowledge to be fact, nevertheless, even in these cases there is something the mind apprehends to be feasible: for when the object of desire lies

any

any thing remote, every step leading to it, nay the very thought of an approach towards it, sooths the mind with a momentary satisfaction, which thought may be in our power, though the object itself confessedly is not: for we have seen that persuasion does not always follow conviction, and as by reading a poem or a novel, so by an operation upon our mental organs, we may sometimes raise a temporary persuasion of things we know to be false. Besides, the holding an object in our thoughts is one means towards attaining it, because that may suggest expedients which did not presently occur, and because the strength of an idea, heightened by our attention to it, urges us to a stronger exertion of our powers. These causes I conceive make people dwell upon whatever appears with an engaging aspect, and keep them still hankering after things they have found unattainable. For present satisfaction being the point continually in view, they flatter themselves with a fond imagination of making advances towards the obtaining of their wishes, where understanding can give them no such prospect, overlooking that disappointment which must necessarily ensue. The mind has a strange knack of deceiving herself with respect to the success of her measures, when the taking them promises some little amusement for the next succeeding moment.

moment. If the idea of something attainable were not part of the essence of desire, there would be no difference between desire and the contemplation of any thing agreeable, which is contrary to experience. I suppose most of us would think it very agreeable to fly about in the air like a stork or an eagle; methinks it would be mighty pretty to glide along with such an easy motion, to transport ourselves suddenly from place to place, to soar in the upper regions, having an extensive prospect of lands and seas below, and varying our scenes at pleasure; yet we never fix our desires upon such amusement, but what hinders us, unless that we cannot raise even a delusive imagination of any thing practicable towards the attainment of it? But should some Dedalus invent a plausible scheme for making wings, we should probably find ourselves very desirous of having a pair, though we sold our coaches for the purchase: and if after many fruitless attempts we were convinced the thing was impracticable, we might still continue to ruminate upon it for a time, and please ourselves with hunting after better expedients upon a bare possibility, though without any hope of finding them.

3. All that has been said above concerning satisfaction, may be applied with a little alteration to uneasiness, which urges us to fly from

from it in the same manner as the other attracts us towards it. Wherefore the schoolmen reckon another passion opposite to desire, which they call Flight, or Avoidance, and has some impending evil for its object: but since whatever appears hurtful we always desire to avoid, since the very escape from mischief affords a sensible satisfaction, and since nature has so befriended us that we never want for amusement, whenever we can keep clear of all disagreeable perceptions, there seems little need of distinguishing between the avoidance of evil and desire of good, the latter being always implied in the former: and the less, because it would require some nicety and labour of thought to make such distinction.

But there is another distinction which, though somewhat nice, we have found occasion to take notice of before, and may find the like again hereafter, I mean the making want a separate species of desire. For when the mind is moved by some object, and exerts herself strenuously in searching for some means of advancing towards it, but none offer, or such only as appear ineffectual upon their presenting themselves, this state of mind I call Want: and may be compared to the gnawings of an empty stomach, whose sides grind against one another, as having nothing to
work

work upon. Therefore genuine desire finding continual issue for its efforts, proves the source of all our enjoyments, but want always torments us with uneasiness. Whenever incompatible desires assail us together, one of them at least must degenerate into want, if it still continue to solicit, and be not quite overwhelmed by its antagonist, wholly engrossing our attention. But though want throws the mind into such a disagreeable situation, yet it may be expedient to endure it sometimes for the sake of a greater future advantage: for many very useful desires not vigorous enough at first to surmount all opposition, and therefore meeting with continual disappointment, yet by being still kept alive, and put often to struggle with a superior adversary, may in time acquire strength to overthrow him. Content I take to be nothing else but the privation of want, which though indifferent in itself, yet a contented state is always a happy state in consequence, because as observed just now, we never fail finding matter of amusement, whenever we can keep clear of all disagreeable perceptions.

4. Desire, as we learn from Mr. Locke, obtains a place in all the other passions, and we may say they are only desire under so many different forms. As this derives its original

ginal from the expectance of satisfaction to come, so the actual possession of satisfaction throws the mind into a state of enjoyment. But possession does not always put an end to desire, but many times excites it, putting the mind upon stretching her mental optics to obtain a stronger view of the object that pleases her, and upon opening the passages of the animal spirits, to admit a larger current that may heighten and prolong the delightful sensation: when this is done with any considerable degree of exertion, it produces the passion of joy. I think we may pronounce the province of this passion extends over the whole system of vessels concerned in exhibiting ideas, or performing voluntary motion, and that it quickens the circulation of spirits throughout all their passages in general, whereas some other passions pour them more copiously upon particular quarters: for we find people very brisk and active in seasons of joy, breaking out continually into wanton and extravagant sallies, unless restrained by decency and reflection. Sometimes joy has been known to rise so high as to produce great disorders in the body, and even extinguish life, too great a redundancy of spirits causing suffocation, like a strong wind blowing against one's mouth and nostrils which hinders the play of our lungs: but
these

these transports rarely happen, nor perhaps ever unless when the channels have been emptied before by some opposite stagnating passion, as grief, or fear, or want. The sight of an only child given over for lost, a pardon brought to a malefactor under the gallows, or a sum of money poured into the lap of a man in utmost distress, may have proved fatal: but then the pleasure comes accompanied with an idea of deliverance from something very irksome before, which gives it a double force. As joy introduces a pleasurable situation of mind, it would deserve encouraging whenever we could, if it were not for some pernicious consequences attending it: for it confines our views within the present to the neglect of our future interests, it disturbs the operation of reason, shutting our eyes against the lights she would offer, and turning a deaf ear against her remonstrances; for the mind, perfectly satisfied with her present condition, cares for nothing else, but rejects every other idea that might interrupt or abate her enjoyment.

5. As the expectance of satisfaction, dependant upon our endeavours to procure it, causes desire, so the like expectance from external causes, when no endeavours of our own appear necessary, gives birth to Hope. It is true, we often find it incumbent upon us to
do

do something ourselves for accomplishing our hopes; but then so far as our own activity extends belongs to desire, hope relates only to that success of our measures which is not in our power; for no man is said to hope that his hunger will be appeased by eating when he has victuals set before him, and there is nothing requisite besides his own act to assuage his cravings. It is commonly reckoned that hope must contain a mixture of fear; and perhaps this is generally the case, considering the uncertainty of events for the most part; but sometimes we have the prospect of a distant good to befal us without any doubt of its arrival, and I know not what better name than hope can be given to this situation of mind; therefore see no impropriety in the expression of a sure and certain hope. I am not quite satisfied that hope ought to be ranked among the passions, as being gentle in its own nature, and never raising emotions unless by means of other passions generated from it. For as a man reckons the reversion of an estate among his valuable effects, and esteems the gaining a title to such reversion an accession of fortune, so the assurance of future good affords a present pleasure: and if the mind exults in the contemplation of that pleasure, or feels an extraordinary flow of spirits arise upon it, this we may call a species

cies of joy. On the other hand, if the promise of distant enjoyment does not instantly satisfy, but begets an eager impatience of possessing it before the time, then hope assumes the form of want.

6. The old philosophers, as we may gather from Cicero, could not settle among themselves, whether to define anger a fervour of mind, or a desire of revenge; which seems to me just as wise a dispute as if they had contended whether Chrysippus were an animal or a man, the one being implied within the other, and differing no otherwise than as genus and species: for custom has appropriated the name of Anger to that particular fervour arising in the mind upon thought of a supposed injury. But there are fervours occasioned by other causes; any pressing pain or uneasiness sets the mind a struggling to throw it off; and difficulties, not apprehended unsurmountable, stir up an earnestness of resolution to master them: therefore it is common when we see people go about any thing in a great hurry and flutter, to admonish them not to put themselves in a passion. And I conceive it is this view of difficulty that gives rise to the violence of anger; for as the party upon whom we would wreak vengeance will naturally oppose it with all his might, a more than ordinary exertion becomes

comes necessary in order to surmount that opposition; and the mind, having found this to be constantly the case, gets a habit of eagerness and vehemence in every thing she does, either tending or preparatory to revenge. Whatever may be thought of other passions, this cannot be born with us, for there are several things to be learned before we come to the idea of anger: nature makes us concerned originally only with our own pleasures or pains; we feel not, and consequently regard not, what happens to other people, until having received hurt from them, and found that our retaliating the like prevails upon them to desist from offending us, we thence learn the expedience of exerting ourselves upon such occasions. Thus the desire of revenge is not a natural but a translated desire, we first look upon it as a means of procuring ease to ourselves, and security from injury; but having often beheld it in this light, the end at length drops out of sight, and desire, according to the usual process of translation, rests upon the means, which thenceforward become an end whereon our views will terminate. We may reckon at least four stages in our progress to the passion of anger: our experience of damage brought upon us by others, of our power to give them displeasure, of the effects of such dis-

pleasure

pleasure to make them alter their measures, and of the opposition we must expect against the exercise of that power. But having by these gradations once brought satisfaction to connect immediately with revenge, it becomes a motive of action which we pursue many times by ways not at all conducive to the end that first rendered it recommendable. For men sometimes vent their wrath upon inanimate beings, although incapable of punishment, or of mending their manners thereupon: and in violent transports of rage beat their heads against a wall, or otherwise punish themselves, thereby bringing on that hurt which it was originally the purpose of anger to remove. Though anger raises a mighty flood of spirits, it does not like joy diffuse them equally throughout the whole system, but forces them in torrents upon the vessels concerned in action, producing sudden violent starts of motion, spreading a heat to the outward parts, and showing more apparent signs of disorder than any other passion: for which reason I suppose it has generally engrossed the name from the rest, for when we call a man passionate we mean that he is prone to take offence and quick to resent, not that he is apt to fear or hope, or grieve, or fall into any other emotion. We may safely rank this among the uneasy passions,

sions, as partaking more of that species we have called want than of genuine desire: for however it may have been said that revenge is sweet, the sweetness does not come until the desire ends by having been glutted; but while the desire subsists, how strong assurance soever it may have of succeeding, there always remains a restless impatience, which, like immoderate hunger, never ceases to torment until it be removed.

7. When danger threatens and appears inevitable, or the means of avoiding it do not yet discover themselves, this fills the mind with fear, which proceeds upon two views; one of collecting a fund of spirits to be ready for use when any method of deliverance shall offer, the other of benumbing or deadening the notice so that when the mischief comes it may affect us the less sensibly: both which are effected by the same means, to wit, withdrawing the animal spirits from the organs of reflection and motion: because the strength of our perceptions, and vigour of our actions depending upon the quantity of spirits employed therein, if we can withold them from flowing upon the mental organs, we scarce feel the pungency of evil befalling us; and if we forbear to spend them in fruitless endeavours, we shall have the greater supply ready to serve us when they may prove effectual.

tual. Therefore, fear overwhelms with confusion; and though people will stare wistfully at a frightful object, they discern little of what they stare at, their ideas being duller than usual: and if the terror rise to a very high degree, it totally stupifies the senses, and causes a fainting. Fear is observed to chill the limbs, crowding the whole mass of blood upon the heart; and as the vital spirits have their circulation too, we may presume it gathers them all to some vessel, which performs the same office with respect to them as the heart does to the blood. But that there is a mighty fund of spirits collected somewhere, appears manifest from the uncommon force they operate with when breaking forth into action. Fear adds wings to our speed; none fight so furiously as cowards driven to despair, and people in a fright have been known to exert double the strength they could muster up at other times with their utmost resolution. I have been credibly informed of a man so lame with the gout, that he could stir neither hand nor foot, who on hearing a sudden outcry of fire in the next house, started up out of bed and ran to the window, but upon finding the danger over, his strength immediately left him, and he was forced to be carried back again. Children and other animals show no signs of fear

at

at their first coming into life; nor can they be supposed capable of any before they have an apprehension of danger, which must come by experience of things hurtful: indeed, they learn very soon to take fright at hideous objects; but then it is not till they can discern the difference between them and others whereto they have been some time familiarized.

8. Shame seems to be a species of fear, having for its object the evil of disgrace: like other fears it fills with confusion, and darkens the ideas; it operates rather by deadening the notice than collecting spirits for future exertion, therefore seems to be occupied chiefly in driving them from the organs of reflection, whose seat probably lies in the head, and discharging them upon the next adjacent parts, which may account for the blushings wherewith it overspreads the countenance. Shame, indeed, often proves a powerful incentive to action, but at such times it takes the form of desire, urging us to do something either for reinstating ourselves in credit again, which we look upon as an attainable good, or for preventing the censure that might otherwise happen, which we consider as an avoidable evil; there is not properly shame until the consciousness of disgrace actually comes, or the mischief is apprehended irremediable, which
throws

throws the mind into a state of want wherein she exerts herself in endeavours to stifle the uneasy reflection, and withdraw her notice from it as much as possible. This is one of the latest formed among our passions, for little children appear to have no notion of it a considerable time: it is so far from being infused by nature that it derives wholly from our intercourse with mankind, nor would ever come to a person who from his birth should be secluded from all society; before we become susceptible of it, we must have gotton some use of language, without which we cannot well be made sensible of the estimation set by others upon any thing we do: and though after having arrived at maturer reflection, we take shame to ourselves for follies that can be known to nobody else, yet are we taught this practice by censures we have found others pass upon us, or we have passed upon them. For as anger, although beginning on hurts received from other persons, will at length sometimes turn upon ourselves, so having got a habit of blaming what we have seen blameable elsewhere, we fall into the like train of thinking with respect to our own miscarriages. There is another emotion of mind, the opposite to shame, that deserves to be ranked among the passions with better reason than Avoidance, the opposite to desire:

for

for commendation agitates the spirits and stimulates to action no less than disgrace. Nor let it be said that the one allures only as implying a removal from the other, for though we sometimes stand so circumstanced as that we must either attain the one, or incur the other, according as we exert ourselves in some thing, or let it alone, yet this is not always the case; for persons already in good credit will bestir themselves strongly to increase it, where there is no danger of censure falling upon them if they were to forbear their endeavours. But I shall have occasion to consider this principle more particularly, when I come to my four classes of motives, of which I have made Honour to be one.

9. But of all the passions, there is none more difficult to be accounted for than grief, which keeps the mind intent upon a troublesome idea, that one would think she should endeavour most strenuously to throw off. It seems to contradict the constant experience of satisfaction being the point the mind every moment pursues, when we find her strangely courting uneasiness, and dwelling upon an object that affords her nothing but torment. I conceive the mind led originally into this absurd procedure by the same view that draws her into that situation we have termed want: for as we have observed under that article, the
holding

holding an evil in our thoughts is one step towards removing it, because they may suggest expedients which did not presently occur, and because the strength of an idea, heightened by our attention to it, urges us to a stronger exertion of our powers. Therefore you find it commonly used as an argument to dissuade men from sorrow. That it can do no good, and that the mischief is irremediable: which shows the general opinion, that when men afflict themselves, they do it under a delusive persuasion of receiving benefit thereby, and that if we can get them out of this notion, they will rest contented. On the other hand, we endeavour to encrease their vexation at evils brought upon them by their own misconduct, because there it may do service by witholding them from committing the like for the future. And our aptness to vex ourselves encreases not a little by our intercourse with mankind: for complaint procuring us the comfort and assistance of others, and our complaints rising in proportion to the pressure we feel, we get a habit of adding to that pressure, in order to obtain the surer and readier relief. For which reason children grow more fretful for being humoured, their fretfulness having proved a means of getting their desires gratified. Thus the mind having found the contemplation of evil, and the encreasing

creasing her sensibility of its pressure, expedient, desire, as is usual in the like cases, becomes translated to the means, and her view terminates upon afflicting herself as much as possible, without prospect of any further end to be attained thereby. When she has often turned the spirits into this train, they will take it afterwards mechanically: for I can admit the doctrine of Hartley's German friend, Stahl, with respect to the mental organs, that motions in them which were voluntary at first, may grow to be automatic; and when this is the case, they will pour in one set of ideas forcibly, to the exclusion of all others. Therefore you see people under great affliction tasteless of enjoyments they were fond of before, incapable of business, and unable to think of any thing but the subject of their grievance: nor can you extricate them from their distress, until by some amusement, or engagement, or danger, or pain, you can turn their spirits into another channel. Nor can it be doubted that there is an earnestness of want in all heavy sorrow, a want to get rid of the uneasiness, how improper means soever may be employed for that purpose, a want to undo what has been done, and to alter past events, which being palpably impossible, the mind works without any subject to work upon, and worries herself with empty strugglings: but if any thing flatters with the promise of a momentary relief, we see how strongly she exerts herself, as in cryings, exclamations, stampings, tearing the hair, and beating the breast, which draw off her attention elsewhere for awhile, and thereby suspend her uneasiness.

10. Though we always find Love and Hatred upon the list, I take them to be not so much passions in themselves, as the aptness of certain objects to excite passions in us: for a man may be said to love what he has not in his thoughts, if we conceive him generally looking upon it with complacence, but he cannot be said to hope, or fear, or rejoice in a thing, whereof there is no idea present before him. Besides, the beloved object may give occasion to opposite and incompatible passions, without making an alteration in our love: which shows it to be something distinct from them, since it can subsist entire under all their various forms without losing its essence. Therefore I apprehend love to be a disposition of mind to receive pleasure from certain things, which disposition nature never gave us, but we acquire it by experience of what has been used to please us: and the idea of this effect being associated with that of the things themselves, the bare contemplation of them affords us delight. But as our pleasures

CHAP. 21.] *Passions.* 115

sures are of very various kinds, so are the affections they generate: for the love of eating, of hunting, of money, of power, of reputation, of virtue, of a mistress, a friend, a child, or a wife, though all called by one common name of love, yet operate differently, and form dispositions spreading into very different branches, how much soever the roots may be similar. I shall not stay to examine all the several kinds of love the human breast is capable of, but confine myself to those which fasten upon our own species.

Under the helpless condition wherein we are born, we stand indebted to the care of others for the continual supply of our wants, and the satisfaction received in such supply, communicates a portion of itself to our idea of the person administering it; therefore a child's first love is its nurse. But this love is of an imperfect nature, being the same in kind with that we entertain for things inanimate, which we consider only as instruments of our pleasure: for though the child will cry if you turn nurse out of the room, it feels the same emotion if you take away its rattle. But after having a little enlarged our acquaintance, and found that every body will not, like nurse, give us the same assiduous tendance upon all occasions, but are more or less willing to oblige us, according as they are at ease in
them-

themselves, or as we can oblige them, then are we ready to do and wish them pleasure, that they may be the more ready to humour us. Yet this is not perfect love, which will suffer no advantage of our own to stand immediately in view. In further process of time, if we find our enjoyments arising chiefly from the conversation or intercourse of one, or a few persons, we practise the like method of engaging them to serve us so frequently, until this end slips out of view, and satisfaction, as we have before remarked in cases of translation, adheres immediately to the thought of doing them kindness. Then it is that love becomes personal, and then arrives at its highest state of refinement, wherein it may be defined the pleasure of pleasing: for I cannot conceive a purer love than that which makes us feel a sensible delight in gratifying another, and in every thing that happens conducive to his gratification, without thought of any other benefit redounding therefrom to ouselves, except that very delight. And this delight is of two sorts, which may be distinguished into Love and Fondness; the latter tends barely to gratify, the other to gratify without doing a disservice, and even to forbear a present compliance for the sake of a real advantage.

Thus the most resplendent love springs originally

CHAP. 21.] *Passions.* 117

ginally from our concern for ourselves, and our own desires, like a rose growing from a dunghill: wherefore Cupid, that is, Desire, was supposed the god of love, and nothing nourishes it so much as reciprocal kindness, and a return of good offices, or rather a ready compliance with our humours; for we are more inclined to love those who humour us, than those who do us good. But as flowers retain no scent of the dirty ground from whence they sprung, so genuine love, although encreased by acts of kindness, carries always a retrospect to those that are past, and does not look forward in expectance of having them continued. But though the natural progress of love be through expedience, yet our converse in society generally shortens the way, for seeing other people love upon receiving good offices, we catch the like disposition by sympathy from them, without needing to travel the usual road. For sympathy takes a nearer compass to arrive at its end than translation, and we sometimes contract a liking to things or persons merely upon finding others fond of them, with no other inducement than the force of example. For the same reason romances tend greatly to infuſe that whining love wherewith they abound, by keeping the mind continually conversant in imagination

among

among persons who talk and act with an amorous extravagance.

11. The strongest connections of love are reckoned to be those of friendship, of the sexes, and of parents towards their children. Friendship we know proceeds from long intimacy, mutual interests, and similitude of temper, which lead friends into the same courses of action, and methods of diversion, whereby they continually assist in promoting their common schemes, and enhancing their common pleasures, until each other's company becomes almost necessary. Nor is it hard to guess at the source of that propensity between the sexes, which has been always assigned as the peculiar province for Cupid to reign in, for he does not pretend to interfere in the affairs of friendship, or parental fondness. The love lighted by this desire too commonly burns with the grossest flame, and is rather of the instrumental kind than the personal; men looking upon the beloved object as a means of gratifying their pleasures, rather than as amiable in itself. Such love, when desire happens to abate, changes instantly into aversion, as was the case of Amnon with respect to Tamar: and these accidents happening oftener than were to be wished, gave occasion to that severe remark of

of the poet, Two things in marriage happy are allow'd, A wife in wedding sheets and in a shroud. And though there may be for the present a desire of pleasing, this is only a borrowed, not a translated satisfaction, which we have observed in a former chapter, rests for a while upon means apprehended necessary for a further end we have in view. Nor perhaps is there the true pleasure of pleasing until by cohabitation, by communication of interests, and partnership in amusements of all kinds, by those graceful acts, as Milton calls them, those thousand decencies that daily flow from all her words and actions, mixt with love and sweet compliance, which declare unfeigned union of mind, we have joined a thorough friendship to love : or at least, unless the prospect of such intercourse occupy the imagination as much as any other idea. If any one would know whether he possesses the genuine pleasure of pleasing, let him consider whether he could at any time forego his dearest pleasures, when he perceives them hurtful, or unseasonable, or disgustful to the party beloved: for if he could not, his passion is to please himself and not another. Love has been usually esteemed productive of our greatest pleasures, and our greatest pains, and which sort of fruits it shall bring forth depends greatly upon the object of our choice :

choice: if the disposition and qualities of that be such as may add friendship to love, we shall reap a plentiful crop of enjoyment; if the contrary, it will yield continual vexation and disappointment; if neither, our life will become insipid and tedious.

Parental affection has been currently ascribed to instinct, and is the only species of it that I remember ever supposed belonging to mankind: but if there were a sense of instinct infused by nature, nobody need remain in doubt concerning the genuineness of their offspring. Husbands would have a sure and ready test to try the fidelity of their wives, for they need only set their children in a circle before them, and by looking round upon each, considering how powerfully instinct operates, they would feel an emotion by which they might easily distinguish their own from those of the gallant: but I never heard of a discovery made this way, therefore we must seek for some other origin of this supposed instinct. I shall not trouble myself to examine how it might arise in a state of nature, though I think it might be accounted for there, without having recourse to a secret impulse: but as we live in society, we see the care of parents so universal, that we derive the like quality by sympathy from others; the notion of children being our own flesh

flesh and blood throws a part of our self-love upon them; we have in view upon our entering into wedlock, the prospect of amusements and comforts expected from them; and receive congratulations from every quarter upon their birth. All these causes make us look upon them as a valuable possession, and begin our concern for them: therefore fathers who bring children into the world clandestinely and unlawfully, wanting these sources, feel less tenderness for them, and many times none at all. The regard we thus entertain at first for our children, urges us continually to provide for their welfare and gratification, and every exercise of our cares encreases our affection: therefore we see people more afflicted for the loss of a child when grown up, than of a new-born babe. For continual tendance alone, from whatever inducement first undertaken, suffices to create a habit of loving. How often do nurses, though hired to the task, show as evident signs of instinct towards their charge as the parents themselves? and how many women feel a kind of parental fondness for the birds, the puppies, and the kittens, they have bred up.

12. It has been noted before, that anger sometimes vents itself upon inanimate beings, and imagination on other occasions personifies them, prompting us to behave towards them

them as though they were capable of receiving benefit or damage, pleasure or pain. We retain a kind of personal love for the towns, the countries, the places which have been the scenes of our enjoyment, after having been long removed from them, and never likely to see them again: we still wish them well, rejoice to hear of their flourishing, and if any calamity befals them, express our sorrow by tender exclamations, in the manner we should do upon losing a friend.

Love, peculiarly so called, must always center in a single object, because that thorough co-incidence of interests, and participation of pleasures, necessary to render it perfect, cannot obtain between more than two persons. Friendship may take in a little larger compass, but can extend only to a few chosen objects: the friendships recorded in history, have always run in pairs, as between Theseus and Perithous, Orestes and Pylades, Scipio and Lelius, Cicero and Atticus. Yet I do not see why there may not be a sincere and hearty love, ardent enough to be reckoned a passion, between more than one friend, as well as a parental fondness for several children, which we know is often the case, and I can confirm upon my own experience: for I have more than one, and had I twenty, if I know my own heart, I could never see any signal good

or

or evil befal any of them without feeling a strong emotion of soul. But love in a gentler degree may diffuse itself to multitudes, to the whole human species, to every thing capable of being the better for it. A good natured man can relish the pleasure of pleasing; whatever subject shall afford him an opportunity of enjoying it, he will be ready to oblige upon every occasion; he rejoices in the enjoyments of others, and makes their successes become his own: but this pleasure does not rise to a passion, so as to render him uneasy whenever the means of gratifying it are wanting.

13. Hatred derives in like manner from the contrary sources to those of love, being produced by some hurt or displeasure received, or the apprehension of an aptness in certain objects to bring them upon us. It may be catched by sympathy, as well as infused by translation, for we are often drawn to detest merely by the strong expressions of abhorrence we see in those we converse with. I cannot subscribe to the notion that men are born enemies to one another, or that nature has given us any constitutional aversions; for I apprehend we are born with a total indifference to all things, until experience teaches us to make a difference between one thing and another, upon seeing the manner in which they

they affect us. Sometimes hatred becomes personal, and then may be styled the pleasure of displeasing: under this disposition men desire and wish hurt to their enemy as an ultimate end, without any prospect of benefit, or effecting a security from danger to themselves. Generally, when people have taken a violent distaste to one or two persons, they behave with more than ordinary civility to the rest of the world : but there are those in whom the pleasure of displeasing extends to all mankind, they take delight in crossing and vexing, and rejoice at the sight of mischief or disappointment, on what quarter soever it shall appear. On the contrary, there are other tempers to whom nothing is so hateful as hatred itself, therefore they never give it admittance, or at least do not suffer it to become personal: and though the sight of detestable qualities has an aptitude to transfer an odium upon the possessor, yet they find means to separate the offender from the offence, and can do him all kind of good offices consistent with the general good, or a necessary regard to their own lawful interests. We have shown before in the proper place, how translation arises from the narrowness of our imagination, which when any purpose requires a number of steps to compleat it, cannot retain the whole line in view, and as it

loses

loses sight of the further parts, desire rests upon those remaining: therefore the proneness to animosities argues a narrow mind, which having found the doing hurt to others sometimes expedient, forgets that expedience, and confines its views to the means which that had rendered desirable. But whoever possesses a large and open understanding, if the giving displeasure appears at any time necessary, will hold that necessity in view, which draws his aversion aside from the person, and carries it forward to those mischiefs which cannot be prevented, without giving such displeasure.

14. Despair, envy, jealousy, contempt, vexation, peevishness, astonishment, and the like, are not distinct passions, but branches or mixtures of those already described, and therefore need no further notice. But there is one situation of mind, causing great emotions both in her and the body, that deserves particular consideration, as having been of late much recommended for uses whereto it seems not properly applicable: which is, that species of joy, called Mirth, expressing itself frequently in laughter. This has been commonly held by our moderns to arise from contempt, upon a comparison of ourselves with something apprehended greatly our inferior. I shall not urge that we make ourselves merry
with

with compositions of mere matter, which cannot come into competition with any supposed excellences of our own; because I know very well, and have observed just now, that imagination often personifies things inanimate, conceiving them at first glance as possessing the qualities and sentiments of men, or as representations of the human affections, or as evidences of blunders in the contrivers of them. But if we consult experience for instances of contempt and laughter, we shall find either of them often appearing without the other. If a man, going to take up something shining upon the ground, discovers it to be a pin, if upon being offered a bribe he rejects it with scorn, if he sees a child endeavour to stop his passage, will he burst into laughter upon the occasion? Contempt and scorn are gloomy situations of mind, and the proud who deal most largely in them are the most solemn and statliest of mortals: besides that a despicable object contemplated ever so long will appear equally so, but a diverting one cannot keep up your merriment for ever. On the other hand, your merry giggling people love best to consort among their equals, to put themselves upon a par with the company, and are less supercilious or disposed to draw comparisons between themselves and others. The sudden appearance of an intimate friend

spreads

spreads a smile over the countenance; the sight of an exquisite dainty, the unexpected offer of an advantageous scheme, sets the voluptuous, the covetous, and the ambitious a chuckling, and would produce a downright laughter, if men had not been habituated to restrain themselves by the rules of decorum: but the situation of mind they then stand in seems the farthest imaginable from a state of contempt. Success of all kinds, if it does not immediately shake the sides, yet renders us more susceptible of mirth upon any little trifling occasion happening to excite it. Who are so easily set a laughing as young children? but what idea of superiority can they be supposed to have? They laugh before they are capable of casting back a reflection upon their own qualifications, much less of comparing them with those of other people. They laugh upon the sight of nurse, or mamma: begin, little child, says Virgil, to show you know your mamma by your smiles: but if they make any comparisons, they must consider nurse and mamma as their superiors and governors. That exultation the mind feels upon an opinion of superiority is a very translated satisfaction derived through many stages: she must have learned the tendency of things to gratify her desires, the propensity of other people to get them away for ministering to their

their own, the contest ensuing upon such occasions, the advantage of greater powers towards obtaining victory, and the reflection of possessing such advantages as of an immediate good; by all which gradations satisfaction must have been transferred to the thought of superiority; a process too long to be gone through in the first stages of life, wherein the proneness to laughter appears evident.

15. Mirth I conceive occasioned by a sudden influx of spirits generally, if not always, turned from some other channel, to which they have been drawn by an earnest attention: and therefore perhaps it is that to make merry is called to divert, as being a diversion of the spirits out of the course they have been strongly thrown into before. For that attention gathers a considerable fund of them appears manifest, from the fatigue and wasting it brings on if continued long, and when some pleasurable idea opens the fluices at once, it lets in so large a flood that reflection cannot employ them at all, having no other business for them than to contemplate that idea, and the superfluity overflows upon the muscles causing the convulsions of laughter. Thus there seems to be three causes concurring to excite laughter when not produced mechanically, as by tickling, by fits of hysterics, or the like: viz. a stretch of attention
loosened

loosened at once, the suddenness of such relaxation, and want of employment for the spirits so discharged upon the mind. Wit consists in allusion, and is commonly said to carry two faces; that on the grave side engages your attention, which upon turning the other instantly lets go its hold: the most diverting humour is that which raises your expectation of something very serious, and then upon breaking the jest cuts it short with an issue very different from what you expected. Nor yet is it always necessary there should be a long preparation to introduce a joke, imagination being extremely agile and quick in her motions, can fix a strong attention upon one object, and turn it off upon another in a moment: therefore a short expression, a single gesture, an arch look, a comical figure, will suffice to create mirth. We learn from Mr. Locke that wit lies in putting ideas together, wherein can be found any resemblance or congruity; to which I may add by way of comment, that the resemblance must be pointed out between things usually esteemed the most discordant, and which contemplated separately would lead the mind into the most opposite trains of thinking: for the quick transition of thought or fluctuation between such distant ideas is what causes your merriment. And the like changeable situation of mind occasions our laughter at the follies and blunders we see committed: for every blunder implies a deliberate endeavour to attain some purpose by means not conducive thereto, and the sight or thought of earnestness and expectation, in the persons so labouring, fills our own imagination by sympathy with the like ideas, which are immediately dissipated upon the reflection of their being ineffectual and nugatory. But I have said the relaxation must be sudden, and employment wanting for the spirits let loose thereby: therefore if the relator of a merry story manages so ill that you see beforehand how it will end, you lose half your pleasure. For the same reason, a story often repeated becomes insipid, and a jest may be worn threadbare: because when you know what is coming, attention cannot run into another channel from whence it might be suddenly diverted. Nor will all kinds of joyful ideas, how unexpected soever, provoke us to laughter: the news of an estate or some extraordinary success befalling us, leads in a train of advantages and pleasures attendant thereupon, which fill imagination with a variety of ideas, and find abundant employment for thought, so there is no redundancy of spirits to run over upon the risible nerves: but a jest presents one pleasurable idea without further consequences, which

which occupies the mind alone, and requires no pains to retain it, or keep out other ideas, but leaves the spirits at liberty to rush into whatever quarter their own impulse shall carry them.

16. If laughter sometimes accompanies a thought of superiority, it is owing to that vanity which too often teaches men a habit of exulting at the sight of folly or infirmity; for the vain having an immoderate fondness for pre-eminence, without either abilities or application to raise themselves above the common level, feel a sudden joy on beholding anything below it. And this aptness to mirth upon such occasions, whatever they may think of it, redounds very little to their honour, as implying a secret consciousness of wanting merit in themselves; for it shews that instances of their superiority come seldom and unexpected, carrying something of novelty and surprise, without which they could not instigate to laughter. A good natured man can smile at indiscretions, without casting back reflections upon himself; and whenever such reflection does occur, I believe it is most commonly an after thought, not so often the cause of mirth, as the consequence: vanity running on to a comparison of our own supposed perfections, which must rather abate the emotion than increase it, by

finding

finding other employ for the spirits: and we find, in fact, that it does make such abatement; every one sees the difference between a hearty laugh of real joy, and a scornful sneer, or a grin, expressing a claim to superiority; the laugh of contempt is a forced laugh, shewing signs of gladness in the countenance, but not making the heart merry, and encouraged not so much to please ourselves, as to vex another.

Contempt being so apt to show itself in derision, hence the making a thing appear despicable and silly, has been called rendering it ridiculous. But ridiculous, although derived from the latin word standing for laughter, does not always imply a quality of exciting even that affected laugh which is the expression of contempt: you shall see men with a very grave countenance go about to demonstrate the ridiculousness of a thing without ever raising mirth in themselves, or expecting to raise it in others: therefore ridiculous is not synonymous with comical or diverting, but rather coincides with absurd or foolish, and tends more to provoke your spleen than your laughter.

17. Upon this view of the nature and essence of wit and ridicule, it seems surprizing to hear them recommended as methods proper for the discovery of truth, and offered

as

as the surest test and touchstone to try the soundness of an opinion: for they tend to alarm the passions, they fill the mind with one single idea, barring her attention against all others, and produce their effects by their manner of placing objects, one setting them in a diverting, and the other in an offensive light. Whereas reason requires a calm and dispassionate situation of mind to form her judgments aright, she wants the whole attention to look round upon every circumstance, and places her objects in all the lights wherein they are capable of standing. But the most surprising thing, is to find the greatest stress laid upon jest and derision by those who make the loudest pretences to freedom of thought: for liberty consists in a thorough exemption from all influence and constraint whatsoever, which may as well be thrown upon us by the allurements of wit and stings of ridicule, as by any other impulse: for they cast a prejudice upon the mind, that cramps and confines it within the narrow point of view they hold their objects in; and he that lies liable to be laughed out of his sentiments, is no more master of his thoughts, than if he were driven by the force of authority or example.

It has been alledged in support of these methods of arguing, that disputants of all
kinds

kinds are observed to employ them, if they have talents that way, and fit opportunities offer for exerting them. But I desire it may be remembered, there are two sorts of argumentation, one by way of rhetoric, and the other by that of logic: the former addresses the imagination, aims at working a persuasion there, and endeavours to interest the passions: the latter appeals directly to the understanding, proposes only conviction, and rejects all kinds of artifice. Therefore, when we have fully satisfied ourselves of any matter upon a full and fair examination, and are only to persuade others who will not hear reason, being hindered by some prejudice or passion, it is allowable to use any contrivances likely to remove those obstacles: but when the business is to inquire into some doubtful point, and such are all to be esteemed during a debate with any sincere and judicious antagonist, none of the arts of persuasion ought to find admittance. I can allow jest and taunt to be useful engines of oratory, but can by no means think them proper instruments for reason to work with: nor do we ever find them employed in the sciences, where understanding alone is concerned. Where is there purer, closer, or clearer reasoning than in the mathematics? but what room do they afford for merriment? Who ever demonstrated a problem

blem in Euclid by ridicule? or where will you find a joke in Sir Isaac Newton's principia? The five mechanical powers, the properties of fluids, the courses of the planets, were not discovered nor explained by sallies of humour and raillery: and though the cycles and epicycles of the ancients are now become ridiculous by being grown out of fashion, they were first overthrown by serious argumentation from the phenomena of nature. Divination, astrology, magic, and the philosopher's stone, afford an ample field for humour and raillery, yet I believe no man who held them upon principle, was ever beat out of his notions by those weapons, without some solid argument convincing to his understanding.

18. Violence and turbulence constitute the essence of passion: the same emotions of soul, when too gentle to deserve that name, are styled Affections. It is not easy to ascertain the precise limits between passion and affection, the difference lying only in degree, nor indeed are they always accurately distinguished, either in discourse or writing; but, strictly speaking, passion is that which causes perturbation and disorder of spirits, throwing its own set of ideas forcibly upon the mind, and not leaving her master of her own motions; a situation very dangerous, as laying us open

to

to every mischief, while the exercise of understanding, by which alone we might help ourselves, remains suspended. Therefore, passion may be styled the fever of the mind, which disturbs and weakens, and cannot continue long, or return often, without pernicious consequences: but affection, like the steady beating of the pulse, actuates and invigorates, and keeps the mind continually alive. For we are every moment, while awake, pursuing or avoiding something or other; and indeed it is necessary we should be so, for were it possible to remain totally unaffected and unconcerned with any thing, there would be no business for volition to do, but we must lie like logs, to receive whatever chance should throw upon us. It is our affections that lay the foundation of prudence, by prompting us to look forward to the future, that multiply our enjoyments beyond those of sensation or appetite, and find work for understanding by suggesting objects to contrive and provide for. Nor are any of them unserviceable, if properly directed, and kept within due moderation: chearfulness preserves health, and renders the common scenes of life pleasurable: hope was esteemed of old, as we learn from the fable of Pandora's box, a salve to assuage the smart of all evils, and supplies the place of enjoyments when we have none actually in

our

our power: caution helps to preserve the good things we have, and secure us against dangers: sensibility of the difference between good and bad usage urges us to apply the proper means for preventing injuries: decency keeps the world in order, nor could society or good manners subsist without it: reflection on cross accidents teaches us to provide against the like for the future: good nature and obligingness double our pleasures by making those of other people our own, and are the channels through which the benefits of society are chiefly conveyed: dislike to things or persons obnoxious secures us against catching contagion, or receiving mischief from them: desire, if not boisterous, furnishes us with constant employment, and gives a glee to every thing we undertake: and want, not rising to impatience, spurs us up to industry and vigilance, and holds us steady in pursuit of useful aims not presently attainable.

19. I said at the end of the last chapter, that the passions were only a stronger sort of habits acquired early in our childhood: from whence of course it follows, that habits must be feebler passions learned later, when the organs being grown tough, become less susceptible of new forms, but having once taken them, are less easy to be thrown out
of

of them again. The force of passion seems to proceed from the wideness of the channels, and that vigorous pulsation wherewith they drive on the spirits contained in them: that of habit from the stiffness of their coats which will not readily close, so as to turn the spirits from their accustomed track. Therefore passion does its work by vehemence and impetuosity, bearing down all opposition; it can only be mastered by a strong resolution, and that not without difficulty; but if you can stop the torrent it leaves you quiet. But habit prevails by perseverance and importunity, it does not bear you down by force, but steals upon you imperceptibly, or teazes and tires you into a compliance; it is easily restrained at any time with a little attention, but the moment you take off your eye it recoils again, and when grown inveterate, is extremely difficult to be totally eradicated. Our little motives are mostly introduced and the manner of our proceeding shaped by habit: it is that gives us dexterity and readiness in every thing we do, and renders our thoughts and motions easy. We see how awkward and troublesome it is to consort with company, or pursue a method of conduct, or perform any work very different from what we have been used to. The tenor of our lives, and success of our endeavours, depends more upon habit than

than judgment: for what avails the knowing what is proper to be done, without an expertness and readiness to compass it? wherefore we cannot employ our understanding better than by enuring ourselves to such ways and practices as may prove beneficial, and carefully guarding against any others encroaching upon us: for if understanding can gain over habit to her service, it will do her work more compleatly, and effectually, and pleasantly than she could herself. Passion grows feeble with age, but habit gathers strength: old people can relinquish any fancy that comes into their heads, without much trouble, but none are harder to be put out of their ways; and in those few desires they have remaining, they show less of the eagerness of passion than the stubborness of habit. But we take notice of their attachments to money, to command, and some other objects, and style them passions because they are few, and engross their whole attention for want of a competitor, not because of any violence, or impetuosity we discern in them. But as passion, affection, and habit, must have some matter to work upon, and the subjects giving rise to them, or recommended by them to our pursuit are infinitely various, it would be endless and perplexing to particularize them all: therefore I shall attempt to reduce them

under

under a few general heads, and can think of none more proper than those four classes into which I had before proposed to distinguish our motives of action.

CHAP. XXII.

PLEASURE.

To Pleasure I might have joined Pain or Trouble, in the title of this chapter, but they being each of them respectively a species of satisfaction or uneasiness, may be treated of in the same manner, that is, both under the former. For as the one by repelling actuates us to almost the same motions as the other by attracting, what I shall observe concerning pleasure will serve equally for its reverse, unless where some particular occasion may require them to be considered distinctly.

Pleasure, like other satisfactions, when taken as a motive, must not be understood of the actual possession, but the prospect or idea of it: for motives do not prompt us to what we have already, which were needless, but to attain something we have not, or to preserve the continuance of something that would

would otherwise slip away from us. Yet as that idea rises from experience of the manner wherein things have affected us, we can only get acquainted with this species of motives by examining from what sources we derive our pleasures.

Nature gives us at first none other pleasures besides those of sensation and appetite, among which may be reckoned that soothing feel accompanying the free circulation of our blood and humours when in health and vigour, or the easy flow of spirits along the mental organs, when in contemplation or pursuit of any thing engaging our attention: and in these internal sensations perhaps may consist all the pleasures of imagination and reflection which we feel in seasons of joy, or hope, or desire, or other agreeable situations of mind. But however this be, certain it is that in process of time, when reflection has learnt its play, it supplies us with a considerable fund of entertainment: the pleasures of reading, of meditation, of conversation, of diversions, of advancement in knowledge, honour, or fortune, belong to the reflection rather than the senses, therefore are styled mental, as the others are bodily pleasures. And the former furnish much the greater share of our enjoyments in our riper years: for if any man will reflect on a day agreeably spent, he will find much less of it taken up in mere sensation than in some pursuit or variety of amusement that engaged his attention. Thus our pleasures, how much soever afterwards multiplied, take their rise from sensation alone, all others being derivative or translated from that original. To instance only in acquisitions of knowledge, which is commonly held sweet to the mind by the very frame of her constitution: but if it were so, every accession of knowledge would engage everybody alike, whereas in fact we find the contrary. What would the mathematician give to know the newest fashions as they start into vogue, or be let into all the scandal and tittle tattle of the town? Or what cares the beau for discoveries in astronomy, or explanations of attraction, repulsion, or other secrets of nature? Though we all have our curiosity to a considerable degree, yet it leads us by various tracts to objects that we have found contributing most to our entertainment: not that we have always any thing further in view than to gratify our present curiosity, but it is the usual course of translation to confer a quality of pleasing upon whatever has often administered to our other gratifications. The most refined pleasures are those that have passed through the greatest number of translations, and therefore stand furthest removed

from

from sense: but before we depend upon them for our enjoyments, we ought to be well assured of our having a real relish for them; for men often deceive themselves in this point, affecting a fondness for refinements they have not; from a secret motive of vanity which induces them to believe themselves possessed of any thing they think will give them credit and reputation.

2. Our pleasures, as well those of the gross as the refined kind, depend upon the constitution and disposition of our machine; some can bear hot weather best, others cold; health and sickness, vigour and weariness, render the same sensations and exercises delightful or irksome. In like manner the gust of mental amusements varies according to the cast our imagination has been thrown into by education, or custom, or habit, according to the humour we happen to be in, to various accidents or circumstances befalling us, or to the satiety or novelty we find in them.

This variety of disposition in mankind to receive pleasure from different objects is called Taste, because like the palate it enables us to distinguish the relish of things, and to discern which of them are savory, insipid, or disgustful. Taste is usually confounded with judgment, of which it is rather the basis than the thing itself: for taste properly denotes

denotes a sensibility of delight in certain objects, and therefore having experienced what has pleased us, we learn to judge what will please others or ourselves another time. Nature may have laid the foundation of taste, but the superstructure is raised by instruction, or conversation, or observation; for we never find it in children, and very rarely among persons confined to the common laborious occupations of life. Not but that all men have their sources of amusement, and therefore in this sense your mechanics and ploughmen may be said to have a taste for bull-baiting foot-ball, the finery of a Lord Mayor's show or diversions of a country fair: but taste is most usually applied to those relishes given by the perfection of art, or good company, or an uncommon sensibility of imagination. Yet we sometimes take it in a larger sense, as when we distinguish between a gross and a refined, a vulgar and an elegant, a false, and a true taste: the latter being such as enables us to receive more exquisite, or more durable pleasures from things, or in greater variety, or as Horace calls it, more sincere, that is, unalloyed with any disagreeable mixture. But there may be an over squeamishness and nicety of taste, which renders the imagination too delicate, and liable to disgust from the common objects continually surrounding it, it, like a very tender skin, that cannot bear the least drop of rain, or breath of air, without suffering, and is rather to be esteemed a weakness than a perfection. Therefore goodness of taste seems to be relative, that which is suitable to one man being not so to another: what good would a fine taste for opera music do him who could not afford to go to it? or of what service would a taste for poetry, rhetoric, or elegance, be to a missionary, who must spend his time among savages? I conceive the best, if not the truest taste, is that which gives a man the strongest and fullest relish of objects and employments lying within his power and suited to his situation and circumstances in life. But if one could cast imagination into any mould one pleases with a wish, I would make the same distinction here as I have done before between desire and want, and would wish to have a taste for the finest productions of art, without any distate of those that fall greatly inferior: for by this means I should have a chance of being sometimes exquisitely pleased, but run no hazard of being ever disgusted.

3. What is called genius I imagine proceeds chiefly from the turn imagination has taken early in our youth: we do not discern when

it begins, and therefore ascribe it to nature; but though nature may have given each of us quicker and stronger, or duller and weaker parts, or made some of our organs more lithesome and sensible than others, yet their aptness to run into this or that particular course of exercise depends upon some accident or lucky hit, or the company we converse with. Mr. Waller supposes, that Great Julius, in the mountains bred, Perhaps some flock or herd had led: The world's sole ruler then had been, But the best wrestler on the green. 'Tis art and knowledge which draw forth The hidden seeds of native worth. A book falling into a boy's hands, an adventure related, or performance he sees, that happens to strike his fancy, the conversation of a servant, or a companion, may lead his imagination into particular trains of thinking, which thenceforward become easy to him, and he cannot strike into others of a different kind without trouble and uneasiness. If example had not at least as great a share as nature in the formation of genius, why should we see different ages and countries produce their several sorts of it peculiar to themselves? and why should men ingenious in any particular way generally arise together in clusters? for we cannot suppose the time when, or place where

where they are born should make such a difference in their constitutions.

4. Beauty is a species of taste: it may be defined an aptness of things to please immediately upon sight; for if they please from a view of something else introduced by them, they are not beautiful, but useful or valuable. But this aptness to please is a relative term, not solely a quality residing in objects, but depending equally upon the cast of our imagination: as the aptness of a shoe depends no less upon the shape of your foot than upon its own make, for that which sits perfectly easy upon one man may pinch another, or may become uneasy by your foot being swoln. We find the taste of beauty infinitely various and variable, the same thing appearing charming to one person, indifferent to another, and disgustful to a third; admired or neglected in the several stages of our lives; courted or nauseated at different seasons, according to the diposition of body, or humour of mind we happen to be in. Therefore nothing is beautiful in itself; those things bid fairest for the title that are adapted to please the generality of mankind: for as the features of all men have a resemblance in some respects, how much soever they may vary in others, so it is with the trains of our imagination. Our frame, our constitution, as well internal as external,

external, our employments in life, our wants, our enjoyments, are in a great measure the same, and our daily intercourse with one another increases the similitude: therefore it is no wonder that some objects are generally beheld in the same light, and appear agreeable to every one. Hence it is we can pass a judgment on beauty even when not affected by it; for having observed what usually pleases, we get a standard wherewith to compare any object we behold, and if it agrees with that we pronounce it beautiful, though through some particularity of our own it does not hit our fancy.

One cannot easily discover that little children have any notion of beauty at all: they will turn away from the sight of a celebrated toast, with all her tackle trim and bravery on, to hide their faces in the flabby bosom of an old wrinkled nurse: nor do they feel any thing of those charms which, as Horace expresses it, inspire desires, and steal a man away from himself. We find the first notions they get of prettiness very different from those of their maturer years. Gewgaws, tinsel, high colouring coarsely laid on, ill-shapen playthings, and figures carrying scarce a half resemblance of their originals, delight them. And though their fancy improves as they grow up, yet they scarce ever gain a relish

lish for the finest performances of art, or works of nature, until taught by care, or led into it by example.

5. Thus our sense of beauty was not born with us, but grows by time, and may be moulded into almost any shape by custom, conversation, or accident. There seem to be four principal sources from whence the efficacy of beauty derives; composition, succession, translation, and expression. The materials of a fine building do not entertain the eye until disposed in their proper places: and a parcel of colours unstriking of themselves may hit the fancy upon being curiously assorted and interspersed together. Symmetry, proportion and order, contribute greatly to the good look of things: but we have already shown, in CHAP. X. that they consist in the correspondence of objects with the trains of our imagination, and the mind must have learned to run the proper lines of separation before she can discern any thing of order or proportion. Order enables us to take in a larger view of the scene before us, presenting a more complex idea, consisting not only of the objects themselves, but of their situations, connections, and relations, with respect to one another. In deformed things there is commonly one or two remarkable parts at which the eye sticks. A lump of lead is neither hand-

handsome nor ugly, because as there is no composition, so neither is there a want of any, but may become either, according to the mould wherein it is formed; when cast into an ill shape, the continuity of parts leads the eye to expect a composition of which it is frustrated.

6. Succession is another spring of beauty, for as in some motions, as in riding, walking, bowling, and the like, which are pleasing at first, become indifferent, and then irksome by long exercise, so it is with our ideas of sensation and reflection, and in a much quicker transition; many that were striking at first, soon grow insipid, and afterwards troublesome; wherefore to prevent cloying, there must be a variety of objects succeeding each other to keep up the play. Order, symmetry, and proportion, furnish great store of variety, without multiplying the subjects whereon it is thrown: in the materials of a fine building, you see there is stone, there is mortar, there is timber, with a few other particulars, and that not without attention and labour; but when skilfully put together, they present a multitude of assemblages readily occurring to the reflection. In the scenes before us the notice, as has been formerly observed, changes continually to different sets of objects, or contemplates them in various lights,

lights, the reflections shifting while the sensations remain the same. Hence in a masterly performance, whether you consider the whole, or the principal members, or parts of those members, or move the eye from one to another, there is always something of composition or comparison presented, which perpetually supplies a fund of fresh entertainment. But mere novelty does not delight of itself, unless there be an aptness in the imagination to take impression of what it exhibits: for as a man would find it extremely uneasy to walk backwards, being an unusual motion, so the mind feels an awkwardness and irksomeness in receiving assemblages entirely different from any she has been accustomed to. A rustic, bred up among wilds and forests, being brought into a fine garden, would see more confusion than ornament there, and though you were to point out the disposition of the whole, and correspondence of the parts, you would not make him so sensible of them as to be affected therewith. Our pleasures are generally the greater for being preceded by pains, or set in comparison with them, and so are our lesser amusements of sight and imagination: therefore an agreeable object is rendered more so by having a foil, and a proper contrast of lights and shades embellishes a picture; for the notice passes to and fro
succes-

successively, between the opposite branches of the comparison.

7. A third source of beauty is translation: whatever has been the occasion of much or frequent delight becomes agreeable in our eye, satisfaction being transferred from the effects to the cause. A person that has delivered us out of some great distress, or helped us in a matter we had strongly at heart, or gratified our desires in many instances, appears the handsomer for it ever afterwards: while the sight of him only introduces a reflection of the good he has done us, there is no alteration in his features, but by degrees the intermediate links of the chain drop off, the pleasure at the end becomes immediately connected with the person, and then it is that his beauty begins; which is often so closely united with his appearance, that we shall like another person the better for resembling him. Thus though Cupid be usually styled the son of Venus, we may say there is another of the name, who is the son of Pleasure, and many times begets a little Venus; for the love we entertain for things upon account of the gratifications received from them, gives them charms in our eyes they had not before. Wherefore lovers think their mistresses, and parents their children, handsomer than others do, because having found continual entertainment

tainment in their company, they are accustomed to behold them with delight. So likewise women conceive an advantageous opinion of the favourite animals under their care, because the satisfaction and amusement they have found in a constant tendency upon them becomes transferred to the creatures themselves. And we see charms that other folks cannot discern, in a place where we have spent our time very agreeably, or found conveniences wanting elsewhere; whence the saying, that home is home be it never so homely.

8. The fourth and most plentiful source of beauty, is expression. The knowledge of this discloses the secret of that commanding majesty, that winning softness, and other graces of the countenance: for the face being a picture of the mind, whatever amiable qualities are discerned there, give a lustre to the features denoting them. Good nature, health, sprightliness, and sense, enable and dispose men to give pleasure to others, therefore the marks of them are pleasant to behold. The force of sympathy has a great influence here, for whatever bespeaks ease, satisfaction and enjoyment in the mind of the possessor, throws that of the beholder into the like agreeable situation: therefore in our description of beauty we commonly employ epithets

thets belonging to the sentiments, as a chearful, an innocent, a smart, an honest, or a sensible countenance. But the language of the eyes and face requires time to be perfectly understood: some turns of feature seem expressive at first, but are afterwards discovered to have no meaning; in others we find a significancy, upon better acquaintance, that did not show itself before. Therefore some beauties striking immediately upon sight, quickly fade away, and cloy; others make no strong impression, but steal upon the heart insensibly by imperceptible degrees. Beauty has the strongest influence upon those of the opposite sex: women are imperfect judges of one anothers persons, because they are not affected by them; they judge by rules, not by what they feel. Though there be one original cause of desire between the two sexes, many subordinate desires of conversation, or other intercourse, branch out from thence, which have not a visible connection with the principal root, and therefore may consist with the purest modesty: now an object expressing all the requisites for gratification, even of those lesser desires, without any obstruction, abatement, or disappointment, is alluring to the sight. And a long intercourse of endearments, and good offices of all kinds, may increase the expression so far as to render the party exhibiting it

the

the most agreeable object one can behold, styled in the language of mankind above two thousand years ago, by way of eminence, the desire of the eyes. Many works of art are esteemed pretty, merely from their expressing a likeness with the works of nature: in artificial figures of men, birds, beasts, insects, trees, or flowers, the eye expects no more than an exact resemblance of the things they represent: wherefore there may be a beautiful copy of an ugly original. The famous statue of Laocoon is admired, though Laocoon himself would be shocking to the beholder: we admit pictures of satyrs, witches, old men with hard rugged features and grisly beards, to hang as ornaments in our chambers, where the real originals would be deemed an eye sore.

9. Beauty of action and sentiment seem to derive wholly from translation, for the good nature, complacence, innocence, chearfulness, patience, and considerateness of others, so continually promote our advantage, ease, and enjoyment, in the commerce of life, that the pleasure felt in these effects is transferred to the qualities producing them, which thenceforward become engaging in themselves, so that we cannot help admiring them in persons at the greatest distance of place or time, from whom we can reap no possible benefit.
But

But that we cannot help being thus moved no more proves us born with such affection, than that you cannot help understanding a reproach cast upon you proves you were born with a knowledge of language. But it has been usual to style acquisitions natural that we were led into by custom and experience, without any care or instruction to convey them, for we are said to speak our mother tongue naturally: and in this construction only we may admit our sense of the amiableness of good qualities to be natural.

From all that has been said above, it appears how little foundation there is for Plato's notion of an essential beauty existing independently of any subject whereto it might belong, and as that was superadded to particular substances it rendered them beautiful. For not to insist upon the inconceivableness of a quality existing without any subject to possess it, or of there being beauty before there was any thing beautiful, we have found that objects, however qualified, please us or not, according to the disposition of our organs, translation, or resemblance casting a lustre upon what had it not before; and that the same thing appears agreeable, or indifferent, or loathsome in the eyes of different beholders: which, if it depended solely upon the qualities of the object, then the opposite qualities

of

of beauty and deformity must reside at once in the same subject.

10. Among our distastes, there is none so visibly dependent upon imagination as that of nastiness: a filthy word, a nauseous comparison, a mere fancy of having touched something loathsome, shall set our stomachs a kecking against the most innocent food. Nothing is nasty of itself, but things become so by being assorted together in unsuitable mixtures: he that should gnaw his glove, and paw the meat with his hands, would be cried out against as a nasty fellow, but if he apply both to their proper places, you have nothing to complain of him. Dirt in the fields, gravel upon the roads, and the carpets upon our floors are not nasty, but whoever should lie down upon either, would be blamed for daubing his cloaths. Nastiness seems to have no opposite, for cleanness is rather a negation of that than a contrary quality, and to make clean implies no more than to remove away filth, without substituting anything else in its room. We often use Neatness to express the middle point between beauty and deformity in objects, and Decency to denote the like in actions or sentiments: a neat little house, and a decent behaviour, is that wherein there is nothing either to engage or offend the eye. Yet these middle points

points incline a little to the favourable side, for there is a degree of complacence in seeing things clean and neat, and persons behave decently about us: but this complacence perhaps is of none other kind than that which frequently arises upon contemplating the absence of any thing that would disturb us.

11. Our tastes varying as much as our faces, make us very bad judges of one anothers enjoyments, for we take for granted that every body must be pleased with what we like ourselves, and according to the vulgar saying, measure other people's corn by our own bushel. Nor are there instances wanting wherein we measure our own corn by their bushel: when we see a crowd of people running to look at any sight, it raises our own curiosity to make one among them, and a dish, or diversion, we find others eagerly fond of, stirs up a longing to partake of the like: but upon trial, we often find our expectation disappointed, and that what may give another great delight, affords us no entertainment.

Nor do we judge much better of our own pleasures, for want of being well aware of their aptness to cloy upon repetition, and to change their relish perpetually according to our disposition of body or mind, or the circumstances

cumstances we happen to stand in: neither can we trust even experience itself in this case, for because a thing has pleased us once, we cannot always be sure it will do so again. The boy who wished to be a king that he might have an officer appointed to swing him all day long upon a gate, took his resolution upon the remembrance of what had given him pleasure; for we may suppose he had often found a supreme delight in that innocent amusement, but little thought that the same continued for hours together would prove extremely tedious and irksome. The like mistake prevails with many after their ceasing to be boys; they find a vast delight in diversions and fancies of several kinds, and therefore eagerly pursue them as inexhaustible sources of enjoyment; not considering that those things please only in the acquisition, or by their novelty, and lose all their poignancy upon growing familiar. Therefore it is one of the principal arts of life to find out such pleasures as are most durable, and least liable to change by an alteration of temper, or circumstances.

12. But if we make mistakes in estimating pleasures singly, we commit more in computing the value of a series of them taken collectively: for we cannot reckon them with the same exactness practicable in our money affairs,

affairs, nor can we tell how many little amusements are equivalent to a great one, as we can how many shillings go to a pound. He that keeps a regular account of his cash, may know to a shilling, what were his receipts, and what his disbursements, in any month of the last year, and how much they exceeded, or fell short of those in any other month; but I defy any man to make the like entry of his enjoyments and disquietudes: if he can tell that such a day was spent more agreeably than such another, it is more than he can always do with certainty, but he can never cast up the exact amount on the debtor and creditor side in any day, nor tell precisely the proportion one bears to the other.

Therefore we are forced to take our pleasures in the lump, and estimate them upon view; as a man who guesses at a flock of sheep by the ground they cover, without being able to count them, and who will do it very imperfectly, until he has gotten an expertness by long and careful practice. For absent enjoyments, whether past or future, being not actually existent, we cannot hold them as it were in our hand to weigh them, but must judge by the representative idea we have of them in our imagination; and we ordinarily determine their value by the degree of desire we feel in ourselves towards them. Besides, the

the mind being constantly attentive to the bettering her condition in the next succeeding moment, it is not, strictly speaking, distant enjoyment that ever moves her, any otherwise than by the desire it raises of advancing towards it, the gratification of which desire yields a present satisfaction.

13. For this reason, intense pleasures engage more with the generality of mankind, than a continuance of gentler amusements; for the latter weighing only by their number, cannot so easily be brought within the compass of a single idea, and when we endeavour to do so, we commonly fix upon one or two of them as a sample of the whole; as a man who would recommend a poem, a play, or any other entertainment, pitches upon a few striking parts for a specimen of the rest: whereas high delights, carrying their whole force in a single point, make a deep impression upon the mind, which excites a desire proportionable to the representative idea left behind. But frequently desire encreases, though the relish dies away upon repetition, hence your men of pleasure retain the former, after having utterly lost the latter, and perhaps receive none other satisfaction from their pleasures, than what arises from the gratification of their eagerness in the pursuit of them. This probably induced Sir John Suckling,

who was a man of pleasure, to say, It is expectation makes a blessing dear: and if he added, Heaven were not heaven if we knew what it were, we may presume it was because he had no idea of any other than the Mahometan heaven, which was not likely to prove one upon experience, how alluring soever it might appear in speculation.

But if we sit down to such careful computation as we are able to make of our enjoyments, we shall find ourselves much more beholden, upon the whole, to those of the gentler kind: for high delights, like high sauces, if they draw no mischiefs after them, at least pall the appetite for every thing else, or create a hankering after themselves at seasons wherein they are not to be had; thus making us pay dear enough for the transient gratification they afford. Yet pleasures of the tempting kind, if properly chosen, have their value, not so much for their intrinsic worth, as for the fruits they produce: for pleasing sensations or reflections rarely come upon us of their own accord, much the greater part of our enjoyment lies in the exercise of our activity, when engaged in some pursuit or employment; but there can be no engagement without an end, which we conceive it would give us a more than ordinary degree of complacence to attain. The

The pleasures commanded by riches, or those expected from eminence of station or accomplishment, spur men on to industry in their several callings and professions. The joy of seeing a piece of workmanship compleated, carries an artist through the toils and difficulties of his work. I find myself not a little encouraged in this my pursuit of the light of nature, by casting back a look now and then upon those rays of it already collected. Even virtue herself receives no small accession of vigour from the contemplation of such few of her beauties as we may have in our possession. Nor need I mention that seasonable recreation enlivens the spirits, gives briskness to the circulation, and renders the mind alert for any exercise: it often prolongs enjoyment beyond the present moment, by furnishing materials to think and talk of afterwards; so that a few days diversion in summer may supply a fund of entertainment for the succeeding winter. Let us not then think pleasures unworthy the attention of a philosopher, since in good hands they may be turned to excellent services.

14. As expectation makes a blessing dear, so by making dear it makes it valuable: the main of our enjoyment depends upon our desires, which take rise from experience of what has pleased us, whence we conceive an

expectation of its doing the like again. But desire generally produces a more plentiful crop than the parent plant from which it sprung, especially in our common diversions, which lie almost wholly in the pursuit, and very little in the attainment. He that at whist should have four honours, six trumps, always dealt him, would lose his whole diversion, because he would have nothing to do but throw down his cards and set up his score. So in bowling, the player minds to deliver his bowl aright, he runs after it, chides it, encourages it, writhes his body into all manner of contortions, as if to influence the bias, and herein consists his entertainment; for the joy of winning the game passes over in a moment, he takes his stake, pockets it, and thinks no more than where to throw the jack for beginning another cast. Many a man has found greater pleasure in planting a tree, and tending, and pruning it, and observing its growth, than he ever did in tasting the fruit: yet the former arises wholly from the latter, for else why might not he plant a bramble as well as a nectarine?

But every pleasure does not keep desire alive alike, nor will every desire return an equal produce of entertainment, which makes the science of pleasure so little understood.

stood. Men run eagerly after the most intense, thinking the more of them they can obtain, so much the better, being deceived herein by their method of computation; for they reckon, like the boy, that if a quarter of an hour's swing upon the gate gave immense delight, five hours swinging must give twenty times as much: whereas the arithmetic to be employed in this science, differs widely from common arithmetic, two and two do not always make four, the second number often operating as a negative quantity, which being added to the former, diminishes instead of increasing the sum. Besides, when we have settled the intrinsic value of our pleasures, all is not done, we must consider other things dependent upon them, and proceed in a kind of algebraical method: such a degree of delight, more by the amusement it will afford us in the pursuit, the pleasing expectation it will raise beforehand, and the soothing reflections it will leave behind; less by the labour we must undergo, the difficulties and hazards we must run to obtain it, the wants and cravings it may create, the disappointments we may meet with, and the mischiefs and inconveniences it may introduce. Thus we find the art of book-keeping in the commerce of pleasure very hard to attain, for besides the difficulty

of

of reducing every species of coin to some current standard, we must make all fair allowances for interest and produce, and take all reasonable charges and deductions into the account: but any tolerable skill we can acquire in this business is well worth the pains of learning.

I have remarked in another place, that our idea of pleasures, like our prospect of visible objects appears duller when they stand at a distance, and grows more vivid upon their nearer approach: and that habit and sympathy take effect by suggesting trains of thought, and methods of action, without the trouble of hunting for them. For there being a degree of complacence in every common motion of the mind, and exercise of our activity, ease and readiness become a species of pleasure, and whatever gives play to our powers, engages us in each succeeding moment, until something more important carries us into another track. From this source, I apprehend derived most of our little motives, influencing our by actions, and under motions, which steal upon us without our perceiving, and shape the manner of proceeding in all our performances.

CHAP. XXIII.

USE.

As the greater number by far of our pleasures spring from one another by translation, so our other satisfactions come to us through the same channel, being derived from pleasure: for nature affects us originally only with sensations excited by the play of our external or internal organs, and objects engage us according as in the various alterations and contextures of our frame produced by education, custom, or accident, they are made to give that play to the organs. But that use bears a derivative value, is implied in the very term, for whatever may have been said concerning things beautiful or laudable in themselves, we never hear them styled useful in themselves, but for something else; that is, so far as they tend to improve our condition, or contribute to our enjoyment, either immediately or remotely, in some respect or other.

Though nature has poured enjoyments around us with an unsparing hand, yet she has not hung them so near within our reach, as that we can pluck them whenever we please:

please: we must do many things before hand preparatory to the obtaining them, we must provide instruments and lay in materials to serve us upon occasion, furnish ourselves with the necessary means for administering to our wants, and take pains in planting and cultivating the tree long before we can gather the fruit. This tendency to supply the means of gratification transfers our desire to things indifferent in themselves, so that having observed them frequently serviceable we can willingly store them up, without view to any particular service they will do us, but upon the general prospect that we shall find occasion for them one time or other. And as the materials of enjoyment many times are no more to be had with a wish than the enjoyments themselves, but require other materials to procure them, hence use grows from out of use: for whatever conduces to the acquisition of useful things becomes useful itself upon that account. Thus, if the accommodations of life are useful for the comfort and delights they continually afford, money is useful too because it will purchase those accommodations; an estate because it yields an annual income of money, a profession because it tends to raise a competency of estate, application and industry because they help to make men thrive in their professions, skill and sagacity

gacity because they render industry successful, experience and learning because they improve our skill and sharpen our sagacity. All that men esteem valuable or think worth their while to pursue, derives its value either directly from enjoyment or from something else first recommended thereby. Riches, power, fame, health, strength, existence, talents, knowledge, accomplishment, luck, liberty, justice, steadiness, become this way objects of our desire.

2. But desire, as has been shown in the last chapter, although the child of pleasure, begets an offspring of the same features, make, and complexion with its grandmother: for the gratification of any desire, by how distant object soever excited, affords a present pleasure proportionable to the eagerness of the desire. Therefore, we see men express great joy according to the ardency of their wishes upon any accession of wealth, or power, or knowledge, or enlargement of their liberty, or discovery of their strength of resolution: and these secondary pleasures take up much the larger share on the credit side of our account after we arrive at manhood; yet even these objects affect the balance more by the engagement of their pursuit or consequences of their possession than by the joy of their acquisition. Wherefore the wisest of men
have

have been ever observed attentive to things useful in preference to things pleasant, because the former contain the seeds of many future enjoyments, whereas the latter can only improve our condition for the present moment: and we have seen a little while ago that pleasure itself does not deserve regard so much for its own poignancy as when it becomes useful by raising an expectation that engages us in a pursuit giving scope to agreeable reflections, or instigates to something more beneficial than itself.

That species of use called convenience visibly bears a reference to pleasure: for though our instruments be inconvenient, nevertheless we may make shift to work with them, but when we have all our implements convenient about us we can compleat our work with more ease and dispatch. The conveniences, as distinguished from all the necessaries of life, serve only to make it run more smooth and agreeable, and to render that an amusement which would otherwise have been a task. He that has all necessaries fully supplied him has every thing requisite for his being, but conveniences superadded enable him not only to support but to enjoy his being.

Desire having passed through many translations we often lose all remembrance of the progress it has made, nor can trace it back to the

the original fountain, which induces us to believe many desires natural and interwoven into our constitution, that derived their influence from certain things conducive to our enjoyments and conveniences. A very little reflection will convince us this is the case with respect to money, which however sometimes looked upon as desireable in itself, and how much soever the covetous man may prefer it beyond all things else, yet nobody can suppose he would ever have had the least attachment for it, if he had never found it serviceable to procure the enjoyments and accommodations of life. But there are other desires, whose derivation is not so apparent and therefore are imagined born with us, or to be propensities infused into the mind, and which break forth into act immediately upon the proper objects to excite them being presented. Of this sort are the desire of knowledge, of liberty, of power, of self-preservation, and many others. I shall examine only two which may serve as samples for the rest: the love of justice, and that fondness for having our own wills discernible more or less in all men.

3. We find justice commonly divided into two branches, called Commutative, directing us to render to every man his due, and Distributive, guiding us in the application of reward and punishment. The first of these
you

you see no appearance of in children, who greedily catch at every thing they can get without regard to the claims of their playfellows: and when they grow up, all the laws, the penalties, the punishments in the world, are little enough to prevent the invasion of property; but the generality of mankind still remain disposed to overreach one another in a bargain, and take all undue advantages whenever they can do it safely. So that since the golden age Astrea resides no more upon earth: even the honestest of men, if they will speak ingenuously, must acknowledge it extremely difficult to preserve a strict impartiality of judgment, in matters affecting their own private interest. Besides, it seems to be agreed among the learned, that nature gave the earth and all its produce among mankind in common, and that property would have had no existence, but for the necessity of it to preserve order and encourage industry with all the improvements consequent thereupon. The view of these advantages inspires us all with a liking to justice, but it is when discerned in other people, and certainly there can be nothing more convenient than that every body should behave justly to us: therefore, no man but would be glad to see justice prevail universally with an exemption only for himself. And though I
doubt

doubt not there are many who would act uprightly although there were no laws nor even hazard of a discovery, to restrain them from the contrary, yet these are persons who have learned to regard the interests of others as well as themselves: so that their principle of integrity still results from convenience, though not their own, but that of other people.

As for distributive justice, we have already seen under the article of anger, how the desire of revenge springs from expedience; and though men of consideration and judgment will often punish but not in anger, they do it from the necessity of punishment to keep the world in order, wherefore, they regard the intention more than the deed, knowing that the use of punishment is not to repair the damage sustained, to which it will by no means contribute, but to mend the manners and direct the intention of mankind to the forbearance of injury. Even the vulgar, though ordinarily prompted by impulse of passion, yet if you would dissuade them from the prosecution or retaliation of wrongs, reply readily, Why otherwise we cannot sleep safe in our beds, or we shall be liable to perpetual insults: which however insincere they may be or ignorant of their real motive, shows that common sense dictates expedience as the only

only plea to justify resentment. If there were a natural and necessary connection between offence and punishment, how could there be any room for mercy? which a person of humanity will always shew whenever it can be extended to the offender, without inconvenience to the public, or detriment to private persons. Nor does our inclination to reward grow from any other root than that of expedience, as encouraging men to repeat the good offices that have deserved it. When we promise a poor man a reward for doing us some particular service, or offer one for the recovery of goods lost, or apprehension of a thief; we have visibly our own ends in view. And the observation that the return of good offices engages men to continue them, is so obvious as to escape nobody's notice, but the convenience found in such returns occurs so continually in the commerce of life, that satisfaction, as customary in translations, becomes connected with the practice, and we get an habitual aptness to retaliate favours as well as injuries, without looking forward to the benefits attending upon so doing. Thus the heartiest gratitude, as I have shown in the proper place concerning the purest love, though bearing the fragrantest flowers, sprouts originally from the earthly principle of self-interest.

4. And

4. And that adherence to what we have once set our hearts upon, so common in the world, issues from the same bed: for our larger actions, by which alone we can help ourselves in our needs, consist of many single acts, which must all tend towards the same point, or they will never form an entire body to compleat the purpose we intended. We cannot walk across the room with a single step, nor help ourselves to a glass of wine by one motion of our arm, nor compass any thing whatever, until our volitions have been accustomed to follow one another in the same direction. This discovers to us the expedience of a steadiness and consistency of conduct, and renders the having willed a thing, a motive with us to will it still, until some cogent reason shall occur to the contrary. Experience indeed might convince us in time, that it is often expedient to change our measures, and comply with the necessity of our situation, but all do not profit by experience: and those are observed to be the most wilful, who have found the least need of compliance, being either such whose strength of body, and hardiness of constitution, have enabled them to resist compulsion, or such as being constantly humoured by persons about them, have used to gain their ends by persisting. But this sturdiness of temper ought by no

no means to be absolutely rejected, being eminently serviceable or pernicious, according to the objects whereto it is directed: when turned the wrong-way, it is called obstinacy, stubborness, and perverseness, when the right, we entitle it steadiness, resolution, and bravery, without which there is no enduring pains, hardships, and difficulties, nor going through with an arduous undertaking, nor indeed compleating any work that requires labour and time. For considering the fluctuating nature of our ideas, it is impossible to keep up the desire, first urging to the task in its full colours, but we should faint in midway upon any fatigue or obstacle intervening, if it were not for the habit of perseverance in what he had once begun. The forming a resolution requires a very different situation of mind from that of executing, in the former we gather as many considerations as we can to fortify our resolves, in the latter we are too busy with the measures, to be taken to admit any further idea relating to our purpose than the strength of resolution, wherewith we had determined upon it. Especially when pain assaults us, it so fills the mind, that we have no room for more than the remembrance of our having judged the thing, to be attained by supporting it, expedient, without any of the foundations for that

judgment

judgment: all we can do further is by an operation upon our organs, to withdraw our notice from the smart and heighten our desire, or want of perseverance in our design as much as possible.

Since then adherence to our purpose proves so signally serviceable upon great occasions, and so continually useful upon common ones, no wonder it becomes the object of desire, in some degree with all men, and gives them vexation upon being crossed, and pleasure upon being gratified. They may not always be able to trace out its reference to use, they know they love to have their Wills, but forget by what steps they fell in love with them: for understanding cannot penetrate into all the private recesses of imagination. In other cases, men are frequently deceived with respect to the influence that use has upon them, self-interest giving a wonderful bias to the judgment, and producing those motives we have called the obscure, because sheltering themselves under cover of more specious reasons, while they too often give the real turn to our behaviour.

CHAP. XXIV.

HONOUR.

As use sprouts from pleasure, so honour branches out from use, and stands one remove further from the parent root, for which reason it is more readily supposed innate, its derivation being not so easily traced: for it never grows to maturity, while adhering to the mother plant, nor until separated from it as an offset, and standing upon its own stem. We are not thought actuated by honour, so long as we have any further advantage or gratification in view, nor until it becomes a motive of itself sufficient to operate upon us, without needing recommendation from any thing else to give it weight. But this does not prove it to be the gift of nature, for we may remember many instances already pointed out of translation, wherein satisfaction has been made to fix so strongly upon things originally indifferent, as to render them powerful motives of action.

Our principle of honour is so far from being born with us, that we should never have acquired it, if we had always been debarred from society. Little children, as they show no signs of shame, so neither do they discover any notion of applause, until being perpetually told that Mamma will not love them, nor Papa give them pretty things, nor Nurse take care of them unless they be good, they learn to look upon the approbation of persons about them as desirable. And when we grow up, we find it so extremely and continually useful to have the good opinion and esteem of others, which make them friendly and obsequious to our desires, that this is enough to give us a liking to esteem, and consequently to those actions or qualities tending to promote it. For reflection and experience leading us by gradation from one thing to another, our desire of approbation throws a complacence upon actions procuring it, and this again makes us value the possession of qualities productive of such actions, although we have no present opportunity of exercising them.

2. Besides, there lies a nearer way for good qualities to arrive at their valuableness: for we find the very sight of them raising an esteem in the beholder, without staying for the benefits to be received from them. Nay, that sight contributes more to give a good opinion of the possessor than the reception of the benefits, and the latter only as an evidence of the former. Whatever enables a

man to do much good or hurt, sets him higher in the estimation of the vulgar, than a disposition to use his powers well: therefore we see great talents, sagacity, strength of body, nobility of birth, and even opulence and good fortune, introduced for topics of panegyric as well as beneficence, public spirit, and industry.

But what is more useful carries away our attention from what is less, therefore we judge of things by comparison, placing our esteem upon those which are excellent and supereminent in their kind; and what we once greatly admired, may be eclipsed by something darting a superior lustre. And our admiration of superiority renders the marks of it subjects of our admiration too: hence proceeds our fondness for titles of honour, splendor of equipage, and badges of distinction: hence likewise majesty of countenance, dignity of gesture, and solemnity of deportment, command our respect, as expressing something extraordinary and excellent within; for where we know the subject exhibiting them possesses nothing more than common, they excite our laughter instead of our admiration. Nor are we unaffected with excellence appearing in beasts, or things inanimate, or the performances of art: we admire the noble mien of a lion, the magnificence of a building,

building, the immense expanse of heaven, the regular courses of the stars, the master strokes of poetry, and sublimity of style, because these objects afford immediate entertainment, by filling imagination with large ideas, or express something extraordinary in the authors and causes of them. And honour, resting chiefly in comparison, teaches us to see an expedience in excelling, for it is not so much matter what we are in ourselves, as what degree we stand in amongst others, which sows the seeds of envy, emulation, and contention for superiority. But as excellence will not produce its effects until made visible, this opens the door to ostentation, vanity, and affectation, which may be observed abounding most in those who have been flattered into an opinion of their having something extraordinary to exhibit, or some agreeable peculiarity in their manner.

3. But the thought of possessing whatever we esteem useful or advantageous, sooths and gives immediate pleasure to the mind: for which reason there is a near affinity between beauty and honour, both delighting the eye instantly upon sight, without reference to those further advantages which first made it recommendable, and love and esteem commonly generating one another, or at least nourishing each other's growth. In visible objects

objects one can more easily discern the distinction than describe it, only we may say that beauty seems to affect the sense alone, whereas admiration more apparently requires the concurrence of imagination. But when applied to actions and sentiments it is harder to know them apart: wherefore the Greeks used the same term to express them both, and though the Latins had a different name for each, yet they applied their epithets promiscuously, distinguishing things indifferently either into beautiful and deformed, or laudable and blameable. But the mind, having a natural propensity to pleasure, loves to solace herself in the contemplation of whatever belonging to her she conceives will do her honour: this engenders pride; which may be called a habit of dwelling upon the thought of any supposed excellences, or advantages men believe themselves possessed of, as well power, birth, wealth, strength of body, or beauty of person, as endowments of the mind.

But our propensity to this as well as other pleasures, produces mischievous effects, too often misleading the understanding, damping industry, and destroying its own purpose by overcharging the appetite. It casts a wonderful bias upon the judgment, inclining men to fancy themselves possessed of advantages
they

they have not, to overvalue those they really have, and to depreciate those of other people. It keeps them so attentive to their own self-sufficiency, as to think it needless to look for any thing further: whereas industry bespeaks a humble mind, more solicitous to make new acquisitions, than to count over those already gained, as not judging them enough to rest satisfied with. And it destroys the relish men find in the possession of good things, by satiating them with the contemplation: for as our bodily members tire upon continual exercise, so our mental organs cloy upon repetition, soon exhausting the sweets of an object, and entertaining no longer than while receiving fresh supplies of novelty and variety. Accordingly the proud reap no delight from their pride, we rather see them more gloomy and discontented than other people; and if they still retain a fondness for reflecting on their superexcellence, it is like the unnatural thirst of a drunkard, which does not draw him by pleasure, but drives him by the uneasiness of his unextinguishable cravings.

4. Is it then never allowable to cast back a look upon any thing wherein we have succeeded well, or upon any advantages we possess? This I do not assert: for the complacence we feel upon such occasions improves

our

our condition, so long as we can enjoy it pure, and whatever pleases deserves our regard, if none other consideration interfere. I see nothing should hinder the boy from swinging, provided he took care to do his lesson first, not to break down the farmer's gate, and to leave off his diversion before it grew tiresome: so neither need we scruple to ride upon any little excellency we may possess, taking only such transient views of it as may afford us a real gust, if we have nothing else to do, and neither injure nor offend anybody, nor harbour a thought injurious or offensive to anybody. Besides, there is a further use beyond the present amusement, in making proper comparisons of things and persons: for the retrospect upon what we have done well, encourages us to persevere in the like conduct, the knowledge of any good things we possess, whets our industry to preserve and procure more of them, and a due sense of our estimation among mankind, withholds us from consorting with persons, or giving into behaviour unbecoming our character. But what comparisons of this kind are proper or not, depends upon a fair computation of the service they will do, or the net income of real pleasures they will yield upon the balance.

5. As honour branches from use, so it takes diverse tinctures, according to the stock whereon

whereon it is grafted. The professions and situations of men in life rendering different things serviceable to them, creates a proportionable variety in their sentiments of honour: the merchant places it in punctuality of payment, the soldier in bravery, the artificer in the compleatness of his works, the scholar in acquisitions of learning, the fine gentleman in politeness and elegancy of taste, the lady in her beauty, or neatness of dress, or skill in family œconomy. There is no man utterly destitute of honour, because no man but finds the expedience of it in some degree or other: nor is there a possibility of living in any comfort or tranquillity under universal contempt. But men's notions of it are widely different and discordant: what one esteems an honour, another looks upon as a folly or disgrace; one values himself upon his sincerity and plain dealing, another upon his art of dissimulation: one upon his patience in enduring wrongs, another upon his quickness in resenting them: though Falstaff ridiculed the grinning honours of the field, yet he scorned to give a reason upon compulsion: every one esteems that highest which he has found turning most to account in the way of life wherein he is engaged, or best promoting his designs, or adding to his enjoyment in the company among whom his
lot

lot has fallen. Which shows that our sense of honour is not natural like that of seeing, for this exhibits the same distinction of colours to all alike, nor ever makes a lilly appear blue to one man, green to another, and scarlet to a third, according to the several ways they have been brought up in, or employments they have followed.

6. Though our estimation of things commonly first arises from the credit they bear with other people, yet the judgments of mankind being so various, obliges us to look out for some other rule to direct us in our observation: for by following what we see admired at one time, we may be thought to pursue trifles or incur censure at another. To avoid the trouble such accidents would give us, we have none other remedy than by hardening ourselves sometimes against reproach, which we see every one ready to do more or less upon occasion: for there could be no steadiness of conduct nor perseverance in any purpose, if we were to veer about with every blast of applause or censure. But as no man would wish to throw off all sensibility, he must distinguish when to restrain and when to give it scope: this teaches him to look inwards upon himself and observe what estimation things bear in his own mind, and the judgments the mind passes in such cases immediately
upon

upon inspection are called the sentiments. I know this term is often applied to opinions concerning the truth or falsehood, expedience or inexpedience of things: as when a man is asked to declare his sentiments upon a point of natural philosophy or a maxim of policy or measure of prudence, the question means no more than to know what he judges most agreeable to reason, or most conducive to the purpose aimed at. But Sentiment being derived from Sense or Feeling, seems more peculiarly applicable to those judgments the mind passes upon matters of praise or blame, which she cannot do without feeling a degree of complacence or disgust in contemplating the subject whereon she so passes her judgment.

One can live but little while in the world without acquiring some of these sentiments, and when deeply rooted by long habit, they become powerful incentives of action. The testimony of a man's own breast when clear and full will bear him up against the reproaches of a whole world; self-approbation when strong and well grounded will support him under hardships, disappointments, and distresses; and the desire of doing something he may applaud himself for will carry him through labours, difficulties, and dangers. You may move any man almost any way by touch-

touching his point of honour, if you can but find out where it lies: but herein and in applying the proper means to affect it rests the difficulty, for perhaps it does not lie in the same part nor look towards the same objects as it does in yourself. We currently pronounce the vulgar void of honour because they want those notions of it instilled into us by education and good company: but if they had not a sensibility of their own they would never be moved unless by blows or something affecting them in point of interest, whereas we find the meanest of mankind as apt to take fire upon opprobrious language or defamation, when they understand it, as the most refined.

7. The generality of men draw their sentiments of honour from those with whom they consort, or from the tendency of things to promote what they most ardently desire: they feel themselves affecting some objects and shocked at others, they neither know nor enquire how they come to be so, but follow the present impulse without further examination. But the studious, desirous to see with their own eyes, and unwilling to trust either the opinions of mankind which they perceive infinitely various and contradictory, or even their own sentiments which they find wavering and clashing with one another,
endeavour

endeavour to fix upon some criterion whereby to distinguish true honour from the false. This has led many into the notion of an essential quality, which residing in certain objects they became laudable in themselves: which quality I take to have been understood by the Kalòn of the Greeks and Honestum of the Romans, to which I know of no word that answers in the English tongue, but it may be described, that which raises your approbation instantly upon being suggested to the thought without reference to any consequences attendant thereupon. If you asked what this Kalòn was, you were referred to the effect it would have upon the eye of an impartial beholder. But several beholders see different appearances in the same object: this it was replied arose from a fault in the vision, for the optics of some are so dimmed and overclouded by the mists of error and prejudice, that, like a jaundiced eye, they cannot see the Kalòn in its true colours. Well, but how shall we know whether our optics be clear and how to rectify them? why, observe the best and wisest men and learn to see as they do. Thus, the whole matter is at last resolved into authority, a method unbecoming a philosopher, for though the examples of wise men be an excellent guide for us to

follow

follow in our conduct, it lets us nothing into the nature of things unless we have the grounds explained whereon they formed their judgment: and as we shall meet with many instances wherein we cannot have the benefit of their example, we shall still remain at a loss how to distinguish the genuine Kalòn from the spurious. Besides, the actions of the wise themselves have been made the subject of controversy, many judicious persons having doubted whether Cato the censor had a just idea of the Kalòn when he persecuted the Carthagenians to destruction, or Brutus, when he assassinated Cæsar, or the younger Cato, whom Seneca pronounces a perfect wise man, when he deserted his post of life at Utica: so that we want some other test to try the dictates of wisdom when mingled among the frailties of human nature in the very best of men.

When such disputes happen, the parties generally recur to some principles they think will be admitted on the other side; and if those are agreed to, it is very well, but what if they be denied? or what if it be asked upon what grounds those principles are founded? I know of none other way to determine the matter than by a reference to use. And so far the old philosophers seem to have admitted

ted this rule as to allow that all things laudable were useful, but then they placed those qualities out of their proper order, for they held that things were therefore useful because laudable, whereas the truth appears to me to be that they are therefore laudable because useful: for I cannot conceive how any practice can be laudable which will never do the least service to the performer nor any body else, nor blameable from whence more good will accrue by following it than letting it alone. All services are esteemed, as well in the eye of the world as in a man's own reflection, according as they are more or less signal: and if temptations and difficulties standing in the way render a deed the subject of greater applause, certainly nothing can be more useful than an ability to surmount difficulties and resist temptations when they would withhold us from any thing beneficial.

8. But if things be laudable because useful, must not use and honour always go together? Is there then no difference between one and the other? If a man entrusted with a valuable deposit by a person deceased, debates with himself whether he shall apply it to the purposes directed or to his own benefit, does not use exhort him one way and honour the other? Certainly they do: but then use must be understood here of what appears
such

such to him, not what is really such upon the whole upshot of the account. We get a habit of looking upon power, profit, and such like, as valuable, and thence contract a desire of attaining them whenever an opportunity offers, but this desire would lead us many times into mischiefs and inconveniences if not withheld by the restraint of honour; or we grudge the pains of pursuing things really valuable, and should miss of them unless shamed out of our indolence: here the sense of honour does us signal service by stimulating when interest wanted sharpness sufficient, and urging to practices, whose use we are not sensible of, as lying too remote for us to discern. Were there a race of men of so penetrating and extensive an understanding as to comprehend at one view all the consequences of every action, and so well regulated a taste as constantly to prefer the greater remote good before the lesser near at hand, they would have no sense of honour because they would want none: for their own discernment would lead them precisely into those very courses which true honour recommends. The necessity of this principle arises from the weakness and narrowness of our capacities; they that are whole need not the physician nor his remedies, but they that are sick, and honour is that remedy which alone can cure the

the disorders and confusions brought upon the world by a too close attachment to our injudicious desires in disregard of the general good, wherein our own is ultimately contained or I may say lies concealed. The voluptuous, who constantly follow whatever appetite or fancy prompts, have the narrowest minds; a prudent regard to interest widens them a little; but a due sense of honour opens the heart and enlarges the soul as far as it is capable of extending. Therefore, the wisest and best of men, as they have ever been observed attentive to things useful in preference to things pleasant, so they give the like preference to the laudable before the useful, and for the same reason; because as use contains the seeds of many future enjoyments, so honour leads to further uses than their wisdom, but imperfect at the best, can always descry.

Now to come as near as possible to my old friends of former ages I shall readily admit that, although things be not therefore useful because laudable, yet they ought therefore to be esteemed useful because of that approbation we feel resting upon them in our own minds. For as we have shown in CHAP. XI. that many truths reputed self-evident were not innate but acquired by experience of facts, nevertheless we may justly employ them as the basis of our reasonings, because the strength wherewith they strike upon the judgment is a good evidence that we had sufficient grounds for embracing them, though now absolutely forgotten and irrecoverable: so when we perceive objects commanding our applause instantly upon inspection, we may rest assured that we ourselves, or those persons from whom we have taken the tincture, have found advantages in them which we do not now retain in memory, nor can readily trace out. The uses we see daily resulting from a principle of honour, are enow to give it a value in the eyes of every prudent person; continual experience testifies that this principle rightly grounded, witholds us from folly, rouzes us to industry, shines through the mists of prejudice, and balances the influence of passion: nor can anybody avoid taking notice how much men's regard for their credit with others, and self approbation within themselves, contributes to preserve that good order in the world, the benefits whereof they want penetration to discern. Therefore we shall do well to follow the dictates of our own heart concerning what is commendable or unworthy, for that will inform us sufficiently for common occasions, if we take care to consult it sincerely and impartially: and when doubts arise, we must adhere to such sentiments as we find estab-

established most firmly, and striking most strongly. I know nothing further we can do, unless we stand in a situation to discern all the consequences and tendencies of the matters under deliberation; and then that which appears least confined to private or present gratification, but most extensively and generally advantageous, will deserve the character of the most laudable.

9. But in computations of this sort, regard must be had, not only to the usefulness of the objects proposed, but likewise to the usefulness of praise or blame towards attaining them: for if there be other motives sufficient to set us at work, commendation were thrown away as being superfluous. This explains why, though honour depends upon use, nevertheless every thing useful is not laudable: because where we discern the use, and are moved by it to exert ourselves, there is no use for honour. Therefore we do not lavish our applauses upon things we find men willing enough to do of themselves, however beneficial they may appear. What is more useful than eating and sleeping? but nobody gains credit by them, for appetite prompts us fast enough without it. Bakers, shoemakers, and taylors, are very serviceable members of society, but who ever rose to honours by exercising those trades?

trades? for why? the prospect of getting a livelihood holds them tight to their work, without any other spur to assist it. But upon boys being first put out apprentices the master finds it useful to encourage them by commendation, because they have then none other inducement to do their duty besides reward and punishment. We chide and applaud our children to make them careful of their money, but when they have gotten a competent habit of œconomy, then honour changes stations, standing as a fence on the other side, to secure them against covetousness,

Hence too we may learn why the most considerate persons honour the intention rather than the deed, for though the usefulness of an action results from the performance, not the design, yet the use of commendation lies only in its operating upon the mind, nor does it at all influence the success any further than by doubling our diligence. Yet a proper estimate of external objects has its use too, as directing us which way to apply our endeavours out of several presenting: for if there were not a credit in having things neat and handsome about us, many men would satisfy themselves as well with groveling always in the dirt, and if there were not a respect paid to eminence of station and fortune,

fortune, even where we have no high opinion of the persons, we should invalidate those rules of good breeding which keep up decorum, and render conversation easy. Hence likewise we may see why honour generally runs counter to profit and pleasure, because the use of it lies in restraining them when they would carry us on to our detriment; and the more forcibly they tempt us, the greater is the merit of resisting them, because we then need a stronger weight to overbalance their influence. The same reason may account for honour resting upon comparison, because use frequently does so too: for as among many things proposed to his option, a prudent man will always choose the most useful, so he will prefer the most laudable, as carrying the presumption of being the most useful. Therefore the desire of surpassing others is always faulty, unless when some real benefit will result therefrom, or there be some good purpose in view, which cannot be attained without it.

10. The desire of honour, like all other desires, gives an immediate pleasure in the gratification, or when moving on successfully towards its object, and this may be reckoned among the uses of honour. But these pleasures are not to be valued according to their intenseness, for high delights of all kinds, though

though they ravish the mind while fresh and new, yet they pall the appetite, and render it tasteless of common enjoyments; nor can they keep their relish long, because our organs are too weak to support the violent exercise they put them upon. But there is a self-approbation, which, being of the gentle kind, throws the spirits into easy motions that do not exhaust nor fatigue, and sooths the mind with an uninterrupted complacence in the reflections she may cast back upon her general tenor of conduct. For as ease, health, and security, afford a degree of actual pleasure, though implying no more in themselves than a negation of pain, sickness, and danger, so there is a real satisfaction in keeping clear of every thing for which others might justly censure us, or we might blame ourselves. This then the wise man will be most careful to attain, as adding more to the sum total of his happiness than the momentary transports of joy, upon excelling in any way whatever. Nevertheless, an ardent desire of doing or possessing something extraordinary has its value, but as we observed before concerning intense pleasures, not so much for its intrinsic worth, or for the gust found in the gratification, as for the good fruits it may produce, by stimulating our industry, furnishing us with employment, and putting us upon useful

useful services we might otherwise have omitted.

11. If there be any meaning in the expression of things laudable in themselves, it must belong to those we find esteemed most universally, or by the best judges, or from which we cannot withhold our applause whenever we consider them in our own minds, though we know not why they so affect us: but our not seeing the benefits resulting therefrom, is no proof of their non-existence. By such tests it behoves us to try our sentiments every now and then, for as we catch a tincture from others by custom or example, without this caution we shall lie perpetually liable to be drawn aside by the glare of false honour from pursuing the true. But when we do employ the method of reference to use, we must carry the reference to all quarters whereto it can extend: for it is not enough to weigh the consequences of the present action, but we must consider what effect our departure from a rule may have upon ourselves at other times, how far it may influence other people to follow our example, when they have not the like reason for doing as we do, and in short all the circumstances that any ways relate to the case. Honour, says Mr. Addison, is a sacred tie, and its laws are never to be infringed, unless when

when more good than hurt will evidently result from dispensing with them: nor must the danger of weakening their authority be forgotten in the account, and if that be considered, there are some of those laws which perhaps a sufficient warrant can never be found for transgressing.

12. Situation and circumstance may cast a dishonour upon what appears perfectly innocent in itself: there are many things I need not name, that every man must do, and therefore will acquit himself in doing, yet every discreet man will choose to do in private, and conceal from the knowledge of others as much as possible. It is well known what irregularities the Cynics were led into by judging of things as laudable or blameable in themselves: for intrinsic qualities cannot be divested by the circumstances of time and place, from the subject whereto nature has united them. A stone will retain its hardness so long as it remains a stone, and air be yielding to the touch always and every where: therefore they made no scruple to commit the grossest indecencies in public, because their adversaries could not but admit the acts they performed were at some times allowable. But if they had judged by a proper reference to use, they must have seen the expedience of decency and decorum, that
what

what becomes one man may not become another, and that the same actions, according as they do, or do not, tend to give offence, or to the breach of good manners, may become blameable or allowable.

13. Much ado has been made of late days about certain moral senses, which nature is supposed to have furnished us with, for the discernment of things laudable or blameable, becoming or ridiculous, as she has with the bodily senses for the discernment of sensible objects: and this notion seems introduced to supply the place of innate ideas, since their total overthrow by Mr. Locke. If we alledge that nature is more uniform in her gifts than we find these moral senses to be, which judge very variously of the same object in different persons, we are silenced with the old pretence, that all who do not see as we do, must labour under some disorder in their vision, by having contracted films before their eyes from error and prejudice. But how shall the moral sense be proved born with us, when we see no appearance of it before we arrive at some use of our understanding, and there are whole nations who seem utterly destitute of it? Our five senses we receive perfect at first, they rather decay and grow duller than improve by time, the child and the savage can see, and hear, and taste, and smell, and feel, as well as

the

the most refined and civilized. Let us then look upon this supposed sixth sense as an acquired faculty, generated in us by the operation of those materials thrown in by the other five, together with the combinations formed of them, and other ideas resulting from them in our reflection. We ordinarily imbibe our sentiments by custom or sympathy from the company we consort with, or from persons whose judgments we revere: therefore the exposing of children, the extirpating of enemies, assassinating for affronts, persecuting for heresy, do not strike with horror in countries where commonly practised, or taught by the leaders. But as all custom must have a beginning, and all judgment some foundation to build upon, let us try to discover what might first bring into credit those objects which the moral sense, when supposed clearest will recommend: and this will appear upon examination to be nothing else besides their expedience, and eminent serviceableness to promote the happiness of mankind. The objects that seem most strongly to affect the moral sense are integrity of justice and restraint of brutal appetites, which we have already seen deriving their value from expedience: and it is remarkable that the mind discerns the beauty of them abroad before she can discover it at home. For as the eye sees

not

not itself, unless by reflection in a glass, so neither can we know our own internal features, unless by beholding the counterparts of them in other persons: therefore if you perceive the moral sense in anybody a little dull, it is common to clear it up, by asking him how he would approve the like behaviour in another towards himself. Which shows that actions have not an intrinsic turpitude necessarily touching the sense, when contemplating them naked, but we must place them in other subjects, where their tendency to bring trouble and inconvenience upon ourselves casts a turpitude upon them; having frequently seen them in this position, we learn to reflect that what appears foul and ugly without doors would do the same within, if we stood at the proper point of view; we then practise the art of removing ourselves to a distance from ourselves, through which channel, we derive that skill of discernment called the moral sense.

Nevertheless, I am not for depreciating these moral senses, on the contrary I wish their notices were more carefully regarded in the world than they are: for their being acquired is no diminution of their value, unless we will despise all arts and sciences, acquisitions of learning, and whatever else we had not directly from the hand of nature; which
would

would reduce us back again to the helpless and ignorant condition of our infancy. Men of the most shining characters and exemplary lives are found peculiarly attentive to them, nor will ever suffer themselves to be drawn into a disregard for them, by the impulses of passion, or temptations of profit. Yet being apt sometimes to gather films and foulnesses, it may not be amiss to examine them at the bar of reason by a jury of their peers; that is, by comparing them with one another, when we have leisure and opportunity to give them a fair hearing, and take full cognizance of the cause: for the presumption lies strongly in their favour, and the burden of the proof belongs to him that would impeach their character. For we may have had substantial grounds for our estimation of things, though we do not now retain them in mind, and the experience of others may have discovered an expedience that we never stood in a situation to discern: therefore whatever appears shocking to our thought, or generally odious in the eyes of mankind, deserves to be rejected, without very evident and invincible reasons to the contrary.

CHAP. XXV.

NECESSITY.

By necessity I do not mean that impulse whereby bodies are made to move and strike upon one another, nor those laws, by which nature carries on her operation in a chain of causes and effects unavoidably depending upon each other, without choice or volition. For I consider it here as a motive driving the mind to one manner of action, when we have the contrary in our inclination and our power: and we hear the term often applied this way, how properly I shall not examine, choosing rather to regard every expression as proper, that obtains currency in the language of mankind.

I have laid down that all our motives derive their efficacy from pleasure, other satisfactions flowing through the channel of translation, either immediately or remotely from that: but then it must be remembered, that under pleasure I comprehend the avoidance of pain, and it is the latter solely that gives rise to the class of motives at present under consideration. In all necessary actions, we have some uneasiness, or displeasure, or

damage,

damage, in view, and some inclination drawing us another way which we should gratify if it were not for such obstacle; and as inclination generally stands for Will, we are said in such cases to act unwillingly or against our Wills, notwithstanding that we perform the acts by our volition, and therefore are no more necessary agents than when pursuing the thing most agreeable to our heart's desire.

2. Thus the motives of necessity have the very reverse for their objects to those of the three former classes, to wit, some pain or disquietude of mind, some detriment to our possessions, or blemish in our character, to which may be added the omission of something pleasant, profitable, or creditable, which we conceive in our power to attain; for whatever we desire strongly we feel an uneasiness in the thought of going without, which uneasiness many times lays us under a necessity of taking all measures to prevent it. To this class belong the obligations of duty, of honour, of justice, of prudence, of the laws of the land, and of fashion: the attachment to professions, application to business, preservation of our persons and properties, checks of conscience, and the greatest part of the influence of our moral senses. For whenever we do so or so because we must, whether the obliga-

obligation be laid upon us by our own fondness for particular objects, or by the judgments of reason, we are actuated by the apprehension of some mischief attendant upon the forbearing it. Conscience particularly acts as a monitor, like Socrates' Demon, never exhorting to any thing, but restraining our desires from the course they would otherwise take, informing us what is right, no otherwise than by warning us against what is wrong: and moral senses, when young and newly acquired, operate by the dread of that compunction we should feel upon transgressing their dictates.

The very term Must implies that we should have acted otherwise, had matters been left to our choice, and indicates a desire subsisting in the mind, which unavoidably degenerates into want upon our being obliged to thwart when we cannot stifle it. Therefore, want being an uneasy passion, necessity always throws the mind into a state of suffering, greater or less in proportion to the degree of want urging us to the course we must not take. But men frequently missapply the term, using it as a pretence to justify what they really like and might have omitted without the least inconvenience: or when there is a real necessity, ascribing their action to that though they were in fact pre-engaged

by

by other motives. For we must remember the motive of action is always something actually in the scale; not every good reason that might move us if its help were wanted, but some object in view, and weighing with us at the instant time of acting. So that we cannot certainly conclude people uneasy when we hear them talk of being obliged to such a particular proceeding: for perhaps there was no obligation, and they only amused themselves, or meant to amuse us, with the pretence of one; or if there were, perhaps they had nothing less in their thoughts, but proceeded upon other grounds. What is more necessary than eating? yet which of us sits down to table upon that motive? we do not need to be told that without victuals we cannot sustain life nor keep our bodies in health, and this consideration might have sufficient influence to bring us to them, if there were nothing else: but appetite engages us beforehand and sets our jaws at work long before necessity can heave itself into the scale. On the contrary, physic, having no other recommendation, will not go down with us, until we throw in the heavy weight of necessity. And in this as well as all other cases wherein the cogency of necessity gives the real turn to our activity, there is an uneasiness corresponding

ponding to the reluctance we feel against complying with it.

But as this uneasiness proceeds from the opposition of contrary desires, if that which occasioned the reluctance can be totally silenced, necessity changes its nature, and becomes a matter of choice, having no competitor to struggle against it: for as when driven by necessity, we should have acted otherwise if that necessity had not occurred, so we should have readily complied with it as a thing desirable, if we had had no contrary inclination which must be thwarted by it. Therefore persons well practised in the ways of honour, take delight in performing the obligations of it, and fulfilling the rules of duty and justice: for though these ties were obligations at first, and still retain the name, they no longer act as obligations, but as objects of desire, nor does the party influenced by them once think of any mischief that would ensue, or any pleasure he might lose upon transgressing them.

3. The bare exemption from evil, often suffices to touch us with a sensible pleasure. the testimony of a good conscience, although implying no more than a clearness from offence, has been ever held a continual feast to the mind. And in common cases, the avoidance of mischief does not operate as a mo-

tive of necessity, where there is nothing to raise a reluctance against the measures to be taken for preventing it. We bar up our doors and windows every night to secure them against robbers, we provide fuel against winter, and send down stores into the country for our summer occasions: there is no pleasure in all this, nor should we do it unless necessary; yet being familiarized to the practice, we do it as a thing customary without thinking of that necessity. The essence of necessary action consists in an unwillingness to perform it; take away that unwillingness and the necessity is gone. There are persons of so happy temper as to bring their minds into a ready compliance with what must be done, and upon discerning that, whatever desires they might have had before for doing otherwise instantly vanish: if we could attain a perfect acquiescence in whatever the present circumstances require, we should escape the iron hand of necessity, we might see which way it drives, and lay our measures accordingly, but should always elude its grasp, and take the gentler guidance of expedience.

Nevertheless, since our desires will not always lie down quiet at the word of command, we can only restrain them from mischief by contemplating the necessity of so doing, and inculcating that idea so strongly

as

as to drive us into the performance of what we could not do willingly: for though it will throw us into an uneasy situation, we must submit to it for the good fruits expectant thereupon; the road to ease and pleasure lying frequently through trouble and uneasiness. It is by this way we first come within the influence of honour, prudence and justice; and the moral senses, as we observed before, begin their operation in this manner, though by a long and steady practice they get the better of all opponent inclinations, and become themselves the sources of desire, which would then prevail with us if there were no necessity to enforce them.

But as necessity by good management may be refined into pleasure, so pleasure by indiscretion may be corrupted into necessity; a constant indulgence of our appetites encreases their cravings while it lessens, and at last totally destroys the gust we had in gratifying them, so that desire, whose office it is to solace and delight us, changes into the tormenting passion of want. It has been often said that hunger is the best sauce to our meat, but this the voluptuary never finds in his dish; and likewise that novelty gives a relish to pleasures, but by hunting continually after a variety of them, we may bring novelty itself to be nothing new. Many run a perpetual round of diversions abroad only because they should be miserable at home; so that while they seem invited by pleasure, they are really lashed on by the scourge of necessity. Therefore if we wish to pass our time easily and agreeably, the worst thing we can do is to make a toil of a pleasure, and the best to make a virtue of necessity.

CHAP. XXVI.

REASON.

Thus far we have been busied in laying our foundation, a toilsome and tedious work, but wherein diligence and an attention to minute particulars was requisite, because we were unwilling to leave any cracks or chasms unfilled, over which our future building might stand hollow: how well we have succeeded in the attempt, and whether we have worked the whole compact with a mutual dependence, and due coherence of parts, must be left to the judgment of others, whose decision in our favour I rather wish for than expect. For, to say truth, it has not answered my own expectation, as wanting much of that compleat workmanship I
am

am well satisfied the materials were capable of: but with regard to the necessity and usefulness of all we have been labouring, I beg the determination of that may be suspended until it shall be seen what uses we can make of it. Let us now begin to raise the superstructure, wherein I hope to proceed with a little more ease to myself, and satisfaction to anybody that may deign to look upon me. We have examined how and upon what incitements men act, together with the tendencies and consequences of their action: let us try to discover from thence how they ought to act. But I am not so fond as to imagine any thing can be done this way so compleatly as to render all further care and consideration of other persons needless: if I can set up the main pillars of morality, and perform the offices of mason and carpenter in erecting the edifice, this is all can be required of me, I may leave it to each particular man to fit up the several apartments according to his circumstances and situation in life: for things calculated for general use, require some pains and circumspection in applying them to private convenience in the variety of cases that may happen.

2. We have seen how the actions of men are of two sorts, inadvertent and deliberate, the former prompted by imagination, and the
others

others by understanding. To imagination belong our combinations and judgments, starting up immediately upon the appearance of objects, our spontaneous trains of thought, our passions, habits, and motives, giving the present turn to our volition. Of what kind all these shall be, or when, or how they shall affect us, depends upon the impulse of external objects, upon experience, custom, and other prior causes: the mind has no share either in modeling or introducing them, and though she acts by her own power without their assistance to invigorate her, yet she shapes her motions according to the directions received from them. There remains only the understanding, in whose operations the mind acts as principal agent, comparing and marshaling her ideas, investigating those that lie out of sight, forming new judgments, and discovering motives that would not have arisen of themselves. It is therefore by the due use of our understanding, or reason alone, that we can help ourselves when imagination would take a wrong course, or proves insufficient for our purposes. To this then we must have recourse, if we would avail ourselves of any thing we have learnt in the foregoing enquiry, because we must employ this to rectify whatever shall be found amiss elsewhere.

3. And

3. And in such employment consists principally, if not entirely, the benefit we may expect from reason, which is necessary to be noted, that we may know wherein she may prove serviceable: for some people require too much at her hands, more than she is able to perform, they want her to actuate every motion of their lives, which is impossible, for her power lies in her authority rather than her strength, she does little or nothing herself, but acts altogether by her inferior officers of the family of imagination: at least, till she takes them into her service, her efforts terminate in speculation alone, and do not extend to practice. Nor can she work, even in her own peculiar province, without continual supplies from elsewhere; for she works upon materials found in the repository of ideas. She never produces a judgment or a motive from her own fund, but holds the premisses in view until they throw assent or satisfaction upon the conclusion. She is perpetually asking, Why is such a thing true, Why is it desirable, but former experience must suggest the grounds from whence the answer will result; for reason does not make the truth nor the desire, but only lays things together whereout either of them may grow. And when she has formed her decisions, she must deposit them
with

with her partner for safe custody against future occasions; who proving ever so little unfaithful, all she has deposited will either be absolutely lost or so weakened in its colours as to become unserviceable. She runs very short lengths, sees very little way at once, therefore must establish rules and maxims for her own guidance, and make over her treasures to imagination as she acquires them, that they may rise spontaneously to serve her afterwards in her further advances towards knowledge. But we ordinarily mistake the province of reason by supposing every thing reasonable to lie within it, whereas that epithet implies no more than a thing that reason would not disapprove. But many very just and solid opinions we imbibe from education or custom without any application to our reason at all: and those we do acquire for ourselves by the due exercise of that faculty, when firmly rooted become the property of imagination: conviction growing into persuasion. They then command our assent without contemplating the evidences whereon they were founded, and that full assurance wherewith they strike the mind instantly upon presenting themselves, is not an act of reason, but of habit or some moral or internal sense, which continue to influence though consideration and understanding lie
dormant

CHAP. 26.] *Reason.* 217

dormant. Were our faculty of reason to be suddenly taken from us, how unable soever we might find ourselves, to make new acquisitions of knowledge or judgment, we should not necessarily lose those already gotten by former exercises of the faculty.

4. But if the office of reason lie within so narrow compass in her own province of speculation, we shall find it reduced to narrower limits when applying her theory to practice; for she is a tedious heavy mover, poring a long while upon objects before she can determine her choice; our active powers will not always wait her leisure, but take directions elsewhere while she deliberates. Besides, there is not always time for consideration; when the season of action comes unexpectedly, we must instantly turn ourselves one way or other, therefore should make no dispatch in business, or must give up the reins to chance, if we had not some rules and measures of conduct ready in store for our guidance: and the principal service our understanding does, is by holding our attention steady to those rules, wherein she quickly tires and faints unless there be some motive of pleasure, or profit, or honour, or necessity, at hand to assist her. And yet in doing this service she performs the smallest share of our work, directing only the main tenor of our conduct; but the component

nent acts whereof that conduct consists must be suggested in train by former practice and experience: for it avails little to know what is expedient or the rules proper for attaining it without an expertness and readiness in practising them. The orator may choose his arguments and select the topics proper for enforcing them, but the figures, the language, and the pronunciation, will be such as he has accustomed himself to in former exercises. The musician may think what tune he will play, what divisions he shall run, or with what graces he shall embellish it; but unless his eye has learnt by use to run currently along the notes, and his fingers along the keys, he will make very indifferent harmony. The business of life goes on by means of habit, opinion and affection, which understanding only checks from time to time, or turns, or sets them at work without adding anything to their vigour, unless by bringing several of them to co-operate together. Reason, as Mr. Pope says, is the card, but passion is the gale; and if there were a necessity of parting with one of them, we might better spare the former than the latter: for though the course of the ship would be very uncertain without a compass, yet without a wind it would not move at all. To lose our reason would make us beasts: to lose our appetites, mere logs.

5. If

5. If there be any instances wherein reason shows signs of an active vigour, they are when we surmount difficulties or endure labours or pains by mere dint of resolution: yet even here every one's experience may convince him how feebly she acts unless seconded by some powerful motive retained in view, and how carefully she is forced to fortify herself all around with considerations of damage, or shame, or compunction. Nor has she even this little vigour naturally, but acquires it by enuring the mind by previous discipline to a habit of perseverance; which when gained, a little time passing in softness and indulgence will divest her of it again. And when with all her care and contrivance she has mustered up a resolution, we know too well how wofully it fails in time of trial, how often it is born down by the weight of pain or passion, undermined by the working of habit, or surprised by some sudden temptation catching her at unawares.

I have remarked elsewhere that if our imagination were rightly set so as to exhibit no false appearances, and our appetites and desires all turned upon proper objects, we should want nothing else to answer all the purposes of life more effectually and readily than we can do now. On the other hand, if our understandings were so large as to
comprise

comprise in one prospect all the tendencies of things so far as they might affect us, and to see the future in as strong colours as the present, we might serve ourselves of that alone to supply all our occasions. But since we have neither of our faculties perfect, we must employ both in their proper offices to make up for each others difficiency. Man has been incompleatly defined a rational animal, he is rather, to use Mr. Woolaston's words, sensitivo-rational, therefore must regard both parts of his constitution: for one can do nothing without the other, and this would run riot and do worse than nothing without continual direction from that.

6. The contrariety and opposition observable in the mind gave rise, as I have already remarked in my first chapter, to the notion of several Wills, within us: for the mind constantly following the direction of her ideas, that state of them immediately preceding her action, we entitle the Will, by a metonyme or sometimes mistake of the cause for the effect. For, if we apprehend every prospect of objects inclining us to act to be really a Will, we shall fall into the absurdity of several Wills, several agents and persons in the same man: whereas it is the same agent, the same power, that acts in all cases, whether we act madly or soberly, whether we deny

or

or indulge our Wills. But, if we take the matter figuratively, this diversity of persons may serve aptly enough to express the disordered condition of human nature, wherein reason and passion perpetually struggle, resist, and controul, one another. The metaphor employed by Plato, was that of a charioteer driving his pair of horses, by which latter he allegorized the concupiscible and irascible passions: but as we have now-a-days left off driving our own chariots, but keep a coachman to do it for us, I think the mind may be more commodiously compared to a traveller riding a single horse, wherein reason is represented by the rider, and imagination with all its trains of opinions, appetites and habits, by the beast. Everybody sees the horse does all the work, the strength and speed requisite for performing it are his own, he carries his master along every step of the journey, directs the motion of his own legs in walking, trotting, galloping, or stepping over a rote, makes many by-motions, as whisking the flies with his tail or playing with his bit, all by his own instinct; and if the road lie plain and open without bugbears to affright him or rich pasture on either hand to entice him, he will jog on, although the reins were laid upon his neck, or in a well-acquainted road take the right turnings of his

own

own accord. Perhaps sometimes he may prove startish or restive, turning out of the way, or running into a pond to drink, maugre all endeavours to prevent him; but this depends greatly upon the discipline he has been used to. The office of the rider lies in putting his horse into the proper road, and the pace most convenient for the present purpose, guiding and conducting him as he goes along, checking him when too forward or spurring him when too tardy, being attentive to his motions, never dropping the whip nor losing the reins, but ready to interpose instantly whenever needful, keeping firm in his seat if the beast behaves unruly, observing what passes in the way, the condition of the ground, and bearings of the country, in order to take directions therefrom for his proceeding. But this is not all he has to do, for there are many things previous to the journey; he must get his tackling in good order, bridle, spurs, and other accoutrements; he must learn to sit well in the saddle, to understand the ways and temper of the beast, get acquainted with the roads and enure himself by practice to bear long journeys without fatigue or galling; he must provide provender for his horse and deal it out in proper quantities, for if weak and jadish, or pampered and gamesome, he will not perform
the

the journey well: he must have him well broke, taught all his paces, cured of starting, stumbling, running away, and all skittish or sluggish tricks, trained to answer the bit and be obedient to the word of command. If he can teach him to canter whenever there is a smooth and level turf, and stop when the ground lies rugged, of his own accord, it will contribute to make riding easy and pleasant: he may then enjoy the prospects around or think of any business without interruption to his progress. As to the choice of a horse our rider has no concern with that, but must content himself with such as nature and education have put into his hands: but since the spirit of the beast depends much upon the usage given him, every prudent man will endeavour to proportion that spirit to his own strength and skill in horsemanship; and according as he finds himself a good or bad rider will wish to have his horse sober or mettlesome. For strong passions work wonders where there is a stronger force of reason to curb them: but where this is weak the appetites must be feeble too or they will lie under no controul.

7. From all that has been said above, as well literally as allegorically, we may learn what the proper business of reason is, namely, to watch over our motions and look out for the

the proper measures of conduct with as much circumspection as the present circumstances of the case shall permit or require. For this there is little need of instruction, but rather exhortation, to prevail on men to exert their faculty; for everybody knows the difference between considerate and thoughtless behaviour. The principal part of her employment, lies in storing the mind with solid knowledge, establishing useful rules of conduct, and above all contracting such habits and desires, as may continually lead the active powers into proper courses. For this last branch is of the most importance, because it fructifies our knowledge by making it practical; nor can any one doubt that the world would receive more improvement by everybody's living up to what they know, than by any encrease of their knowledge whatever; and that they do not live up to it, can be owing to nothing else besides bad habits and inordinate desires. But every rule and every desire must have some purpose to drive at, and it becomes reason to examine the propriety of the purpose as well as conduciveness of the measures towards obtaining it: this commonly leads to some further end first recommending that purpose to our choice, and that many times points out another end lying still beyond, and so on without

out limitation. For the most part we stop at a few general principles which we have found most universally received or esteem valuable in themselves, without knowing or without remembering what first discovered to us their value: and this method may serve well enough for common use. But the studious in their seasons of leisure and contemplation, endeavour to carry back their researches as far as they can push them, and penetrate quite to the fountain head: but being sensible that reason muts come to a stop at last and arrive at something which had a recommendation prior to any that she could give it, they strive to find out what is that First or Ultimate end, for first and last here are the same thing, which nature has given for our pursuit, and from which reason must deduce all those principles and rules of action she recommends. And as there has been great variance upon this point, it will deserve a particular consideration, for which I shall appropriate the next ensuing chapter.

CHAP. XXVII.

ULTIMATE GOOD.

For so I choose to translate the Summum Bonum of the ancients, as much and as unsuccessfully sought after as the philosopher's stone, rather than call it the Chief Good as it is vulgarly termed. For the enquiry was not to ascertain the degrees of goodness in objects or determine what possessed it in the highest pitch beyond all others; but, since the goodness of things depends upon their serviceableness towards procuring something we want, to discover what was that one thing intrinsically good which contented the mind of itself and rendered all others desirable in proportion as they tended directly or remotely to procure it. Good, says Mr. Locke, is that which produces pleasure, and if we understand it thus strictly, in the true original sense, our enquiry were vain: for then the very expression of good in itself would be absurd, because nothing good could be ultimate, the pleasure it produces lying always beyond. But it is customary to call that good which stands at the very end of our wishes, and contents the mind without reference to any thing further:

ther: and in this common acceptation the term will be applicable to our present purpose.

2. Upon perusal of the chapter of satisfaction and those of the four classes of motives, whoever shall happen to think they contain a just representation of human nature, need not be long in seeking for this summum bonum: for he will perceive it to be none other than pleasure or satisfaction, which is pleasure taken in the largest sense, as comprising every complacence of mind together with the avoidance of pain or uneasiness. Perhaps I shall be charged with reviving the old exploded doctrine of Epicurus upon this article, but I am not ashamed of joining with any man of whatever character in those parts of it, where I think he has truth on his side: though whether I do really agree with him here, is more than I can be sure of, for I find great disputes concerning what he called pleasure. If he confined it to gross sensual delights or imaginations relative thereto, as his adversaries charged him with, and the bulks of his followers seem to have understood him, I cannot consent to shut myself up within such narrow limits: for though these things may afford a genuine satisfaction sometimes and when sparingly used, yet it is to be had more plentifully elsewhere.

Therefore, being regardless whether my sentiments tally or no with those of Epicurus, I shall not trouble myself to examine what he really thought, but endeavour as far as I am able to explain what this satisfaction is which I suppose, the summum bonum or ultimate end of action. And this I cannot do better than by referring, as I have done before in the chapter upon that article, to every man's experience of the condition of mind he finds himself in when any thing happens to his wish or good liking; when he feels the cool breezes of a summer evening or the comfortable warmth of a winter fire; when he gains possession of something useful or profitable; when he has done any thing he can applaud himself for or will redound to his credit with persons he esteems.

3. But to consider satisfaction physically, it is a perception of the mind, residing in her alone, constantly one and the same in kind how much soever it may vary in degree: for whether a man be pleased with hearing music, seeing prospects, tasting dainties, performing laudable actions, or making agreeable reflections, his complacence and condition of mind will be the same if equal in degree, though coming from different quarters. But this complacence, and indeed every other perception, the mind never has unless

excited

excited in her by some external object striking upon her bodily senses or some idea giving play to her mental organs. We have supposed there may be some certain fibre whose peculiar office it is to affect the mind in this manner, and our organs please or not by their motion according as, in the natural texture or present disposition of our frame, they stand connected with this spring of satisfaction. Whether there really be such a particular spring or no is not very material to know, for if we could ascertain its existence we cannot come at it either with the finger or surgeon's probe so as to set it a working for our entertainment. Since then we cannot touch this spring directly, we must endeavour to convey an impulse to it by those channels that nature has provided us with for the purpose: for common experience testifies that there are variety of sensations and reflections qualified to excite satisfaction in the mind when we can apply them. But our attention, usually reaching no further than to these causes, for if we can procure them the effect will follow of course, we give the name of pleasure to those sensations and scenes of imagination which touch us in the sensible part: hence pleasure becomes an improper term to express the summum bonum by, because objects or ideas that have pleased, may not do so again; therefore if we

were

were to recommend it as the end of action we might be misunderstood, or mislead some unwary person already inclined that way into the pursuit of a wrong object; for pleasure in the vulgar acceptation will not always please. If Epicurus understood it in this sense, I renounce communion with him as a heretic; but if by pleasure he meant the very complacence of mind generated by agreeable objects of any kind whatever, I cannot refuse him my assistance against all opponents; and the rather for fear this may prove the only point whereon we shall ever have an opportunity of joining forces together.

4. Nor can it be doubted that satisfaction is proposed to our pursuit by nature, when we reflect how universally and perpetually it engages all mankind, how steadily volition follows the prospect of immediate satisfaction, as has been shown in the foregoing enquiry, if one may be said to show a thing that was before sufficiently manifested by Mr. Locke. The man and the child, the civilized and the savage, the learned and the vulgar, the prudent and the giddy, the good and the wicked, constantly pursue whatever appears most satisfactory to them in their present apprehension: and if at any time they forego an immediate pleasure for sake of a distant advantage, it is because they conceive a greater satisfaction

tion in the prospect of that advantage or uneasiness in the thought of missing it. Therefore, those who can content themselves with the enjoyments of to-day without feeling an actual concern for the morrow, will never be moved to action by any thing future, how fully soever they acknowledge the expedience of it: and when pain rises so high as that the mind cannot find any contentment under it, it will overpower the best grounded resolutions. Neither is there any more room to doubt of satifaction being the ultimate end than of its being a natural good, because all other goodness centers in that, the gratifications of pleasure, the rules of prudence and morality, are good, only as they tend by themselves or in their consequences to satisfy the mind: one may give a reason for all other things being good, but for that alone no reason can be given, for experience not reason must recommend it. Why is knowledge good? because it directs us to choose the things that are most useful: Why are useful things good? because they minister to the supply of our wants and desires. Why is this supply good? because it satisfies the mind. Why is satisfaction good? here you must stop, for there lies nothing beyond to furnish materials for an answer: but if anybody denies it, you can only refer him to his own common sense, by asking how he
finds

finds himself when in a state of satisfaction or disquietude, and whether of them he would prefer to the other.

In short the matter seems so clear that one may be thought to trifle in spending so many words to prove it: and after all, what is the upshot of the whole but to show that satisfaction satisfies? a mere identical proposition adding nothing to our knowledge, but the same as if one should say that plenitude fills, that heat warms, that hardness resists and softness yields to the touch. Yet as trifling as the proposition may appear, Mr. Locke has bestowed a great deal of pains in proving the value and efficacy of satisfaction: nor have there been wanting persons of no small reputation with whom such pains were necessary, who out of their extravagant zeal for virtue denied that all other pleasures conferred any thing towards bettering the condition of the mind. Had they pronounced them cloying, unstable, often delusive of the expectation, and productive of greater mischiefs, they had said right and enough to answer their main purpose: but this would not do, they insisted that when we see a man actually pleased with trifles, wanting nothing else, but fully contented with the condition of mind they throw him into, nevertheless he was miserable at the very instant of enjoyment without regard

to

to consequences. What is this but undertaking to prove that satisfaction does not satify, which whoever can accomplish may rise to be a Cardinal, for he need not fear being able to demonstrate transubstantiation. Our divines talk more rationally when they admit that the pleasures of sin may satify for a moment, but are too dearly bought when purchased with disease, shame, remorse, and an incapacity for higher enjoyments.

5. One remark more concerning the summum bonum, viz. that though a noun of the singular number, nevertheless it is one in species only, containing a multitude of individuals. For our perceptions are fleeting and momentary, objects strike successively upon our organs, and ideas rise incessantly in our imagination, which thereby throw the mind into a state of complacence or disquietude, corresponding with the manner of their impulse, which has no duration: therefore satisfaction cannot continue without a continual application of satisfactory causes. This gains another name for the summum bonum, and makes us entitle it Happiness, which is the aggregate of satisfactions. For though this term be sometimes applied to the enjoyment of a single moment, and then is synonymous with satisfaction, yet it more generally and properly
denotes

denotes the surplus of successes a man has met with or may expect over and above his disappointments: if the surplus be any thing considerable, we pronounce him happy; if his disquietudes greatly exceed, we style him miserable. Ovid understood it in this sense when he laid down that we can never pronounce a man happy before his death, because the fortune of life being uncertain, whatever enjoyments we see him possessed of we can never be sure they may not be overbalanced by evils to come: and Milton the same, in his apostrophe to our first parents, Sleep on blest pair, yet happy if ye seek not other happiness and know to know no more. But sound sleep, being a state of insensibility, is capable neither of satisfaction nor uneasiness: therefore the sleeping pair were happy only in respect to that ample store of unmingled pleasures lying in reserve for them against they awoke.

Thus happiness relates to the whole tenor of our lives, but multitudes of our actions do not reach so far as to affect our condition so long as we have our being: this breaks happiness again into smaller portions corresponding with the length or extent of their influence. It may be all one after dinner whether I eat mutton or chicken, but if one will please me better during the time of eating and

and the indulgence will do me no harm, why should not I take that I like best? When we lay out a day's diversion by some little excursion abroad we regard what will entertain us most for the day, notwithstanding some trifling inconveniences of sloppy roads or indifferent accommodations at a paltry inn. If we take a house we consider, not what will be the most easy for the first month, but most commodious during the whole lease. And when a father puts his son to school, he might supply him with more enjoyment at home than can be expected during the seven years of schooling: but he considers that learning will enable him to pass his life afterwards more agreeably and usefully. Thus upon several actions proposed to our option, that is always the best which will add most to our happiness as far as its consequences extend.

6. Our satisfactions come sometimes from causes operating of their own accord, as upon change of weather from chill or sultry to moderate, or upon hearing joyful news unexpectedly; but for the most part we must procure them for ourselves by application of the proper means. Now since we are prompted to use our activity by desire, since the good things occurring spontaneously would have been objects of our desire had we known of them

them beforehand, or our intervention been wanted, therefore may justly be styled desirable, and since desire of itself renders objects satisfactory which would otherwise have been indifferent; therefore it is the first rule of happiness to procure the gratification of our desires; nor shall I scruple to recommend this as the proper business of life. Let every man by my consent study to gratify himself in whatever suits his taste and inclination, for they vary infinitely: one man's meat is another man's poison; what this person likes the next may abhor; what delights at one time may disgust at another; and what entertains when new may grow stale and insipid afterwards. Our appetites and fancies prompt us fast enough to this gratification, to choose objects suited to our particular tastes and to vary them as we find our relish change: but the misfortune is that desire often defeats her own purpose, either by mistaking things for satisfactory which are not, as when a child goes to play with the flame of a candle; or by a more common mistake apprehending gratification to lie in a single point, whereas this, like happiness, consists in the sum aggregate of enjoyments. He that indulges one desire to the crossing of many others, ought no more to be thought pursuing gratification than he can be thought to pursue profit

profit who takes twenty pounds to-day for goods that he might have sold to-morrow for forty: a true lover of money will reject it when offered upon such terms, and a true lover of gratification who knows what he is about will reject it upon the like. Therefore there is no occasion to persuade men out of their senses, and face them down that gratification adds nothing to their satisfaction, no not for a moment: on the contrary, we may exhort them to pursue it as a thing most valuable, and therefore to pursue it in the same manner as they would other valuable things, that is, not to take a little in hand in lieu of more they might have by and by. Any trifle that hits our fancy suffices to content the mind, and if we could enjoy it for ever with the same relish, it would answer our whole purpose; for I know of no weariness, no satiety, no change of taste in the mind, these all belong to the organs bodily and mental. When a glutton sits down to a well spread table with a good appetite, if he ever has any, he possesses as much of the summum bonum as can be obtained within the time; and if he had victuals continually supplied him, a hole in his throat to discharge them as fast as swallowed, and nothing in the world else to do, he might attain it compleatly; but this cannot be: yet if he can

prolong

prolong appetite beyond its stretch by high sauces, until he has overcharged himself, still I can allow him in a state of enjoyment during the repast, for he has a desire, and he gratifies it. But has he none other desires that will solicit him by and by? has he not a desire of being free from sickness of stomach, or distemper; nothing else he wants to do with his money; no diversion, no business that requires alertness of spirits, no regard for his credit, the good word of his friends, or his own peace of mind; if he has other desires that must suffer by indulging this one, he is a very bad accomptant in the article of gratification. Thus the very interests of our desires sometimes require self-denial, which is recommendable only on that account: nor would I advise a man ever to deny himself, unless in order to please himself better another time.

7. Since then our desires mislead us so grossly, sometimes mistaking their own intention, and at other times starving one another, let us have recourse to reason to moderate between them, and to remedy the inconveniences they would bring upon us: and this, upon observing the opposition among them, will quickly discover that there are two ways of attaining gratification, one by procuring the objects we desire, the other by accom-

accomodating desire to the objects before us, or most convenient for us upon the whole. Either of these methods would answer our purpose, if we could pursue it effectually: were it possible to command every thing with a wish, and supply fuel to our desires as fast as they start up, still varying their objects, as they themselves vary; or could we carry our heart in our hands, moulding it like wax, to the shape of every circumstance occurring, we need never feel a moment's uneasiness. But neither of these is possible, many things that would please us, lie out of our reach, some of them never to be obtained, others only now and then, as opportunity favours, but the greater part of them satiate, before desire abates: on the other hand, there are some natural desires we can never totally eradicate, some necessaries, without which we cannot sustain our bodies in vigour, nor our spirits in alertness, to serve us upon any occasion. Therefore we must drive the nail that will go, use our understandings in surveying the stock of materials for gratification, either generally or at any particular time in our power, and examining the state of our desires, which among them are most attainable, or least contradictory to others, or what we can do towards bending them to the ply most suitable to our convenience.

The

The former of these methods, that of procuring objects to our fancy, is the most obvious, therefore most commonly practised. We see men run eagerly after whatever their present desire urges them to, in proportion to the strength of their inclination; yet even here they must often call in consideration to their aid. For our pleasures, even those of them which are attainable, do not always hang so close within our reach, as that we can gather them whenever so disposed, but there are many things preparatory to the obtaining them; materials to be provided for supplying them, skill to be learned, dexterity to be acquired for the making and properly applying of that provision. This gives rise to the common rules of prudence, to all arts and sciences, directing or enabling men to make advances in fortune, honour, elegance, or other principal object they have set their hearts upon, and supplying the world with the conveniences and entertainments of life. The preparatories to pleasure, will by translation become themselves objects of desire sufficient to move us, without the reference they bear to their end; and it is necessary they should, or else we must miss of the benefit they will do us. For as a traveller must not keep his thoughts constantly intent upon the place he wishes to arrive at, if he would make any dispatch in

his

his journey, but having once taken the right road, fixes his eye upon the nearest parts of it as he goes along: so neither can we always contemplate the enjoyments we are providing for ourselves without interrupting our progress. Our capacities are too short to hold the whole line of our pursuit in view, but we must rest upon some part of it most convenient for our present direction: nor indeed could we always see to the end of our line if we were to strain ever so much, therefore must trust to others, or to our own former determination, for an assurance that it will lead us the way we would wish. Thus happiness, although the ultimate end of action, yet is not always, perhaps I might say very seldom, our ultimate point of view: for our road lies through lanes and hedges, or over an uneven, hilly country, where we can see very little way before us: nay, sometimes we must seemingly turn our backs upon it, and take a compass round in the plain beaten track, to avoid impracticable morasses, or other obstacles intervening. Hence we may learn why pleasure is so deceitful a guide to happiness, because it plunges us headlong forward through thick and thin, fixing our eyes upon a single point and taking them off from the marks leading to that aggregate of satisfactions whereof happiness consists. Wherefore he that resolves to please himself always will scarce ever do so, for by perpetually indulging his desires he will destroy or lose the means of indulging them.

8. For the skill of providing materials to gratify our desires, we must consult common prudence and discretion, or resort to the professors of arts and sciences, containing the several branches of it: but the other method of gratification by managing the mind itself and bringing desire to the most convenient ply, belongs properly to the moralist; whose business lies not so much in informing you how to procure what you want, as how to forbear wanting what you cannot have, or would prove hurtful to you. But want cannot be removed without aid of some other want; for as you can never bring a man to assent to a proposition unless by means of some premisses whereto he does already assent, so you can never bring him to any desire, unless by showing the connection it bears with something he already desires. The desire of happiness would suffice for this purpose, if we had it stronger infixed than we find in our breasts: but though all have this desire, so far as that they would be willing enough to receive happiness, if they could get it upon asking for, yet, being an aggregate, and therefore always in part at least distant, they prefer the present gratification of other desires before it.
Therefore

Therefore the moralist will begin with striving to inculcate this desire of happiness into himself and others as deeply as possible. But since this can hardly ever be done so effectually as one would wish, for we can never raise so vivid an idea of remote objects, as to equal those standing close to us, he will examine all other propensities belonging to us in order to encourage those which are most innocent, most satisfactory, most compatible together, and best promoting his principal aim. These he will endeavour to render habitual, so as that they may start up to the thought uncalled, and gather strength enough to overpower others he wishes to eradicate. As we cannot upon every occasion see to the end of our proceedings, he will establish certain rules to serve as landmarks for guiding us on the way. These rules, when he has leisure and opportunity for mature consideration, he will build on one another, erecting the whole fabric upon the basis of summum bonum before described. But because their reference to the ultimate end cannot be continually kept in mind, he will enure himself and everybody within his reach, by such methods as he shall find feasible, to look upon them as good in themselves, that they may become influencing principles of action. The outer branches of these

these rules, calculated for ordinary occasions, will of course vary according to those occasions or to the tempers, abilities, situations, and needs of different persons, to particularize all which would be endless and impracticable; but there are a few general rules universally expedient as being the stem whereout the rest are to grow. The first seems to be that of habituating ourselves to follow the dictates of judgment in preference to any impulse of passion, fancy, or appetite, and forbear whatever our reason disapproves as being wrong: for there is nothing more evident than that the knowledge of right and wrong can do us no benefit while resting in speculation alone and not reduced into practice, which it can never be unless become habitual, and striking with the force of an obligation or an object of desire.

CHAP. XXVIII.

RECTITUDE.

WE hear much of an essential rectitude in certain things, but before we attempt to judge of their essence it will be expedient to settle with ourselves the purport of the he word Right, for we shall be likely to reason very indifferently without understanding the terms we employ. Right belongs originally to lines, being the same as straight in opposition to curve or crooked. Everybody knows a right line is the shortest that can lie between two points so as to touch them both, and the nearest approach from any one to any other given point is along such right line. From hence it has been applied by way of metaphor to rules and actions, which lying in the line of our progress towards any purpose we aim at, if they be wrong they will carry us aside, and we shall either wholly miss of our intent, or must begin again and take a longer compass than necessary to arrive at it: but if they conduct effectually and directly by the nearest way we pronounce them right. Therefore the very expression of right in itself is absurd, because things are rendered right by their tendency to some end, so that you must take something exterior into the account in order to evidence their rectitude. Rules are termed right upon a supposition of their expedience, and so are actions too for the most part: when a man digs for hidden treasure we say he has hit upon the right spot if he pitches his spade just over where the treasure lies, though perhaps he did it by guess: but since we are often uncertain

certain of our actions we apply them to some rule in order to determine their propriety. Hence action has another source of rectitude, namely, its conformity with rule, and consequently may chance to be right or wrong according to which of the two sources you refer it: for our rules being generally imperfect or built upon probability, we may act right, that is, conformable to them, and yet take a wrong course with respect to the design we had in view. If you look over the hands at whist and see the party upon whose side you have betted lead his ace of trumps when the adversary has king alone, you will be apt to cry out Right played! because it suits your purpose best of any thing he could have done; yet perhaps he might play wrong according to the rules of the game. What if you see him playing on sundays? you may perceive he plays his cards extremely well, yet if you are a conscientious man you will condemn him for acting wrong: but playing is acting, so then he acts right and wrong at the same instant. What becomes now of the essence of rectitude, when the opposite essence resides in the same subject? Can the essence of things change without any alteration in themselves, but as they are compared to this or that particular object, or set in various lights? Besides that actions perfectly innocent,

cent, having neither essence regarded nakedly in themselves, may derive it elsewhere: nothing can be more harmless than wagging your finger considered in itself, yet if the finger rest against the trigger of a loaded musket, and a man stand just before, you cannot do a wronger thing, and why? not because of any thing contained in the essence of the action, but because of the fatal consequences attendant thereupon. Nor are rules less liable to vary their rectitude, which constantly follows expedience and changes with the change of persons or circumstances. Suppose you lay down for a rule, When you want provisions go the east; this may be a very good precept for those who live to the westward of a market-town, but when carried to villages on any other point of the compass loses its essence.

2. It must be owned that this essential and intrinsic rectitude is not attributed to all rules, but to those only supposed invariable and general, not confined to particular cases. I know of none better entitled to this character than that recommended at the close of the foregoing chapter, to follow reason in preference to passion and appetite: yet one may question whether this be in fact perpetual, for what rule is it to a young child not arrived at the use of his understanding, or to a

man

man who has lost it through age or distempers? Or if there were a man whose appetites were so happily turned as to fix always upon things beneficial, our rule would be wrong, because reflection and consideration would retard the speed of appetite and interrupt it in its operations. But this case being never likely to happen upon earth, we will admit the rule to be invariable; still its rectitude flows from the condition of mankind, which may be looked upon as a permanent circumstance attending them through the whole line of their existence. So then all rules whatever as well general as particular become right, not from any thing essential or in themselves, but from their reference to happiness, and the situation either natural or accidental of the party to be directed by them.

3. Though I said just now that the conformity to rule was a second source of rectitude in actions, yet this conformity does not so much constitute as discover their rectitude. Could we always see the certain consequences of our conduct we should need no rules, for our own sagacity would be a sufficient guide: but since our ultimate end is not perpetually our ultimate point of view, as lying beyond our ken, we want certain marks to direct us in our approach towards it. The rules of
life

life are those marks hung up by observing men for the benefit of themselves and others travelling the road: but nobody supposes a mark to carry any essential intrisic goodness. Thus rules draw their goodness from the shortness of our views and narrowness of our capacities, and bear a reference not only to the good end whereto they conduce, but likewise to the need we stand under of a conductor. As people make further proficiency in any art or business they employ the fewer rules, and in things quite familiar to them they use none: like carriers jogging on continually in the same road with whom posts of direction lose their quality and become no direction at all. To tell a man that when he walks he must step one foot first and then the other were no rule, for he does it of his own accord; but what is nothing can have no essence and contain nothing.

4. But it may be objected that actions sometimes receive a rectitude from their conformity to rule when they do not answer the purpose intended by them. A good man, failing in the success of his endeavours, will find great consolation in reflecting that he had acted right, that is, had laid his measures justly and executed them punctually. But let us remember that the good man aims

at

at happiness rather than pleasure, that is, at the greater sum of satisfactions preferably to the less, and though he misses his purpose in the present instance by following his rule, yet he shall attain it more compleatly in other instances by the like adherence. Your gamesters have two sayings current among them, one that the cards will beat anybody, the other that the best player will always come off winner at the year's end. So how much soever fortune may influence our success in the game of life, yet she is not so unequal in her favours but that prudence and steadiness will always succeed in the long run better than folly and inconsiderateness. The consolation under disappointment of measures rightly taken rests upon this bottom, that as acts of conformity to rule strengthen and evince our habit of adherence to regular conduct, the possession of this habit conduces more to our happiness than any little success we might have gained by a lucky misconduct: and we may reasonably esteem ourselves put into a better condition upon the whole by performing those acts of conformity than we should have stood in had we omitted them. Therefore whenever we can discern the inexpedience of our rule, and may depart from it without lessening our own regard for it or those of other people, we always deem this

an

an excepted case: and if it be true, what is commonly held, that there is no rule without exceptions, then there is no rule which may not become wrong in some instance or other.

5. Let us now trace out if we can the origin of those epithets Essential and Intrinsic, and examine how they first came applied to rectitude of rules: for we cannot but suppose there must be some good foundation for the use of terms we see currently used among learned and judicious men. There are some rules which respect the qualities of objects wherewith we have any concern, and of course must vary according as those objects change their position, or others succeed in their room, or as we have or cease to have a concern with them: these we style occasional, being calculated for particular occasions and relating to the situation wherein we happen to stand. Others take their rise from the make and constitution of man, and therefore cannot change with any change of place or things external, because we can never remove ourselves from ourselves: these are called essential as being founded on the very essence of human nature. Thus, lay in a stock of coals in summer, is a very proper rule of family œconomy here in this climate, where the coldness of our winters renders such a provision necessary; but if we

were

were to inhabit the torrid zone, this rule would lose its rectitude. But look before you leap, is a rule calculated upon the observation of human nature, wherein appetite would continually hurry on to mischief if not restrained by consideration: therefore this rule will remain right everywhere and always so long as we continue to be human creatures, that is, sensitivo-rational animals. The former I take to be of the occasional kind and the latter essential: and a very proper distinction it is, as instructing us which to prefer when they happen to come into competition. Nevertheless, the essence belongs, not to the rule, but to the object whereon it is grounded.

6. The idea of right in itself I conceive arose from observing that our rules grow from one another, their rectitude depending upon the rectitude of those whereout they spring; and that some of them may be rendered right or wrong by authority, custom or compact. It was right some years ago to import and wear cambric, but now it would be wrong, because the laws have prohibited it: it was right among our ancestors to appear in public with ruffs, slashed sleeves and high hats, but now wrong, the fashion being altered: it might have been right yesterday for me to have resolved upon taking a long journey of pleasure, but
if

if I have since made a solemn appointment to meet a neighbour here at home, it would be wrong to disappoint him. These things are rendered right or wrong by their conformity or contrariety to the higher rules of obedience to the legislature, of decency and good manners, and of fidelity to our engagements, without which there can be no order nor agreeable converse, nor dependance in the world: but because we do not always discern, or at least not think of their expedience, we entitle them right in themselves; whereas the rules receiving their sanction from them we do not call so because we can see to what they owe their rectitude. This distinction likewise is of great use because it helps to discover the proper objects of authority, custom, and compact, for what carries a strong intrinsic rectitude they cannot alter: no laws, nor general practice of a country, nor private engagement can make it right to commit murder. I said a strong intrinsic rectitude, for there are various degrees of it, and rules carrying a higher degree may supersede those of a lower. Surely the rule of self-preservation must be acknowledged right in itself, yet the laws of every country oblige men to neglect this by compelling them into military service, and I never heard such laws
absolutely

absolutely condemned by the speculative as unrighteous. And when intrinsic rules interfere, that ought to carry the preference which conduces most largely to happiness, wherein not only the present expedience is to be considered, but likewise the danger of invalidating a rule and the greater mischiefs that may ensue thereby: which make such cases many times extremely difficult to determine, there being so many distant consequences to be taken into account.

7. Thus I conceive those rules essentially and intrinsically right of whose rectitude we are well satisfied or find no controversy made, although we do not discern from whence that rectitude flowed; and these rules are of signal service for trying others of an inferior kind by an application to them: therefore, I am not for discarding the terms, but giving them their due weight and setting them upon their proper foundation. For some men carry them a great deal too far by supposing them to imply something valuable contained in the exercise of a rule without reference to any thing further: as when they place the wisdom of Regulus's choice of a certain and cruel death rather than breaking faith with his enemies, in the sole act of conformity to the rules of fidelity abstracted from consequences.

quences. If Regulus did right, it must be not for any value in the naked act but upon supposition that he acted more for his own happiness in the sequel than he could have done by any breach of faith, for we can hardly think he acted more for his present ease. I know of nothing absolutely good besides satisfaction, but since there are many actions not apparently satisfactory or sometimes the reverse, which yet tend to procure an encrease of happiness, rules are the marks directing us to the choice of such actions: and the highest rules are those which answer this purpose most generally and effectually. We meet with persons sometimes who, perceiving a character of rectitude in their rules, will not suffer you to ask why they are right, but stop your mouth with the repetition of a necessary and essential rectitude: such may be very honest and worthy men, and if their principles be good and their practice conformable, they certainly deserve that character, but to talk in this strain upon a serious enquiry or contest with an opponent is talking very unphilosophically. For no rule is right without a reason that renders it so, nor are the clearest of them above examination; nay an examination now and then is adviseable, they being apt to warp with common use or contract rust and dross with lying by, and

if

if their purity and sterling be doubted of, there is none other so certain way to try them as by the touchstone of expedience.

CHAP. XXIX.

VIRTUE.

VIRTUE has been always esteemed something habitual: our first advances towards it were styled by the ancients an Inchoation of virtue, or as we may call it the embryo or seedling not yet arrived to perfection. A drunkard who abstains from liquor once or twice does not instantly commence a sober man, nor do we think him entitled to that appellation until he has so mastered his fondness for tippling that it disturbs him no more. Thus virtue we see is a habit: it remains to fix on some characteristic whereby to distinguished it from other habits. The most obvious definition is that of a habit of acting rightly: but this upon examination will be found much too large, as taking in other things which do not belong to the subject we would define: for though we must acknowledge every act of genuine virtue to be
right,

right, yet every right action is not an act of virtue. It is certainly very right to eat when we are hungry, sleep when we are weary, put on boots when we ride a journey, and a great coat when we must walk abroad in the rain: so is the habit of taking things with the right hand rather than the left, speaking when we are spoken to, crying out when somebody treads upon out toe: but these are never looked upon as instances of virtue, nor have they any other concern with her than that she does not disallow them. The next definition occurring is a habit of contradicting any inordinate desire or impulse of passion; but against this their lies two exceptions. One that there are people whose natural temperament or manner of education inclines them to be temperate, chaste, industrious, generous, or obliging, without any efforts of their own: now it would be hard to deny these qualities the title of virtues, and imprudent not to propose them as such to the imitation of other persons. The other that this definition seems not to suit with virtue at all unless in her imperfect embryo state wherein she is not herself: for after the opposite passion being compleatly mastered, there remains nothing for her to contradict. Can we suppose then that virtue loses her essence the moment she has gotten it? or were there a man who had conquered all his passions, should we deem him destitute of every virtue because he possesses them all? Let us try then once more and call virtue a habit of pursuing courses contrary to those pernicious ones that passion or appetite generally lead men into: we shall now save the credit of natural good qualities and those imbibed insensibly from custom, together with the benefit of their example to the world, and secure the prize to all who have compleated their conquest. Nor shall we contradict the old observation, that the paths of virtue are rugged and thorny at first, but lead in a delightful champaign country: whereas did virtue consist in opposition alone, she could accompany her votary no further than through the thorny paths, but must quit him as soon as the champaign opens. This definition I believe contains the idea of virtue most generally entertained, and will serve best for common use: for those courses which virtue would recommend being beneficial, let us encourage the practice of them by any means we can, and bestow our applauses upon them in whatever manner acquired. If a man be affable and courteous, and ready to help his neighbours upon every occasion where wanted, it is all one with respect to the world and to his own pleasure of mind in the exercise of those qualities,

qualities, whether he had them from nature or good company, or gained them by his own good management and industry. Under this notion of virtue it will appear capable of variation both in kind and degree; for as many evil courses as there are into which men stand liable to be drawn by their passions and desires, there will be so many opposite virtues: and as every habit gathers strength by exercise, it will enable a man more and more to resist temptation in proportion as it strikes deeper root. The man may be sober at home, who cannot forbear excesses among a jovial company: or may have common honesty, though he wants that total exemption from the bias of self-interest which would denominate him strictly righteous.

2. Yet it still remains a question whether we ought to satisfy ourselves, much less can please everybody even with this last definition; for it may be asked, What merit is there in following the bent of inclination or torrent of example when they chance to carry us in a right course? Does not the province of virtue lie solely in controuling the passions and surmounting difficulties? at least is she not stronger and more conspicuous in the conquest of an adversary than when she has none to contend with? When we see a man bear slander and reproach with a becom-

ing patience, does it not heighten our opinion of him to hear that he was of a warm violent temper, bred up in a country remarkable for being choleric and testy? Remember the story of Zopyrus, the physiognomist, who pretending to know people's characters by their faces, some of Socrates's scholars brought him to their master, whom he had never seen before, and asked him what he thought of that man. Zopyrus after examining his features pronounced him the most debauched, lewd, cross-grained, selfish old fellow he had ever met with; upon which the company burst out a laughing. Hold, says Socrates, do not run down the man, he is in the right I assure you: for I was all he says of me by nature, and if you think me otherwise now, it must be because I have in some measure corrected my nature by the study and practice of philosophy. Now does not this story manifest a higher pitch of virtue in Socrates than he could have attained had his stars befriended him with the happiest turn of constitution?

To these queries I shall answer, there is a particular species of virtue, which we may call the habit of following the dictates of judgment in preference to the impulse of fancy or appetite, and therefore may well enough fall within our definition, and if it were

were possible to be attained in full perfection would subdue all other desires, so that it could not then consist in opposition, having none to struggle against. This I acknowledge to be the most excellent of the virtues, as most generally serviceable to influence the practice, and being the root whereout we might raise all the others: for if we had this habit in any considerable degree, it would supply their places and quickly bring us into such of them as were wanting. Therefore when we behold a man persevering in a right course against the bent of nature and stream of example, we know he must have an ample portion of this higher virtue, which redounds more to his honour than any of the inferior kind. But I see no reason why the superior excellence of this virtue should destroy the merit of all the rest. Silver may be worth having though not so valuable as gold: and whatever tends to mend our manners, to the benefit of society, or our own convenience, does not deserve to be despised though something else may tend more eminently to the same purposes. If a man be made honest by self-interest to preserve his customers, it is better than that he should not be honest at all: if he keep himself sober for his health's sake, still it is a point gained: if he learn activity and perseverance in difficult undertakings
from

from a love of fame, it is likely he will do more good to the world and find more engagement for his time than if he sat still in indolence. Therefore I am for storing up as many of these inferior virtues as possible by any means we see feasible. As old Gripe said to his son, my boy, get money; if you can, honestly; however, get money: so would I say to any body that will hear me, Acquire good qualities by your desire of rectitude, if you can; however, acquire them. Yet notwithstanding what I have been saying here, I think we ought to make the love of rectitude our principal care, to strengthen it as much as in us lies, and keep it in continual exercise by rectifying the frailties of our nature and turning those inclinations that still point towards an improper object.

3. The stoics, as far as I understand of them, would allow none other virtue besides this of rectitude: therefore they held all exercises of virtue and all offences equal and alike, robbing an orchard as criminal as breaking open a house or betraying the most important trust. For they said that right action without regard to consequences being the sole proper object of desire, so that the wise man would not forbear housebreaking out of fear or shame or because it hurt his neighbour or any other consideration, except because

because it was wrong, every departure from this rule showed a want of such desire or at least an influence of other desires: he that quits his rule of right to steal a cauliflower, shows that he has not an abhorrence of wrong doing purely as such, therefore when he travels the right road it is by accident, and if he abstains from robbing a house, there must be some other motive that withholds him. I think this doctrine of the equality of crimes is now quite out of doors, and therefore we need nor trouble ourselves any further about it. But they held some other tenets that we still hear of now and then, as that virtue is good in itself and only desirable, that it is the ultimate good, making the possessor invariably happy: and I think some of them denied that it could be acquired, but must be implanted by nature, or that the party possessing it could ever lose it.

4. As to the unacquirablenes of virtue, this somewhat resembles Whitfield's day of grace, which being not yet come or being once past, no man can attain to righteousness. But if we look back upon human nature, there will appear no colour to suppose ourselves born with an idea of right or that it ever comes upon us at once. Our senses first put us in action, and upon observing what objects please them we get a desire of those objects:

in

in our further progress we find it often necessary to make long preparation for obtaining the things we desire, but the measures we take sometimes succeeding and sometimes failing, we learn by observation to form rules for our conduct, and thence get the idea of right, by which we understand no more than that such a measure will lead us surely to any purpose we have at present in view: thus if we would obtain the favour of tyrants, obsequiousness and flattery may be the right way. But this is not rectitude considered as a virtue, which we know nothing of until having experienced that our desires thwart one another, that it is expedient to restrain them, and that the exercise of such restraint in adherence to the dictates of judgment meets with commendation from others and the approbation of our own breast, we then look upon the Honestum as a mark directing us to what will conduce most to our happiness, and at length as an object of immediate desire: and when this view appears in the highest pitch of colouring imaginable, and becomes steady so as never to vary nor fade, then, if ever the case happens, I conceive a man compleatly possessed of the virtue of rectitude. Thus we see the desire of the Honestum is a translated desire, drawn originally from our others by a prudent regard for the greater number of them

them in preference to any particular one that may solicit at present. Nor can it be doubted without contradicting experience, that a man's progress in virtue may be quickened by instruction, exhortation, example, and his own industry, or that after having in some measure attained it he may receive further improvement by the same means. There may be a particular time wherein virtue first manifests herself, and so there is in the manifestation of most other habits and acquirements. If you converse every day with a man from his beginning to learn any art or language, you will become able in some one moment to pronounce him a master of it: yet for all that, his skill was growing gradually all along from his first entrance upon the rudiments; nor perhaps did he make a larger progress in that day when you took notice of it than in any other before, or than he will do again by further use and practice afterwards. And as we gain habits by use so we may lose them again by disuse: therefore it is a very dangerous position which some have maintained that the saint can never sin; it were much safer to take Saint Paul's caution, Let him that thinketh he standeth take heed lest he fall.

5. Whether virtue be good in itself may be determined by referring to the last chapter but one, wherein it appears that satisfaction, the

only

only intrinsic good, lies in our perceptions: action is only good as it applies the proper objects for raising those perceptions, and virtue, which is a habit or disposition of mind, is good only as it leads into such actions; so that virtue stands two removes from the summum bonum. There are some pleasures fully contenting the mind which come upon us by the operation of external objects without any care of our own to procure them: if we could have a continual and uninterrupted supply in this manner we should have no use for volition at all, and were our appetites so rightly set as to put volition upon every thing most beneficial for us we should have as little use for virtue, which is good for nothing else but to rectify the disorders of our nature; but that is enough to make its value inestimable though not intrinsic. But it will be said there is a satisfaction in the very exercise of virtuous actions, this I grant, but then it must be to those who have a taste for virtue; and there is the like satisfaction in gratifying every other taste. The virtuoso finds it when catching a curious butterfly, the proud finds it when flattery sooths his ear, the covetous when driving an advantageous bargain, the vindictive when taking measures to satiate his revenge. Perhaps you will say there is a secret misgiving and compunction attending the performance

of

of unwarrantable actions: I believe there would be in you or me, because I hope we have some seeds of virtue in us; but the consummate villain, who has none of these, feels no remorse to embitter, no reluctance to lessen, the pleasure of any wickedness his vicious inclinations prompt him to; so then in this respect he has the advantage of us. But it is the fairest way to compare both parties in those instances wherein they gratify their respective desires. If you and I can at any time command our passion by the authority of reason, as I hope we sometimes do, we find an immediate content and complacence of mind: if the hardened wretch goes on successfully in any wicked attempt he has set his heart upon, he finds an immediate content and complacence of mind: therefore thus far the case of both is similar. You will ask whether, if the thing could be done with a fillip, I would be content to change my situation with his? By no means, for it is in my power to act right always, unless where my judgment happens to be doubtful; but it is in my power to gratify my other inclinations only now and then as opportunity favours. When I act right I am providing for my future enjoyments; when I act wrong I am doing something that will cross my other desires or bring mischief upon me. If I take one course I shall

shall find frequent occasion to reflect with pleasure on having pursued it; if the other, I shall find perpetual cause, if not to repent, at least to rue sufficiently for my misconduct. Thus the advantage of virtue over vice and trifle does not lie in the very act, but in the consequences. The pursuit of either will please each man in proportion as he has a relish to it: but one relish prompts to take in wholesome food, the other to that which will bring on sickness of stomach, painful distempers, and perhaps utter destruction.

6. Were virtue the ultimate and only desirable good, she would have nothing else to do besides contemplating her own beauties: she could never urge to action; because action must proceed upon a view to some end, and if that end were not desirable the action were nugatory; but such contemplation is so far from being our only good that one may question whether it be a good at all. I grant the satisfaction felt in acting right makes one considerable part of virtue's value, but then it must be such as arises spontaneously, not forced upon the thought. Should a man do nothing all day long but reflect with himself, How I love rectitude! how happy am I in the possession of virtue! you would hardly think the better of his character for this practice. Such contemplations as these,

these, I fast thrice a week, I pay tythe of mint, annise, and cummin, I give alms of all I possess, are more likely to engender spiritual pride and bring mischief upon a man than to prove his virtue or ensure his happiness. Besides, the confining virtue to the satisfaction of possessing her destroys her very essence, which consists in the efficacy she has to set us upon exerting our active powers, which cannot move without an aim at something better to be had than gone without: and when the good man enters upon an undertaking though the satisfaction of doing right might urge him to resolve upon it, yet our capacities are too narrow to admit of his carrying this reflection throughout! when he comes to the performance he will be too busy in pursuing his measures to think of any thing else; but must fix his desire from time to time upon the several objects as he goes along. He reaps none other benefit from the rectitude of his design, during his engagement in the execution of it, than that his conscience does not check, nor his moral sense disturb him, which is a mere negative benefit. Nor would virtue find materials to work upon if she could find nothing else desirable besides herself; she does not make her objects desirable but chooses those already made so to her hands, whose prior value recommends them to her option:

option: were there no difference what befals us, it were wholly indifferent what we did, for every manner of acting and even total inactivity would become equally right. Where would be the difference between setting a man's house on fire, and running into to extinguish the flames? or why does virtue urge you to the latter, unless because you think the security of a family, and preservation of their property desirable things? If you knew them to be virtuous persons, I suppose you would not be the less forward to assist them: but why may you desire to do what virtuous persons ought not to desire should be done? and if they may desire to have it done, the desirableness has no relation to their virtue, which would continue the same whether burnt out of house and home or no, nor would suffer diminution though they were to perish in the flames, but must arise upon some other account. I would not willingly drop a word to abate our love of virtue, for I think it cannot glow too strong, so long as we preserve it pure and genuine: but you know I have distinguished between love and fondness. Let us not then be so fondly enamoured with our mistress as to allow nothing valuable elsewhere, for there are other objects desirable previous to her recommending them: nay, she herself would never have become desirable had it not been for them, for why should I ever desire to do right, or whence come

come by a satisfaction in so doing, unless from a persuasion that it is better for me, that is, productive of more good, to act right than wrong?

7. We will now examine whether virtue will make the possessor compleatly and invariably happy; or, in modern language, whether of the two kinds of evil, physical and moral, the latter alone be really such, and the former only in imagination. For my part, I can see none original evil besides the physical, were there none of that in nature there could be no such thing as moral evil, for we could never do amiss if no hurt could ever redound from our actions, either to ourselves or any body else. Could you steal a man's goods without endamaging his property, without depriving him of something useful, without taking off the restraint of honesty from your own mind, or shaking the authority of those rules which keep the world from disorder and confusion, why need you scruple to do it? Were it possible to murder a man without pain, without abridging him of the enjoyments he might expect in life, or might assist in procuring for other people, and without setting an example that might occasion the murdering of others not so circumstanced, where would be the immorality of the deed? But since these are wild and impossible suppositions, and that moral evil constantly leads some way or other,

directly

directly or remotely, into physical, therefore it is an evil most strenuously to be avoided.

8. The question we are now upon commonly produces another, namely, whether pain be an evil, or only rendered so by opinion: because it being never pretended that virtue would exempt a man from all pain, while this remained an evil, she could not perform her engagement to ensure him perpetual happiness. In the first place, let us observe that pain appears an evil to young children, before they can be supposed to have contracted any erroneous opinion, so there remains no doubt of its being sometimes an evil not of our own making; and if we may afterwards render it harmless, merely by thinking it so, then it will follow that we can change the nature of things by our opinion of them, which surely no philosopher will assert. The truth seems to be, that we may sometimes help ourselves against the pungency of pain, not by pulling out its sting, but by turning it aside from us. It was observed at the close of the chapter of sensation, that our frame is of a very complicated texture, the influence of objects passing through many stages before they arrive at the seat of perception, where only they can affect us: now if pain can be stopped in any part of its passage, we shall receive no hurt from it. The mind sits retired in kingly state,

nothing

nothing external, not even the bodily organs can approach her, but they deliver their message to the mental organs, and if these officers do not transmit it to the royal audience, it is the same as if never delivered. But the mental organs do not stifle messages out of wantonness, they only drop them when engaged by something else picked up in the family: therefore when painful sensations do not gall, it is by means of some other idea occupying our notice, and sheltering us from their sharpness. Certain it is we can all upon occasion support a small degree of pain without uneasiness: young ladies will bear it for their shape, a beau for the neatness of his foot, a common labourer for his sustenance; sometimes diversion will beguile it, business lull it asleep, fear banish it, revenge despise it, wilfulness, eagerness after pleasure, or the love of rectitude overpower it. In all these cases there is a withdrawing of our notice from the pain, and turning it upon other objects, either by presenting those objects, or by an operation of our own upon the organs, in which latter case, the moment we remit our efforts the pain pinches again. In like manner, affliction may be rendered easy by suggesting topics of consolation, or encouragements for enduring it, or diverting the thoughts into another channel. But it does not prove a burden a burden not galling in its own nature, because you can shrink away your shoulder from it, or thrust in something soft between: and while you can thus keep off the pressure of the burden, it is no wonder you are of opinion it is easy. Therefore we may admit it true that pain is no evil to those who do not think it so, because they think it none who do not feel the smart: but opinion must follow fact, and cannot make it; nor can you alter your opinion, without an appearance at least, of evidence, but merely by willing it. However, it may be of excellent service to entertain a good opinion, if you can, beforehand, for nothing like a strong assurance to help us in exerting our strength for applying the proper means to relieve ourselves: when Virgil said of his competitors for the naval prize, that they could because they thought they could, he did not mean that success was nothing more than opinion, but that their confidence spurred up their activity to a higher pitch than they could ever have raised it without. If any man can attain so ardent a desire of rectitude as shall overbalance all attacks of pain, it is happy for him, but he may allow us who have not such an effectual remedy in store, to call it an evil: and if he can master it so far as to keep it from stinging him, yet I suppose it will require his whole

CHAP. 29.] *Virtue.* 275

whole efforts, so that he will have none to spare for other occasions wherein he would wish to employ them, and in this light it deserves some bad appellation, let him choose his term to express it by.

9. The desire of rectitude, like other translated desires, cannot subsist without continual exercise in actions tending to the gratification of it: therefore virtue alone, how compleatly soever possessed, cannot ensure happiness, as being unable to ensure its own continuance without the concurrence of fortune supplying opportunities of exerting it, which are the food necessary for keeping it alive and vigorous. This probably induced some of the most extravagant zealots for virtue to maintain the lawfulness of suicide, when fortune was so averse that there was no sustenance for virtue to be had. And even in its most flourishing state, it gives more or less delight in proportion as things fall out well or ill: for how much soever the virtuous man may comfort himself under disappointment of his endeavours to serve his neighbour with the reflection that he has done his best, yet I suppose he would have been still better pleased had the success answered his intention: and if he sees a distress he knows not how to relieve, will he not feel an additional joy upon the proper means being put into his hands?

hands? Could he say to any one imploring his assistance, Look ye, friend, I'll do my best to serve you, because it is right, but I do not care two-pence whether you reap any benefit from my services or no: were he capable of saying this, it is hard to conceive how he could have any spice of benevolence, and as hard to conceive, how without benevolence his virtue could be compleat. So that were there two persons alike consummately virtuous, the one destitute of all materials or abilities for doing good to mankind, the other amply provided with both, this latter would pass his life more happily than the former. Besides, as we have remarked before, there are many right actions requisite for the sustenance and support of nature whereto we are prompted by appetite, in these virtue has no concern unless negatively to forbear restraining us from them; if the moral sense does not check, if the Demon does not warn, this is all that appetite desires, for she wants no assistant nor conductor: and he must be of an uncommon make, different from all other men, who will never eat when hungry, nor lie down when sleepy, until urged by the motive of its being right.

Now, during the performance of these actions, the virtuous man must be happy, or else he would have gaps in his happiness, which

which it would be woful heresy to allow; but during such performance, he receives no benefit from his virtue, her influence being suspended, for he does the same and feels the same as the sensualist: therefore he is beholden in part at least to nature for his happiness in giving him appetites, the sources of these enjoyments, and to fortune for supplying him with materials for satisfying his appetites.

10. But how mighty matters soever may be justly ascribed to perfect virtue in the highest idea we can form of it in speculation, I fear such perfection is not attainable among the sons of men: the highest pitch we can rise to will not set us above all approach of evil; pain will gall, labour will fatigue, disappointment will vex, affliction will torment, when they cannot overcome us; so that we owe more of our enjoyment to nature and fortune than to virtue. There are people with a very moderate portion of virtue, no more than just to keep clear of turbulent passions and destructive vices, who, being placed in an easy situation of life, pass it more agreeably than others of far superior merit, forced to struggle perpetually with disease, poverty, contradiction, and distress. Much less will it appear upon an impartial survey, that every man's share of enjoyment in the world bears an exact proportion

portion to the measure of his virtue. Nor yet do the strongest instances of virtue prove always the scenes of greatest enjoyment: for we must remember that uneasiness sets our activity at work as well as satisfaction, and the love of right sometimes operates by the uneasiness of departing from it. If we have desires which we cannot banish from our thoughts, urging us strongly to do wrong, but the moral sense threatens with shame, remorse and mischief, it acts as an obligation, laying us under a necessity of fulfilling it: and we have shewn in the proper place that necessity always throws the mind into a state of uneasiness. For aught I know, this might be the case of Regulus: I would not detract from his merit, nor pretend to dive into the exact situation of his thoughts, therefore shall suppose what I conceive possible in theory, that he might feel so strong a satisfaction of mind as overbalanced the pain of the tenters. But suppose another person not quite so happily disposed, yet he might have a violent abhorrence of infamy, self-reproach, and breach of faith, and the uneasiness of falling under what his soul abhorred, might prevail upon him to undergo any torments for escaping it: he might still expect uneasiness in the tentered cask, nevertheless, might choose it as the lesser evil, and in so doing he
would

would act right, and what all men of honour and probity would applaud him for; yet this less evil remains still an evil, and he, while under it, in a state of suffering. Nor is it a just inference, that whatever all wise men approve, and the moral sense clearly recommends, must necessarily be an act of enjoyment; for wise men and the moral sense regard the whole of things, therefore will recommend a present diminution of happiness, for a greater encrease of it to be obtained thereby. We may sometimes fortify ourselves against pain and self-denial by the dread of infamy or compunction, and holding the force of our obligations strongly in view, when we cannot raise an immediate satisfaction in our proceeding: therefore, it is for the interests of virtue that we should, upon occasion, put ourselves into the iron hand of necessity; she will pinch us sorely while she has us under her clutches, and all that time we shall be very virtuous, and yet very uneasy.

11. Thus we see that virtue cannot secure us uninterrupted enjoyment, for there are other causes contributing to procure it; but though the condition of men does not always answer to their degree of virtue, yet I conceive every particular man will be more or less happy in proportion as he acts right. Life has been compared to a game, and we know the cards will beat anybody, but he that

that plays them carefully, will do more with the same cards than another who throws them out at random. The gifts of nature, education, and fortune, are the cards put into our hands: all we have to do, is to manage them well by a steady adherence to our judgment. Therefore virtue, taken in the largest sense, as including every right conduct, as well upon small as great occasions, may well be styled the only thing desirable, as drawing all other good things in our power after it; for though there be others valuable, yet Seek ye righteousness first, and all these shall be added unto ye. In common language, a thing is called desirable for its consequences, therefore this, on which all good consequences we can procure depend, may well deserve that epithet: we may have other desires, but they need be only such as arise of their own accord, or the present occasion requires, but upon this alone it behoves us to take pains in fixing our desire, because it will direct us to encourage or restrain our other desires as shall be most for our benefit. And things are said to be good in themselves, when they have a natural tendency to our advantage, without regard to reward or applause, or other adventitious benefits attending them; so virtue may be termed good in itself, although bringing no honour nor profit, nor

any

any thing else we desire, because it will lead us into a right behaviour most conducive to purposes we shall hereafter desire, and furnish us with pleasing reflections that will abundantly repay the trouble we are at in pursuing it. In like manner, Happy, in vulgar acceptation, as when Milton pronounced the sleeping pair happy, does not stand confined to the instant time of speaking, but like an estate which denominates the owner rich, though at present quite low in pocket, it relates to the whole stock of enjoyments belonging to a man. Thus virtue, which we may look upon as an estate, yielding an income of happiness, may well entitle the possessor happy, although the rents may not happen just now to come in: and, as a man, having his all, amounting to a hundred pounds, in his pocket, would be glad to exchange condition with one of large fortune whom he finds at a distance from home without ready money or credit; so a prudent man, deficient in virtue, would think it a happiness to be placed in the condition of one possessing it in an eminent degree, though at that time not in a state of enjoyment. In the sense herein last described as, being the most obvious, one should naturally understand those expressions of virtue, being the one thing desirable, good in itself, and making the possessor invariably happy; and I

believe

believe the persons who first employed them, meant to be so understood, wherein they carry a just and useful meaning. Therefore, I am not desirous of discarding or contradicting them, nor shall I hesitate a moment to agree with Socrates, that it is happier to receive an injury than to do one: but, as some of his followers, ancient and modern, men of deeper thought than judgment, have strained them to an extravagance, I was willing to endeavour restoring them to their proper and genuine signification. This is one of those transmutations spoken of in the introduction, whereby valuable and excellent truths, which have been debased into error and falsehood, may be transmuted back again into their original sterling.

12. I apprehend several advantages accruing from our resting the merit of virtue upon this true and solid basis, its usefulness: for if you talk of an essential and independent goodness, few can discern it; if you appeal to the judgment of the wise, many think themselves wiser; if you tell them that every act of virtue affords greater immediate enjoyment than the practice of vice, they will not believe you, nor do I know how they should, as it contradicts their experience; so you will have your principle to battle for, before you can deduce any thing from it. But we proceed upon a postulatum that will readily

dily be granted, for nobody can deny that he had rather have his desires gratified than crossed: we need only exhort men not to forget their absent friends, nor to neglect such desires as they may have at another time, for the sake of one or two at present uppermost in their thoughts: so the door stands open before us, and we shall be willingly admitted to go on in showing the necessary connection of virtue with gratification. A second benefit of referring virtue to use is, that it helps us to rectify our notions of it, to interpret our rules, and teaches us which of them to prefer when they appear to clash: for our moral sense, though the best guide we have, is not always to be trusted; education, custom, prejudice, and human frailty, will sometimes set it to a wrong point, and when suspicions of this kind arise, there is no surer way of trying the justness of them than by examining whether the courses, we find ourselves prompted to, tend more upon the whole to the encrease or diminution of happiness. Many of our rules may be understood variously, but when this is the case, that construction, which appears evidently the most conducive to general convenience, ought to be chosen as the truest: nor is it scarce possible to apply a rule always properly, or know what circumstances require an exception, without under-

understanding the drift and design of it: and when two of them interfere, we can never determine the preference so well as when we can clearly discern which of them it would be most dangerous to break through. For a third advantage of frequently tracing out the good consequences of virtue, we may reckon that it will give us a better liking of her, and greater confidence in the rules she dictates; for by consideration and continual observation of their tendency, we shall often discover an expedience we could not at first descry, and shall more readily entertain an opinion of the like expedience in other cases where we cannot discern it. Whatever practices have the general approbation of mankind or our moral sense urges us earnestly to, though seeming needless or inconvenient, in our present apprehension, will then carry a strong presumption, sufficient to persuade us of their being beneficial, and we shall pursue them by desire, not necessity; that is, not as an obligation but as our interest. This seems the readiest way to conduct us to a love of virtue for her own sake, for having once gotten our thorough confidence and esteem, wherever she appears she will become our ultimate point of view, which we shall follow without looking for any thing beyond, and this we may do without supposing her

the

the ultimate end of action, for we have seen before that these two are often different.

CHAP. XXX.

PRUDENCE.

I GAVE warning in the introduction, that I might sometimes seem to shake the main pillars of morality, but should never do it, unless when I conceived them slid off their original bases, in order to restore them to a solid and durable foundation. I hope I have not been found failing of my promise; for though in the last preceeding chapters, we have appeared sometimes to turn our backs upon rectitude, and take the gratification of every man's tastes and inclinations for our ultimate end, yet, at the close of them, we have left virtue in a recommendable light sufficient to engage the attention of every reasonable person, as being justly entitled to be called good in itself, the one thing desirable, and capable of making the possessor happy, in the proper and genuine meaning of those expressions, when not strained to unwarrantable lengths, but understood as common sense
would

would lead us to understand them. We have likewise endeavoured to ascertain the province of virtue, which does not extend to every thing right; for our appetites prompt us to many right things, the sensualist doing the same in some instances as the righteous: therefore, the office of virtue lies in watching over their motions and instigating to such right actions, from which our other inclinations would lead us aside. But this description of virtue being thought too general, your ethic writers have distinguished her into four principal branches, Prudence, Fortitude, Temperance, and Justice, which they call cardinal virtues, from a Latin word signifying a hinge, these four being the main hinges whereon all inferior virtues and particular rules of conduct hang. The first of these in order they reckon Prudence, as being the chief, and, in effect, comprehending the other three, which relate to the removing three certain obstacles in our nature most apt to disturb and stop us in the exercise of prudence.

2. Before we enter upon a particular consideration of this cardinal virtue, it will be necessary to observe, that there are two kinds of prudence which may be distinguished, as evils have been, into physical and moral. The former consists in knowing the best measures to be taken upon any occasion, and depends

depends upon sagacity, quickness, and strength of parts, or upon experience, instruction, or the opportunities we have had of advancing our knowledge: this we may reckon a valuable endowment, but can by no means be ranked under any class of virtues, for we find it conspicuous in persons overwhelmed with vice and debauchery. But moral prudence, with which alone we have concern at present, consists in making the best use of such lights as we have, not in the number or clearness of them; for virtue lies solely in the right application of our powers, and may reside with those of the narrowest, as well as the largest extent. Were a man wholly void of moral prudence, to be invested with it at once in the most eminent degree conceivable, he would not become a whit the more knowing for the acquisition: it is true, at the year's end, he might advance considerably in knowledge, because he would omit no opportunity of improving it, but he would not instantly discern a single truth more than he did before, unless, perhaps, by dispelling the mists of some passion that might just then prevent him from taking notice of what he knew well enough already.

3. If we survey the transactions of mankind, we shall find there is a discretion much more valuable than knowledge, as being
more

more generally serviceable and carrying on the affairs of life more compleatly and clearer of mistakes. Your men of fine sense, having lost their common sense, get nothing by the exchange: they will work wonders sometimes in matters happening to suit their talents, but know not, or regard not, how to apply nor conduct them, or commit some egregious blunder that overthrows all the good they have done: they perform excellent service under proper direction, but plunge into some quagmire when left to themselves: they can give the best advice to others, but through some whim or oddity let their own affairs run to ruin. On the other hand, we see persons of very moderate capacities, who, by a discreet management of them, pass their life with more comfort to themselves and credit among their neighbours, than others of far superior endowments. They know the extent of their talents, and do not aim at things beyond their reach. They regard the propriety of their design as well as of the measures of executing it: no less carefully considering what they shall do than how they shall compass it. They attend to all the notices of their judgment, never fondly fixing upon any one point to the overlooking of others. They are ductile and flexible, never striving obstinately against the stream, but
ready

ready to seize every light that shall break in upon them, and to lay by their design or change their measures as occasion varies: yet steady to their purpose, so as not to waver with every sudden start of fancy. Willing to play a small game, rather than stand out, and always making some progress when they cannot run extraordinary lengths: yet not backward to quicken their pace and enlarge their schemes, whenever they find it safe and feasible. Their conduct is uniform and consistent throughout, if they cannot perform great undertakings, what they do is compleat and free from fatal mistakes, one of which may do more mischief than a great deal of sagacity and diligence can afterwards repair.

4. Now this discretion discoverable in the ordinary behaviour of some person is not the moral prudence we seek after, yet seems to be the root giving birth to it, and communicates its own complexion and flavour to the fruit: for persons having practised this happy manner of proceeding in the common affairs of life, will follow the same when they come to have an idea of virtue; they will use their whole understanding, regard all the rules of rectitude, and proceed upon a judicious love, not a fanciful fondness for virtue, regarding all her interests so as to hurt none of them by too eagerly pursuing others. It is a virtue, says

says Horace, to escape vice, and the first step to wisdom is made by getting clear of folly: and we know where else it is recommended, not to confine our eyes so closely to what things we ought to have done as to overlook what things we ought not to have left undone: therefore they will be more solicitous to avoid acting wrong, than to act remarkably right, nor think that the omission of common duties can be compensated by works of supererogation. I do not say that moral prudence is incompatible with great accomplishments, on the contrary, it will improve them to the utmost, employ them most usefully in services whereto they are fitted, and appears most conspicuous in the management of them: nevertheless it may subsist without them, or be wanting where they abound, being a distinct quality of itself. It does not always accompany the most glowing zeal, nor give birth to the most shining performances: as Horace says, we may pursue virtue too intensely, that is, when we pursue her with passion, not with judgment. It is not the disquisitions of the closet, excellent discourses, or profound speculations upon the nature of right and wrong, nor yet single acts, how exemplary soever, but the general tenor of a man's conduct, that denominates him virtuous. As thought and consideration contribute

bute greatly to encrease and clear up the lights of our understanding, one should be apt to imagine, that those who think most carefully upon the subject of righteousness, should be the most righteous persons, but this is no certain rule; for men may contemplate for ever without making use of their discoveries, which then tend only to enlarge their knowledge; wherein we have seen virtue does not consist, but employs it only as an instrument for effecting her purposes. And there are persons of lively tempers and little enured to study, who cannot think intensely at all, yet do not want discretion to steer them right in all the variety and quickness of their motions. In most common instances it is easy to see at a glance what is the best step to be taken, the characters of our duty being printed so large, that he that runs may read them: and if men would use themselves constantly to follow their present judgment, when clear and vivid, they would make greater progress towards rectitude than by any other exercise of their faculties whatsoever.

5. It is not easy to pronounce upon actions, or distinguish precisely, when they proceed from the virtue of prudence, and when not; for we have seen the rectitude of actions consists either in their conduciveness to the purpose intended, or in their conformity to rule:

but men sometimes act very right upon wrong principles, or adhere to their rule, because no temptation starts up in their thought to draw them aside; in neither of which cases their prudence can be inferred from their acting prudently; for their taking the right course is luck rather than virtue. Nor are we compleat judges even of our own prudence, because having no better method of estimating it, than by reflecting back upon our past conduct, we cannot retain in mind the secret motives that may have actuated us, much less tell what unlucky turn of imagination might have led us another way. Therefore, as I said before, we may judge best of ourselves or others from the general tenor of conduct, rather than from any particular parts of it how shining soever. Yet this will not ensure us against mistakes, for our leading principle or ruling passion, as it is called, which gives the general turn to our actions, may have been inculcated by others, or taken up upon hazard, and we been led by good fortune into a right course of behaviour, without having ever examined whether it had that tendency, or discerned the reasonableness whereon it was founded.

6. Neither is it an easy matter to settle the exact idea of this cardinal virtue we are speaking of, so that we may know what to look for

for when we go to pass our judgment. It is not knowledge nor acuteness of parts, nor clearness of understanding, nor largeness of information, nor goodness of principles instilled, for it should be something entirely our own; but all these depend upon other causes. It may seem, at first sight, to lie in the exercise of our reasoning faculties, because most of the miscarriages in life proceed from inconsiderateness and hasty determination; but then it lies as much in quickness of following the lights of reason, whenever they shine out clear: for to stand thinking when we should be acting, or hunt after speculations when something lies ready at hand for us to do, were not much less imprudent than never to think at all. Since, then, it is so difficult to describe, and when we seem to have laid our finger upon it still it eludes our grasp, let us endeavour to place it in several lights, that one may supply what shall appear wanting in another. I conceive, then, prudence will enable him that has it compleatly, to keep the mental organs open and watchful, hearing the whispers of the moral sense amid the clamors of passion, and discerning the feeblest glimmerings of reason through the glare of fancy; so that every object in the prospects glancing before him, whether the scene contain more or fewer of them, will be seen in its true shape,

shape, and his notice will instantly turn upon that which is most proper. For our doings being all made up of single momentary acts, volition perpetually following the fresh ideas thrown up by imagination, must take their denomination from that of their component parts: therefore if the steps be prudently taken, the whole progress must needs be so too; but if they be not, we may still chance to steer the right course while nothing occurs to mislead us, but our success will be owing to the goodness of our lights rather than to the soundness of our eye. Nor does this vigilance or openness of the mental eye depend wholly upon industry and the intense application of our optics, they help to improve it when deficient, or on the contrary may sometimes do hurt by confining it to one narrow point, but when once acquired, it becomes a habit operating spontaneously, rather using application as an instrument to effect its purposes than wanting it as a spring to put itself in motion. Whoever could attain this habit compleatly would never act in the dark nor at random; for though his lights might be faint he would distinguish which of them were the clearest, he would find an opportunity for doing something in every situation of circumstances, and would discern what is feasible as well as what is desirable. It would direct
him

him which of his several faculties to exercise, when to deliberate and when to execute, when to suspend his judgment and when suspension were needless, when to exert resolution and when to comply with the occasion, when to bestir himself and when to receive whatever ideas occur. In short, he would act with the same uniform tenor throughout, as well in trifles as matters of importance, and though he might sometimes take wrong measures through ignorance, his every motion would be right with respect to his degree of knowledge or present information.

7. In another light we may consider prudence as a disposition of mind to regard distant good equally with present pleasure, estimating both according to their real not apparent magnitude: like the skill we have of discerning a grown person twenty yards off to be larger than a child sitting in our lap, although the latter take up more room in our eye. Nature first moves us by sensations of pleasure or pain, experience soon teaches us that pleasurable sensations will not always come of themselves, but we must do something to make provision for obtaining them, hence spring our desires and passions. Upon further experience we learn that desire often leads into mischief, this gives rise to the moral sense admonishing to restrain desire
when

when pointed the wrong way: but there being an ease in gratifying and a trouble in crossing it, the contest in these cases lies between expedience and pleasure, and to choose constantly the former is an effect of prudence. For as wordly prudence engages a man upon every occasion to improve his fortune rather than get a little ready money in hand: so moral prudence will incline him always to prefer that which is best before that which will immediately please his senses or gratify his desire or his indolence.

8. The third light wherein I shall endeavour to place our virtue is that of a readiness in following the dictates of reason: but by reason we must not understand here the act of reasoning; for that, in many cases, might be imprudent, but those treasures which we have shown elsewhere reason deposits in the storehouse of ideas, that is, such notices occurring from time to time to our judgment as were formerly the produce of careful consideration or have been examined and approved thereby. The bare possession of these treasures renders a man more knowing and many times a more useful member of the community, because the deed does the service not the internal disposition of the performer; but it is the readiness in following them instantly upon their appearance that constitutes him a perfectly

fectly prudent man. For our active power must take some turn every moment, and if the present judgment does not operate, the turn will be taken imprudently, though no damage may happen to ensue. This readiness depends upon a happy cast of imagination, representing the dictates of reason as satisfactory, for volition ever moves towards that point where satisfaction appears connected, and is not influenced by a conviction of the understanding until it becomes a persuasion too and an object of desire: therefore prudence is no more than a steady, habitual desire of acting reasonably, generated by a thorough persuasion that in so doing we shall act most for our advantage; for nothing else can give birth to such a desire, because all desires not natural must derive by translation from those that are.

9. Hence it appears that this cardinal virtue must have had a beginning, owing its rise either to natural constitution inclining some men to be more observant than others, and rendering their imagination more pliable to receive persuasion easier from conviction, or to accidents teaching them discretion from their own miscarriages, or to instruction and example. The growth and progress indeed depends chiefly upon our own care and industry,

dustry, but then we must be prompted to use that care and industry by some consideration already in our thoughts, and the first act of prudence we ever exerted must have had some prior motive exciting us to it, which was suggested by our other desires. Whether as the nature of man is constituted it may be lost again when once arrived to perfect stature we cannot certainly know, having never seen an instance of such perfection among us; yet it seems hard to conceive how the habit of following reason can subsist after reason itself is totally lost and all the characters imprinted by her obliterated by age and distempers: but we find by woful experience, that such degrees of it as man can attain may be lost again by despondency, or uninterrupted prosperity, or too great security, or evil company or other causes. Nevertheless, it is the most durable possession we can have, as being untouched by many outward accidents that may deprive us of all others, and warning us against the approach of whatever might endanger it: and the most valuable, for though it cannot ensure us perpetual success, it will help us to the greatest measure of all other valuable things in our power to obtain: nay, if we believe Juvenal, we shall find no deity averse if prudence be not wanting.

10. This

10. This virtue of prudence constitutes the essence of moral wisdom, of which some in former ages have entertained very absurd and extravagant notions; supposing the wise man beholden to himself alone for his wisdom, placed above the reach of fortune to hurt him, and master of all arts and sciences from the highest to the lowest, even to the making the cloaths upon his back, the shoes upon his feet, and the ring upon his finger: wherein they confounded wisdom with capacity, which are manifestly different, the one consisting in extensiveness of knowledge, the other solely in the due management of such as we have, be it more or be it less. Therefore there may be the greatest folly where there is the most knowledge, and upon that very account: for if two persons take the same improper course together, he will be deemed to act most imprudently who best knew how to have acted right. If a man unacquainted with a wood takes a country fellow for his guide, who knows all the paths and turnings perfectly well, but will needs push on the nearest way through the thickest part until both are entangled in the briars, it is easy to see that the charge of folly lies wholly at the door of the guide, and for this very reason because he knew better than the other. Besides, by placing wisdom

in

in science, they overthrow the wise man's claim to the sole merit of it, making it to depend upon the natural endowments of body or mind, and accidental advantages: for not to mention the necessity of instruction, leisure, and quickness of apprehension, to render knowledge compleat, I suppose they would hardly pretend that a man born blind could ever make himself perfect in the art of painting, or science of optics.

11. But neither, when we understand wisdom in the proper and genuine sense, can the possessor claim it as entirely of his own creation, for it grows out of common discretion, being the same quality carried to the greatest length human nature can contain: but this depends upon an observant, though perhaps not always a thoughtful temper, upon good guidance or example, and upon lucky accidents: for men often learn discretion from their own misconduct, when the mischiefs of it happen to be so obvious that they cannot but take notice, and so galling that they cannot fail of remembering them. And he must have an uncommon degree of self-conceit, who can persuade himself that he should have acted with the same discretion he does, had he been born with a dull apprehension, and strong sensations, or bred up among the savages in America. I know some affect to cry up the

barbarous

barbarous nations, as furnishing instances of as great soundness of judgment as is to be met with among the most civilized: I shall not deny that such instances may be found, because having no acquaintance with those nations, I cannot disprove them, but we must remember that discretion proceeds from observance of temper, incidents touching the notice, instruction, or example, and any one of these causes may sometimes operate so favourably, as to supply the place of the others.

Let us now suppose the sage possessed of perfect wisdom, yet is he secure that he shall always retain it? Why yes, it is always in his power to act according to the circumstances of every situation that shall happen. I grant it, but this is no answer to the question, for so it is in the power of the unwise: but our power takes its turn, or in other words, volition is determined, by the motives and ideas present in the thought, and what ideas, or in what colour shall be presented, depends upon the state of the mental organs, so that any little change in their texture might destroy the best disposition of mind, or turn it into the worst. Now who can know the whole composition of man so thoroughly, as to pronounce certainly, that no external causes may operate to work a different texture in our organs? It may perhaps be alledged, that the
mental

mental organs have a separate mechanism of
their own, independent of the bodily, so that
though their play may be suspended or varied,
according to the different action of the latter,
yet no disease nor accident happening to the
grosser parts, nor impulse of outward objects
can alter their texture. Whether the case be
so in fact, or no, is more than I can tell, but
admitting it true, still is the wise man beholden
to nature for having framed his composition
in two such distinct compartments; and he
owes the preservation of his best property to
the laws she has kindly provided for securing
it against damage from that part of his mechanism which does not lie under his absolute
command. Neither is he little beholden to
fortune for supplying him with materials and
opportunities of exercising his wisdom, which
render it more serviceable to others and productive of enjoyment to himself than it could
be without those assistances.

12. But whatever condition the consummate wise man may stand in, we who only
make distant advances towards his perfection,
cannot pretend to self-sufficiency, nor claim
the merit of every little success we meet with
as all our own: for we find our pittance of
virtue improve and kept alive by exercise, but
when this exercise is interrupted for want of
proper subjects to work upon, or our minds
thrown

thrown off the hinge by cross accidents, or our discretion beguiled by temptations, we perceive ourselves retarded, if not thrown backward in our progress. Let us then acknowledge our obligation to nature, as well for the good she has already done us, as for the continuance of it by her salutary establishments and own ourselves dependent upon fortune for the favours we may still hope for at her hands, leaving however, like wise generals, as little to her disposal as possible: and nothing will better put us in a way of being befriended by her when favourable, or shelter us from her attacks when she proves out of humour, than such degree of moral prudence as we are capable of attaining.

CHAP. XXXI.

FORTITUDE.

Of all the obstacles standing in our way, when disposed to act right, none operates so powerfully as fear: other passions beguile or tire us out, but this stops us short in our career; therefore the conquest of this passion has been made one of the cardinal virtues. It is is not easy to fix upon a proper definition of this virtue, at first thought one should be apt to call it a habit of fearlessness, but every absence of fear is not courage: for it may proceed from ignorance of the danger, as when a child goes to play with the muzzle of a loaded musket; or it may arise from an insensibility of temper, for there are people who see their danger, but want feeling enough to be touched by it. Now we must acknowledge this insensibility a very useful quality to the public, for without it, perhaps, we could not properly man our fleets nor recruit our armies: yet is it so far from deserving the name of virtue, that it seems scarce compatible with the principal of them, I mean prudence, which grows out of caution, and ever keeps it in company throughout all her proceedings. Besides that, we find fear a necessary engine to restrain many inordinate desires and unruly passions that would else make strange havoc and disorder in the world: and if the intrepidity of pirates and banditti could be wrested from them, it would be much better both for themselves and all others within their reach.

2. This fearlessness of temper depends upon natural constitution, as much as any quality we can possess, for where the animal system is strong and robust, it is easily acquired, but

when

when the nerves are weak, and extremely sensible, they fall presently into tremours that throw the mind off the hinges and cast a confusion over her. Nor are the changes in our disposition of body without their influence: old age abates the spirit, men have their ebbs and flows of bravery, and some distempers bring a mechanical terror upon the imagination. It has been observed, that courage may be partial, dauntless to some objects, and gone upon the appearance of others: Mr. Addison tells us he knew an officer who could march up to the mouth of a cannon, but affrighted at his own shadow, and unable to bear being left alone in the dark. Such contrariety of character must have been owing to impressions taken in his youth; and indeed courage as well as timorousness may come by sympathy and imitation from the company wherewith men consort: the recruit becomes intrepid by the dauntless looks and discourses of his comrades, and their taunts upon cowardice, he improves better this way, than he could do by all the lectures of philosophy aided by his own utmost industry. Courage, from whatever cause arising, may be ranked under those inferior virtues mentioned at the beginning of CHAP. XXIX. which spring indifferently from nature, education, custom, or our own diligence: nor is it the less intrinsically valuable, because sometimes turned to mischievous purposes, for the best things corrupted become the worst. It gains admiration and applause more than any of the rest, for fear being the most difficult passion to overcome, therefore the conquest of it deserves to be most honoured, because honour, as we have already seen under that article, belongs not only to things the most useful, but to those where the honour itself will be of the greatest use: as it certainly will here, for nothing carries men so effectually through danger as a quick sense of honour, which therefore has always been looked upon as the necessary qualification and distinguishing characteristic of a soldier. Yet courage to deserve the name of virtue, in any degree, must be habitual, not owing to insensibility, for the danger must be seen but despised, nor accidental, or accasioned by the prevalence of any passion. Some folks are mighty valiant in their cups, others in the heat of resentment care not what becomes of themselves so they can but wreak their revenge, others again, eagerly bent upon some foolish desire, will run any hazards to gratify it: in all these cases their courage is not their own, but cast upon them by another agent working upon their organs, and is rather a mark of stupidity, or weakness of mind, than of bravery.

3. From

3. From what has been observed above, we may gather the true notion of fortitude, and having seen what it is not, may more easily discover what it is. The contempt of danger, when owing to the want of apprehension, thoughtlessness, or to some other idea forcibly occupying the thought, carries no merit at all: when the effect of constitution, education, or the desire of applause, and become habitual, it deserves the name of virtue, and our commendation as such: but to entitle it a cardinal virtue, it must be a branch of prudence, which we have seen consists in discerning all the lights of our understanding as they present from time to time before us. Therefore he that possesses fortitude compleatly, will enjoy a perpetual presence of mind; nothing will ruffle or discompose him, but he will proceed in an equal tenor, not having his seasons of failing, nor particular objects to start at, the dread of shame will no more disconcert him than other evils, he will regard consequences in order to take his measures accordingly, but rest wholly unconcerned at the event, he will suffer no idea to intrude upon him against his liking, and will have the absolute command of his notice to fix it upon any point he judges proper. Etymologists derive virtue from virility, supposing it to denote a manly strength and vigour of mind: now vigour will naturally

exert

exert itself in throwing off every thing displeasing or unwelcome, and as a concern for sinister events, further than requisite in directing us to provide against them, and the dazzle of objects preventing the sight of others that lie before us, are what everybody would wish to avoid, when ideas intrude forcibly upon the mind it proves her infirmity and inability to resist them. Thus the being master of our thoughts, having the perfect use of our discernment, and all that authority over our mental organs which they are capable of obeying, constitutes prudence; and that branch of it relating to terrible ideas is understood by fortitude, which though not the less for being aided by nature, custom or other causes, yet is not compleat until it can operate without them.

4. But in order to render this command of our ideas compleat, it is necessary that present evils should be no more capable of discomposing us than the apprehension of them at a distance; for if we can face danger while aloof, but shrink under mischiefs when actually falling upon us, it argues a feebleness of our ideas rather than the strength of our mind. Therefore patience has always been esteemed a species of fortitude, enabling us to bear pain, labour, indignity, affliction, disappointment, and whatever else is irksome to human nature.

nature. I will not undertake to determine whether these may be rendered quite harmless, so as not to hurt at all, yet if there be any salve to prevent their galling, patience is certainly the thing, which whoever possesses compleatly, if he cannot escape suffering by them, yet he will be able to divert his thoughts in great measure upon other objects: for he will never be thrown off his basis, nor permit them so to obscure the notices of his judgment, as that he cannot find something proper to be done upon the present occasion, which may in part, at least, engage his attention. Nay, he will very often prevail to fix it wholly upon the measures of his conduct, in which case, he will relieve himself entirely, for when we can forbear attending to uneasiness, it vanishes, which made some imagine it lay solely in opinion. When the mind has gotten this habitual command over her motions, she will exercise it I conceive, for I can do no more than conjecture, with ease, freedom, and readiness, and without variation. But for us learners in the art we must expect to meet many difficulties, which we cannot surmount, nor hope to make any improvement without frequently exerting our utmost resolution: nor should we disdain to avail ourselves of example, company, shame, argumentation, or any other helps that may
advance

advance us forward. But to make the most of our resolution, it will be requisite to know the strength of it, that we may not put it upon more than it will perform: because repeated ill success may drive to despair, and damp the spirits instead of raising them. It will be expedient to take all opportunities of encreasing what little courage or patience we have, to examine in what particulars we are defective, and what feasible methods we have of remedying that defect, thus keeping our resolution in continual exercise! for every habit and every power of our nature gathers strength by being exercised. With such good management, and a vigilant, but judicious use of the strength we have, we shall be continually advancing forwards by little and little: and the acquisition of any of those inferior virtues spoken of in § 2. will bring us so much nearer to perfection, for if it were possible to attain every one, I imagine the aggregate of them all would make that fortitude we are in quest of.

5. Intrepidity in the day of battle, is not the only species of courage, for I suppose many a brave officer might not be able to walk upon a wall like our common bricklayers; which shows he has not an absolute command over his ideas, since some of them will intrude so far upon his judgment as to make him throw himself down for fear of falling. The art of walking

walking upon walls is scarce necessary for those who do not intend to follow the trade of a bricklayer, for they may find other objects whereon to exercise their resolution to better advantage, therefore I do not recommend it anybody to learn until he has compleated himself in all other branches of knowledge: but I apprehend the ideal sage, having a perfect mastery over his imagination, would upon occasion run along the ridge of a house as securely as he could upon the same tiles ranged along his chamber floor; and would likewise, where it were necessary, bear any filthy discourse, noisome smell, or nastiness besmearing him, without squeamishness or offence to his delicacy. But besides natural terrors which may seize anybody upon first trial, before they have hardened themselves by custom, there are others which gather like rust upon the imaginations of particular people, making them distrust their own senses, and afraid that some sudden impulse should drive them upon extravagant actions, though they have never yet done any such, and have the strongest intention to avoid them. I know a very sensible man, who once scrupled to take a bank note into his hand for fear he should throw it into the fire: another unwilling to go near a precipice, lest he should have an inclination to throw himself down. I have
heard

heard of a lady that terrified herself when going a visiting, with a notion that she might tumble down on entering the room, or say something very rude: and I myself when a boy, having occasion to retire to some private corner, have been sometimes grievously disturbed, lest I should be still in a room full of company, and only fancied I had left them. I am apt to suspect there are more of these whimsies in the world than one hears of, for people are shy of betraying their foibles, and it is but by chance after being very intimate, that one gets any such confession out of them. These little distempers of mind may proceed from too great intenseness of thought; for as hard labour brings a trembling and weakness upon the nerves until refreshed by rest, so the organs of attention being overstrained, become unable to resist whatever fancies start up in its way, and I believe your hard students if they take notice will find more of this disturbance after a series of close application, or having been much alone than at other times: but if it be thought that ladies and children cannot be supposed to hurt themselves this way, let it be remembered that they too sometimes puzzle their brains as much though not upon the same subjects nor in the same manner as great scholars. The like effect may spring from a custom of making uncommon

sup-

suppositions, which the studious sometimes necessarily and sometimes needlessly give into, or the habit of building castles in the air, that others often divert themselves with: for, by these practices, we teach imagination to paint her figures as strong as the real objects exhibited to us by nature. Another source of the same stream may rise upon taking too much of the pillow, for sleep protracted longer than necessary will not be sound; but in dreams, volition remains inactive, all being carried on by the spontaneous workings of our organs, which having thereby gotten a habit of moving themselves, will afterwards throw up dreaming thoughts amongst our waking ones so strongly, that we shall scarce be able to know them asunder. I would recommend it to persons labouring under this infirmity, to observe whether they do not find it trouble them less upon those days wherein they happen to have risen early. I do not know that the believers, in a free will of indifferency, are more subject to these fantastical disturbances than other folks, yet one may well wonder why they should not, for upon their principles the danger would be real, not fantastical: because what avails it to have our senses, our judgment, and discretion, if, by our elective power, we may annex the idea of Best to whatever they warn us most clearly against? How can

can we depend upon our subsequent behaviour corresponding with our precedent, if volition be determined by nothing antecedent, nothing exterior to the will itself? In short, take away the influence of motives, and all before us becomes contingent, doubtful and hazardous.

But whatever causes give rise to such apprehensions, they certainly indicate an impotence of mind, that has not a command over her ideas, nor can turn her notice upon any spot she pleases in the scenes of her imagination. One cannot expect a remedy in this case so much from reason as resolution, or rather care and vigilance; for authority grows by custom and every power gathers strength from exercise: therefore it is expedient to accustom ourselves to choose out of the ideas before us for our inspection, to thrust away those that would intrude upon our notice, and to discern the degree of evidence sufficient to work assurance. It has been made appear in Chap. xi. that absolute mathematical certainty was not made for man, therefore whoever looks always for that, must hang in perpetual doubt and obscurity.

6. There is likewise a courage of assenting, as well as acting, for it cannot be denied that men may cramp themselves in their deliberations for fear of discovering a fallacy in something

thing whereof they have conceived a favourable prejudice: and certainly, without a freedom of thought, there is very little advance to be made in our researches after truth. But then it ought not to be forgotten that there is a difference between courage and rashness, between freedom and change of servitude: for if we run deeper into one prejudice by flying eagerly from another, we shall not much enlarge our liberty. Therefore, it behoves us to join caution to our bravery, without which, it will not be genuine; to look around us, observing every quarter from whence an undue influence may fall upon us; to examine all sides calmly and impartially, and give a just weight to the presumption that our prejudice may have been founded upon solid reasons formerly discerned by ourselves or others, though we cannot now recover them.

7. Neither is patience confined solely to the endurance of pains and labours; those whose situation exempts them from such trials, may yet find subjects whereon to exercise this branch of fortitude. There is nobody but meets with disappointments, cross accidents, contradictions and interruptions, as well in business as diversion, and if we could bear these without ruffling, it would certainly be gaining a valuable point. For my part I often envy the patience of hackney coachmen

coachmen sitting whole hours in all weathers upon their boxes, tradesmen waiting behind their counters, and servants attending in anti-chambers liable to be called upon any trifling errand at every touch of the bell: were I in their situation, restrained from employing myself as I liked, and unable to enter upon a train of thought, because expecting every instant to have it broken, I should be miserable: but though I would not choose to pass my time in idleness, I should be glad to bear it when forced upon me unavoidably. While I am poring with the microscope upon objects lying within the light of nature, if a billet rolls off the hearth, or my servant comes in abruptly with a message, I cannot help fretting and vexing a little inwardly: this I acknowledge to be a failing, and would wish to receive all events with tranquillity and evenness of temper, pursuing my little engagements without anxiety and breaking them off without discomposure. For virtue is valuble all over; if we cannot obtain large portions of her yet every little scrap will repay the trouble of acquiring, as containing a source of enjoyment, and adding something to our estate in the fund of happiness.

CHAP. XXXII.

TEMPERANCE.

There have been heroes intrepid in dangers and indefatigable in labours, despising death, wounds, and hardships, who yet have been shamefully overcome by luxury and all kinds of wanton desires, made slaves to popular applause, or to some favourite mistress. For besides the dread of approaching, or pressure of present evil, there is another obstacle against the influence of reason by the allurement of pleasure, either in prospect or fruition; and it no less requires an exertion of vigour in the mind to secure her against being drawn off her basis by the one than driven by the other. Therefore the habit of resisting pleasure and controuling desire has been justly reckoned a cardinal virtue, called by the name of Temperance. Nor does it less deserve a title to one of the four principal places than fortitude, as being more generally useful for all ranks and conditions of people and more difficult to be attained compleatly. For many persons are not in a situation exposing them to much danger or labour, nor of a constitution subjecting them to acute or frequent pains, and so

may

may pass through life well enough although somewhat deficient in courage or patience: but there is no man without desires, and no man whom they will not lead astray from the paths of reason if he has not power to restrain them. Nor perhaps is it harder to subdue terror effectually than pleasure: the one requires a stronger resolution, the other a more constant vigilance. Pain and danger assault us rarely, their attacks are furious but generally short, if you can sustain the first onset the business is done, or should they renew the charge they will do it feebler after every repulse until at length they cease to be formidable: but desire brings a numerous host into the field, put one enemy to flight and another presently succeeds in his place, if they cannot master you by force they will weary you down by importunity, if they find you invulnerable in front they will detach a regiment of secret motives to take you in rear, so that you may be brought to the ground without knowing from what quarter the blow came. Therefore you must continually keep upon your guard and bestir yourself without respite, which demands a larger fund of vigour to perform than any sudden starts of resolution, as it shows more robustness to carry a weight for miles than to pull out a wedge at a jerk. Besides that intestine enemies

enemies are always accounted the most dangerous, and though pleasure sometimes allures with outward objects, it oftner tempts by desires that have found harbour in the breast: and the most judicious persons have always esteemed the conquest of oneself the most important and most glorious of victories, which a man may most justly applaud himself for however the world may think otherwise.

2. According to my notions of temperance it is not confined to restraining the solicitations of appetite or what is usually called pleasure, but extends to habit, passion, humour, and whatever else would entice us away from following our judgment: therefore covetousness, ambition, resentment, extravagant joy, sanguine hope, thirst of knowledge, and even zeal for virtue, when not conducted by reason, are species of intemperance, as well as luxury, debauchery, and indolence. Pleasure is most dangerous in the season of youth, when the organs are vigorous, sensations strong, and every allurement presents with the charm of novelty: in our riper years there is generally some ruling passion, either of advancement in honour or fortune, encrease of knowledge, or other particular aim, that captivates the mind, and instead of obeying the command of reason

presses

presses it into its service: and the intemperance of old age shows itself in an attachment to our own ways and humours upon the most trifling occasions. But education, custom and constitution, raise a different set of ideas in each man; therefore it behoves him to examine his condition of mind, and set himself most carefully to guard that quarter where he perceives the greatest danger threaten.

3. As desire not only entices by the delight promised upon gratification, but when opposed often degenerates into want, which arrives by the uneasiness of missing the thing desired, therefore temperance must call in patience as an auxiliary to assist her; and we find the uneasiness arising upon a delay of desire vulgarly styled impatience. He that cannot forbear hankering after pleasure lost, nor support the trouble any little importunate habit may give him, will make no progress towards mastering them; for whatever ground he may have gained by repelling the first attack, he will lose it all again upon the second. And sometimes, I believe, men give way for fear of this uneasiness when it might not have proved insupportable: so that a little courage and confidence in our strength is very helpful upon these occasions.

4. Of

4. Of all the propensities that take us at unawares none are more dangerous than indolence and pride, or vanity, because none are more universal, and none more sly in making their approaches covertly: a man can hardly fall into excesses of debauchery without being sensible of them; but he may be vain or idle without ever knowing that he is so. Laziness seems to be the very opposite to virtue, for as this consists in exerting the vigour of the mind to discern the lights of our judgment when overshaded by other ideas, he that could keep this vigour perpetually alert would never fall into any error of conduct. But there is a love of ease in us all that makes people often bestir themselves prodigiously in the prosecution of some fond desire rather than be at the pains of overcoming it, and gives birth to the violence and impatience of passion, which wants to have the purpose aimed at by it presently attained that the business may be over. And, perhaps, laziness may lie at the bottom of all pride and vanity, for there is much less trouble in persuading ourselves we possess accomplishments we have not, in contemplating those we have or displaying them to public view, than in improving them, or acquiring new ones. He that is always diligent in advancing forwards, will scarce have time for more than a transient

sient look now and then upon the progress he has made, much less will he stand pointing out the length of it to every passenger he sees in the way. But vanity is so deeply rooted in us by education, by example and sympathy, and assails on so many quarters, that no wonder we can never guard against it effectually: we are taught to judge of ourselves and our possessions of any kind by comparison with others, to despise or overlook what we have not, and value ourselves upon any trifle peculiarly our own. The spectator tells us of a young lady whom he found one day hold up her head higher than ordinary, and wondering what could be the occasion, her sister whispered him that she had got on a new pair of silk garters. One would think virtue should secure a man most effectually against all vain imaginations; but there is a pride of thinking oneself and a vanity of appearing virtuous: nay some have been proud of their humility and contempt of pride, as witness Diogenes when he trampled upon the fine tapestry brought by Plato from the court of Sicily. But until a man can discover all the secret recesses of his heart, and restrain his fondness for contemplating or displaying any supposed perfection, he will not have attained compleatly the virtue of temperance.

5. Nor

5. Nor is moderation less necessary than courage to ensure a true liberty of thought. Men esteem themselves free-thinkers because they can think anything, but I do not hold them really such unless they can likewise forbear to think anything. It has been often observed there is a certain enthusiasm in poetry, and perhaps there is a degree of it though not so much observed in argumentation and most prose compositions. The neat structure of an hypothesis, the shrewdness of a discovery, the acuteness of an observation, the charm of novelty or pleasure of overthrowing a vulgar error, will sometimes transport men beyond themselves: one sparkling thought will eclipse all others their judgment presents, and a secret inclination cast a glare of evidence upon any notion that favours it. There are other restraints upon our freedom besides pusillanimity, and in order to think perfectly free we must learn to think soberly as well as boldly: for courage and caution, like two antagonist muscles, serve to keep one another from drawing the mind awry, if either of them have lost its tone, the party may be said to labour under a paralytic disorder.

6. Some seasonable austerity and self-denial will be found expedient or rather necessary for us all to practise: for we have not

such strength of mind as to surmount all opposition, therefore must endeavour to weaken the enemy by entering the lists against him as often as we can do it safely, and by so doing we shall add vigour to our own resolution which always gathers strength by exercise. This consideration will engage us sometimes to deny innocent desires that we may have it in our power to restrain them when hurtful. For the same reason we ought to keep a guard upon our thoughts as well as upon our actions: for there is an intemperance of imagination that engages men to dwell upon fantastical scenes of power, or gain, or revenge, or unwarrantable pleasures, under a notion of their being harmless, because they do not immediately break forth into act. But, when we reflect upon what has been shown before in the course of these enquiries, how great a sway imagination has, in shaping our behaviour, it will appear extremely dangerous to let that take a wrong turn: for it may steal upon us insensibly and give a wrong turn to our conduct when we are not aware; at least it will abate our relish, for other employments wherein we might spend our time to better advantage.

7. But self-denial is an evil considered in itself, wherefore, those are not to be heeded who would persuade us into a life of austerities

ties without regard to any good purposes to be effected thereby: for happiness, that is, content and solace of mind, is our proper aim, nor does present enjoyment ever deserve to be rejected, unless for the sake of some greater enjoyment to be had in exchange for it. There is no good merely in crossing and afflicting ourselves, but self-denial becomes recommendable, for the ease it will procure us, by breaking the force of those desires that would interrupt and teaze and torment us perpetually with their importunities. Our business is not to extinguish desire, without which there could be no pleasure in life, no choice among objects before us, nor glee in any thing we undertake, but to prevent it from being troublesome: and while we have unruly desires belonging to us it is necessary to travel the rugged road of self-denial in our progress towards the wise man's tranquillity. For I conceive the consummate sage, if there were such a one upon earth, would never practise self-denial, because he would not have an opportunity, his desires lying under such controul, as never to raise an opposition for him to struggle against: not that he would be without desires, on the contrary, I imagine he would abound in them more than we do, receiving delight from them in many things we should count insipid; but they would

hang

hang so loose about him, as to let go their hold the instant an object appeared improper or unattainable, to leave no secret hankering behind nor ever degenerate into want like the sheep who they say, is never thirsty, unless when he sees water, so his appetites would prove sources of pleasure to him, but none of pain. And why should we think such a disposition of mind impossible when there is scarce any of us, who do not possess it in some little degree? We can sit down with desire to a party at cards when proposed, or content ourselves without it, if not agreed to: we may eat fruit with good appetite in summer, and take pains in planting trees to procure it, without wanting it in winter: we can bestir ourselves lustily in forwarding schemes of hunting, or bowling, or dancing, or other diversion, when they fall in our way, and rest fully contented with our situation when they do not. So that we have nothing to do, but improve a faculty we already possess, and extend our authority gradually to all our other propensities, whether of profit, or honour, or building, or equipage, or curiosity, or knowledge, or whatever else would raise an intemperance of desire. The secret of happiness lies in having a multitude of engagements fitted for every occasion that can happen, so that some or other of them, may constantly give

give us an appetite for employment, but none that shall disturb us when we judge it necessary or proper to break them off.

8. As self-denial helps to bring desire under controul, so indulgence must needs have a contrary effect, adding vigour to the adversary and enfeebling ourselves: it is throwing the reins upon the horse's neck, which will quickly make him grow unmanageable. Wherefore, it behoves us to be cautious of our most innocent desires, lest by indulging, we render them habitual, and instead of inviting which is their proper office, they will drag us forcibly along: nor shall we ever recover our liberty, without a more painful self-denial than had been otherwise needful. Nor do intense pleasures deserve the value too commonly set upon them; it may be a man's misfortune to have been too highly delighted, for it will often destroy the relish of his common enjoyments, or fix so strong an impression upon the fancy, as shall obliterate all other ideas, and make him perpetually restless for a repetition: so that whoever seeks to be highly pleased, runs a hazard of being seldom pleased, and passing the greatest part of his time in disquietude and impatience. Many persons, especially young folks, make pleasure their sole aim whenever they can get the command of their time, in those intervals when the restraints

straints of their superiors are withdrawn, imagining they shall enjoy the more by how much the more assiduously they pursue it: but this is a fallacious way of reckoning, for pleasure is an errant coquet, flying those who court her most servilely and showing herself most gracious to those who bear the greatest indifference towards her. She makes forward advances to the unwary to bring them to her lure, but when she has gotten them fast in her fetters, she uses them scurvily, allowing them no rest in her service and feeding them only with delusive expectations and stale scraps of enjoyment, that have utterly lost their savour. Nor indeed is it in her power, were she ever so kindly disposed, to give a solid and lasting enjoyment; for those pleasures your men of pleasure hunt after, owe their gust merely to their novelty and the vigour of youthful blood and the freshness of the organs, but our organs can supply no more than a certain portion of entertainment, for when much employed in the same way, though they may still perform their work, yet they lose that sensibility in the exercise, which they had originally. Therefore, he that makes intense pleasure his whole business, is like an extravagant heir, who squanders away his whole patrimony in a year or two, and leaves himself nothing to live upon afterwards besides

sides poverty, want, and distress. Hence we may see the benefit of this cardinal virtue, Temperance, which will debar us no pleasure we can have at free cost, but rescue us from those that would make us pay more for them than they are worth, will open to us many sources of delight the voluptuous never taste of, and secure us an estate for life in such enjoyments whereof our nature is capable.

CHAP. XXXIII.

JUSTICE.

There is one particular desire, that of appropriating whatever we can get to ourselves, and following our own pleasure without regard to the hurt it may do other persons, which prevails so universally and strongly among mankind, and which, indulged, causes such disorder in the world, that the restraint of it has been thought worthy to be made a cardinal virtue, distinguished by the name of Justice. It is easy to see that justice owes its being to society, for it could have no place were each man to live separately by himself, or had he not in any instance a

power

power of endamaging the possessions, infringing the liberty, or abridging the enjoyments of his fellow creatures. Were men just now brought out of such a state, and placed upon this habitable earth, every one would naturally take of the good things scattered around him, whatever he wanted for his present occasion; when he went to do the same a second time, he might often find that somebody else had taken away the things he wanted before him; this would put him as often as he had an opportunity, upon securing as many of them as he could get together, to provide against the like accidents for the future; from whence springs self-interest, the desire of gain, and covetousness. But as others would do the same, the public stock would be soon exhausted, the fruits all gathered from the trees, and the desire of engrossing would then prompt men to invade one another's hoards: whence must ensue trouble, vexation, and contention, and much waste must be made in the struggle, to the great damage of them all. These inconveniences being severely felt, would teach them to see that their true interests lay in restraining their own desires within such compass, as might bring them compatible with those of others, and they would form rules for securing to each man the share of his blessings that

nature

nature had poured out among them. But it being obvious that the gifts of nature may be improved by labour, nor indeed can fully supply our wants without it, and there being no encouragement for any man to labour, if all the rest were to share the fruits of it with himself, they would find it necessary that all should enjoy the produce of their skill and industry in severalty, without interruption from others: and this would lay the foundation of property. But as it may often lie in a man's power to work out some advantage for others or for the public, and the security of property would be no encouragement with him so to do, because the fruits of his labour in this case would not redound to his own benefit, they would see the expedience of a compensation or reward, to serve as an encouragement for performing such services. On the other hand, some would still employ their strength or cunning to encroach upon their neighbour's properties, or through mere wantonness, or resentment, or other unruly passion, would endamage them in their persons or possessions: this would show the necessity of punishment to restrain such outrages. And as vicious inclinations, according to their strength would require a greater or less restraint to curb them, therefore punishment would be apportioned to the hein-

ousness

ousness of the offence, of which the greatness of the mischief done, would be deemed an evidence when the inward depravity could not otherwise be discovered.

2. Were mankind reduced to a state of nature, I imagine they would gradually fall into notions of justice by such steps as those above described. But we being born into settled communities, having regulations already established, take them as we find them, with the sanction of authority annexed to them, without penetrating into the sources from whence they derived. Yet if we were to suppose all reward and punishment, all law and honesty, banished from among a people, there would be nothing left to guide them besides self-interest, appetite, passion, and humour, and it is easy to see what wild doings, what havoc and distraction, these would introduce. Since then we find so manifest a necessity of justice to secure the happiness and tranquillity of life, we need seek for no other foundation than utility, whereon to build our obligation to support it. Many laws are calculated for the particular convenience of the people to whom they are given, and would be unjust because inconvenient if transported into other countries. The duty of subordination and obedience to higher powers, arises from the benefits of union: for it being impossible that all
indivi-

individuals should agree in their measures of conduct, or stand in a situation to judge of them, if the authority were not placed in a few hands a nation could never act as one man to repel the invasions of an enemy, nor execute any one undertaking that required the concurrence of numbers. Therefore, though it be possible that governors may command things inconvenient, yet it is not justifiable to disobey them, because of the debility that must ensue upon loosening of their authority. Just as a man, who should find a troublesome twitching in his muscles, would do very wrong to destroy the tone of them: for he had better bear the present uneasiness than lose the use of his limbs. It has been commonly said, the worst kind of government was preferable to anarchy: wherefore the consideration of that preference will prove a tie upon every prudent man to submit to such government.

3. Nobody will deny there is a natural justice distinct from the legal, and must be presupposed before men can pay a proper submission to authority: for whoever obeys the law for fear of incurring the penalty is not a just man, he only deserves the title of just who would deal honestly, and forbear offending, although there were no terrors hanging over to compel him, and who does not think

of

of the penalties annexed, but acts upon a motive of principle. Where this principle is wanting, the best contrived laws cannot wholly supply the deficiency; for they being calculated for general use, it is impossible to shape them so exactly as to suit all the variety of cases that may happen, therefore there wants some other clue to direct us when to pursue, and when to abate the rigour of justice. Besides, there are many ways by which men have it in their power to affect one another in matters where the law does not, and perhaps could not interfere, particularly in the application of applause and censure: in all these cases they can have no other guidance than the law of their own minds binding to the observance of certain rules, founded originally upon utility, though not always, or rather very seldom, carrying a visible connection therewith. We have seen under the article of honour, that praise and blame belong properly to those objects whereto the annexing them will do greatest service. Reparation for damages tends to the security of property, preventing retaliation, and answering as a penalty to restrain mischievousness and heedlessness. The labourer is worthy of his hire, because it cannot be expected men should labour without it: and the shopkeeper ought to be paid for his goods, because else there

would

would be an end of all commerce and industry. Merit and demerit of all kinds, arise from a right understanding, and prudent regard to our own interests; and the very term Deserve, implies that such a particular treatment will be most expedient upon such or such a behaviour.

4. Thus every species of justice, as well public as private, as well commutative as distributive, rests upon the basis of utility: but what causes the mistake upon this matter is, the double sense of the word utility, as distinguished into real and apparent; for in philosophical consideration, it is understood of that which upon the whole amount of consequences tends most to advance a man's real happiness, but in vulgar language it stands for that which exhibits the clearest prospect of advantage or profit. If we look back upon the chapter of use, we shall find how pleasure transfers satisfaction upon things instrumental or preparatory to the procuring it, from whence grow the principle of self-interest, and many desires of things conceived beneficial or conducive to our purposes. Now if we take this self-interest, and the gratification of these desires of utility, it is certainly quite different from justice as standing generally at the greatest variance with it; he that deals honestly when not compelled either

by

by the fear of punishment or censure, and without this, he cannot claim a title to honesty, manifestly forgoes his interest for the sake of justice. But our ultimate end of action is not always, or rather very rarely our ultimate point of view, for our faculties being too scanty to look forward to the journey's end, we set up certain marks whereon to fix our attention from time to time for our guidance on the way: some of the first of these marks are the rules of interest, profit, convenience and worldly prudence, but they proving often insufficient, we find a necessity of other marks in the rules of honour and justice to rectify their mistaken directions.

I am well aware that each of us singly, learns our honesty by instruction or sympathy from others, but then it can scare be denied that those, who first set the example, did it from observation of the mischiefs attendant upon a too close attachment to interest. If we could constantly see to the end of our proceedings, and compute exactly the whole produce of enjoyment and suffering to be expected from them, we should want no other rule than that of preferring the greater distant good before present pleasure, for our own advantage would guide us sufficiently in all parts of our conduct; but since we cannot look so far, and interest frequently leads astray from

from its own purposes, we have need enough of the restraint of justice to keep us from being beguiled by it, and led out of the road to real utility, which we often miss of through too great eagerness for the apparent. It may be remarked, that honour and justice abound more in rules than any other principle of action, because lying further removed from pleasure, we can seldomer discern the connection therewith, and consequently stand more in need of direction. But rules will stand us in no stead without a propensity urging strongly to practise them, which propensity, in the present case, is styled the moral sense or conscience: wherefore it behoves every man to cultivate or improve this moral sense or conscientious regard for the obligations of justice to the utmost, and adhere to it without reserve against all the solicitations of interest. The proper office of justice lies in restraining our selfish desires: a thorough righteous man, will never suffer any of them either to draw him privily, or hurry him forcibly upon actions for which his heart may afterwards misgive him or which his mortal sense warns him to beware as unlawful, although he may not directly discern their inexpedience. It is true he may sometimes mistake and forego his lawful advantages needlessly, but the possession of a strong moral sense is more valuable than any present benefit he could receive from its weakness; and he may look upon these inconveniences in the light of troubles naturally attending an estate, which no man would throw away for the sake of escaping them.

Therefore it is much the safer side to be too scrupulous than too remiss, especially for young people. Tully used to reckon exuberance a good sign in a young orator, and say he loved to find something to prune off. The moralist may say the same with respect to his scholars, that he loves to see the moral sense vigorous and redundant, affording something to prune off; for it is much harder to nourish up a weakly plant than reduce one that is luxuriant. The expedience of justice lies through so many stages, that it is difficult to trace them, but the inconveniences of over strictness are easier manifested, nor will fail to discover themselves upon a little experience. But though the moral sense ought to master desire, it ought not to prevail over reason; therefore whenever upon a full and fair examination, we find our rules tend to greater harm than good, we must alter or dispense with them, and since they are liable to error, it will behove us, as often as a proper opportunity offers, to try them by a reference to use. This will prevent their running into extravagances,
and

and give us a better opinion of them; for by frequently observing the benefit of justice, we shall become intimately persuaded of its expedience at other times when we do not discern them: which will teach us a confidence in our moral sense, and make us look upon the laudableness of an action, as a certain evidence of its usefulness.

5. As we are mighty fond of personifying every thing, even the creatures of imagination, abstract notions, and whatever we can express by a noun substantive, it is common to consider the law either of the land, or of nature, as a person, having perception, volition, design, desire, and passion. In this light, if we look for what design the law must be supposed to have, we cannot well conceive any other than the preservation of property, the security of life, limb, peace, liberty, and all other requisites for enjoyment, that may be destroyed or lessened by the behaviour of men to one another. But all design tends to something future, the past being no object of power or contrivance: hence it is plain the law carries always a prospect forwards, and only casts a retrospect behind, in order to take her measures for providing against the time to come. The reparation she awards for damages sustained, manifestly relates to the future convenience of the party aggrieved, for if he be satisfied by being rein-

stated

stated in the possession of those materials for enjoyment he had before the offence committed, or receiving an equivalent that will answer his purposes as well, the law is satisfied too. But it may often happen that the offender is not able to make reparation, or the injury, as in cases of murder or maiming, is of a nature not to be repaired or compensated : under these circumstances the law will not be supposed to design impossibilities, and can only have in view the preventing the like injuries for the future, by such punishment as shall be judged sufficient for that purpose. So that in reality punishment is not inflicted for crimes committed, but as a remedy against those which might be committed hereafter; and guilt is rather a direction than a motive for taking vengeance. And that this is so, will appear more evident when we reflect that natural justice restrains the thoughts, desires, and intentions of men, as well as their out- outward actions: nor do the laws sometimes scruple to punish for the intent where no mischief has been actually done. Conspiring to defraud, assaulting with intent to rob or ravish, are deemed misdemeanors; lifting up a latch in the night time with design to commit burglary, forging or knowingly publishing a forged note, are made felony; imagining the the death of the king, is high treason. And if

an

an overt act be required to convict the delinquent, I believe every one, who knows the nature of right and wrong, will admit that the overt act adds nothing to the delinquency, but is only necessary to prove it, because we cannot dive into the thoughts of men, nor judge of them otherwise than by their actions. Were there a man to whom the hearts of all others should lie open, and a discretionary power entrusted, to do as he judged reasonable, he would not think it unjust to apply such punishment for the most secret evil designs, as he conceived effectual for preventing them from breaking forth into act.

6. But to pursue our idea of personality in the law; as we all look upon the defeating of our designs as a damage, and the law designing the peace and security of those under her protection, therefore every hurt brought upon individuals, is considered as an injury done the law itself, for which she will require such satisfaction as can be made, that is, such adequate punishment as may deter the offender or others from repeating the offence, and reinstate her in her power she had before of protecting: this brings punishment under the idea of a reparation or satisfaction for damage done, not indeed to the party injured, but to the law; for when the offender has undergone the chastisement allotted him, he is said to have

have satisfied the law and to stand right again in court. Then as in ourselves satisfaction becomes often transferred from the end to the means, particularly in resentment where we think of nothing further than wreaking our revenge, and in pursuits of honour or power which we do not follow for their uses but to gratify our present desires of them, we conceive the same passions to prevail and the same narrow views to obtain in the law, which animadverts upon delinquents for her own satisfaction rather than for the sake of the community under her charge.

7. This custom of conceiving the law to have interests of her own to serve, and the detestation which arises instantly in the hearts of the best and wisest men upon the thought of heinous wickedness, has given rise to the opinion of an immediate and essential connection between offence and punishment, which is supposed due to the former without taking any other idea into consideration. I shall readily agree that in taking measures for punishing we need consider nothing further than the degree of delinquency, for being well satisfied our rule is right we need not, nay cannot, constantly look forward to the reasons inducing us to believe it right; and so we depend upon the 47th of Euclid as a certain truth without running on to the demonstrations

tions convincing us of its being true: but if we search for the foundation of justice, though here too we shall find a connection, it will be hard to trace it out unless by the intervention of two links lying between, I mean, the power of men still to hurt one another, and the tendency of punishment to make them change or withhold them from executing their evil intentions. Were mankind to be suddenly placed in a situation which should render them incapable of ever more receiving damage from others, or their dispositions of mind so changed as that they should never more think of doing acts of injustice, I believe every good man would vote for a general amnesty of all former misdemeanors, because the remembrance of them would be needless in one case and useless in the other.

If the connection between offence and punishment were natural and necessary, submission and repentance could never dissociate them, for the nature of actions cannot be altered by any thing subsequent; but repentance, answering the purpose intended by chastisement, takes away the use of it, and thereby dissolves the connection: therefore when severity appears necessary as a warning to others, that they may not expect to come off upon the like easy terms, the just man will not accept of repentance: thus we see
justice

justice disarmed upon becoming needless, and the sword put into her hands again upon the further prospect of necessity.

And the same cause extends her province beyond the limits naturally belonging to it, by warranting her sometimes to take vengeance upon the innocent for wrongs wherein they have had no share: for this is the case of war, wherein the goods and possessions of private persons are invaded for injuries received from the state. I know that in national transactions all the members of a community are looked upon as constituting one person, and in this light you take revenge upon the person that injured you: but this is only an imaginary personality, very useful for pointing out the measures of national justice, but by no means supporting it as a foundation. If the French king has fortified Dunkirk, or encroached upon our colonies in America, in breach of treaties, you cannot charge the merchant trading from Martinico with any faithlessness or badness of heart upon that account: so justice stands here separated from delinquency and every spice of evil intention, for you esteem it lawful to seize his effects by way of reprisal. But why do you judge it lawful? because you cannot right yourself otherwise: so necessity makes the justice; for were it possible to come at the governors

governors directly without touching the subjects, no righteous man would think the latter method justifiable, notwithstanding any supposed identity of person between them.

8. Were the justness of actions essential and inherent, whenever the rules of justice clash, as we find them sometimes do, that which must be superseded must abate something from the justness of the other: for the case is so in matters of profit or pleasure. If you lay out a sum of money to make an improvement of greater value upon your estate, you are certainly a gainer: yet could you procure the same improvement free of charges your gain would be greater. If you might partake of some very agreeable diversion by going five miles through very dirty roads, it is worth your while; yet could you have it without that trouble I suppose you would like it better. But suppose two men in different parts of a field near a river, alarmed by the cry of some person drowning, one has a path to run along, but the other cannot go to help without trampling down his neighbour's corn, which you must allow to be an unjust action considered in itself, nevertheless I conceive the strictest casuist would acknowledge the merit of both equal: so the lesser rule bears no intrinsic value to be subtracted from the greater, for the expedience of abstaining from

from another's property is taken off by the higher importance of saving a man's life.

9. Nor do the obligations of truth and fidelity rest upon any other basis than expedience: it is easy to see that were truth banished the world there could be no intercourse among mankind, no use of speech; if you asked anybody's direction upon the road you might as well let it alone, for you could gather nothing from their answer if there were no truth in men. Were all falsehood wrong as such, why are poems and novels suffered? why do moralists invent fables wherein they introduce beasts talking, gods appearing in the air, and the moon desiring to be taken measure of for a suit of cloaths? But when fiction may serve some good purpose and does no hurt, the wisest do not scruple to employ it. Did the bare form of an agreement create an obligation to perform it, no circumstances whatever could render it invalid. Are then all those suitors unrighteous who apply to our courts of equity to be relieved from their contracts? or are the courts iniquitous in decreeing them relief? But were there no faith among men, no regard to their engagements, anybody may see with half an eye what stagnation of business, what mutual diffidence and confusion must ensue; and it is the avoidance of those evils that gives them their sanction: therefore, when

when the rigid observance of compacts manifestly tends to greater mischiefs than could be avoided thereby, no righteous judge, having authority so to do, will scruple setting them aside. Nevertheless, this does not justify a man in breaking his engagements whenever he finds it detrimental or inconvenient to keep them, for our views are so narrow that we cannot always see all the consequences of our actions, and rules are the marks hung out to direct us to an advantage we cannot discern: therefore the wise man will adhere inviolably to his rules though he cannot discover their expedience; for he will look upon the manifest injustice of a thing as a stronger evidence of its being detrimental than any appearance that may arise to the contrary; yet an expedience there must be or the rules will not be right. For justice is the minister of reason though it ought to be the master of action: and it is one thing to establish rules of conduct, but another to show the foundation of them. When a man is to act he ought to consult his ideas of justice, and follow whithersoever they direct without reserve or looking to any thing further; but when we enquire why justice is recommendable, it behoves us to trace out the reference it bears to happiness; for without this it will be hard to prove the obligation to it, and this being once clearly

clearly evinced it would want nothing else to give it all the influence that could be desired.

This method seems to have been attempted by the old philosophers, but they stopped short in the midway, as we may learn from Cicero, who was no philosopher himself, but an elegant reporter of the Greek philosophy, where he endeavours to show the prudence of Regulus's conduct in Lib. iii. Cap. 27, 8, 9, of his Offices; for he tells us those are to be rejected who would separate utility from justice; because, says he, whatever is just or honestum is therefore useful. This is giving the ladies' reason, It is so because it is; for he does not vouchsafe a word to prove why it is useful. That every thing just is really advantageous I shall not deny, nor that the practice of justice is the surest road to happiness, but I must deny that this is a first principle or self-evident proposition, or to be discerned without much thought and consideration, for I know that in many cases the contrary appears upon first sight: therefore it had become a philosopher, especially such a powerful artificer of words as Cicero, to have laid open the fallacy of this appearance and shown the intermediate steps by which justice leads to utility. He might have had an ample field to expatiate upon in the benefits and necessity of justice to the welfare of mankind. He might have showed that

that the Roman commonwealth rose to that pitch of grandeur they shone in by a strict fidelity to their engagements, and that they afterwards began to decline and fall into confusion by their oppression of the provinces taken under their protection, and their selfish endeavours to encroach upon one another's rights. He might then have gone on to prove the good of every individual contained in that of the public, and thence concluded that Regulus, all things considered, acted more for his own advantage in submitting to the torments he underwent than he could have done by any breach of faith whatsoever. As for his rhodomontade that the brave man looks upon pain as a mere trifle, this overthrows his other assertion, because it seems to admit that if pain were an evil it might justify the breach of engagements: and indeed we, who take it for such, commonly do admit it as an excuse when in a degree we conceive intolerable. When a sum of money is sent for a particular purpose, justice certainly requires it should be disposed of according to the owner's directions. Suppose then the party carrying it attacked on the way by ruffians who threaten him with some grievous mischiefs unless he will deliver it them: if he be perfectly honest, and at the same time possessed of the stoical fortitude so as not to value pain at a straw, he will bear the

the worst they can do to him rather than betray his trust: but suppose the messenger were a weak and fearful woman to whom violent ill usage were really terrible, I believe none of us would think it the least abatement of her character for honesty if she yielded to her terrors. So that justice is not so necessarily connected with use, but that a greater evil on the other side may separate them, and in that case the action ceases to be just: wherefore utility constitutes the essence of justice, but not justice that of utility.

10. But though justice be not utility, nevertheless it ought to be esteemed the certain mark and evidence of utility, and an intimate persuasion of its being so, will fasten desire upon it as upon an ultimate point of view without needing any thing beyond to recommend it. Whoever has this desire so strong as to counterpoise all other desires, possesses the cardinal virtue here treated of: and whoever has not this desire at all, cannot be called an honest man in any degree, though he may do honestly for fear of punishment or prospect of advantage. Therefore if a righteous man be asked why he fulfills his engagements, though to his own manifest detriment, he will answer, because it would have been unjust to have failed in them; for he wants no other motive to induce him, and if the querist

querist be righteous too he will want no other reason to satisfy him. But if he be asked further why he esteems justice a proper motive of action, and he be a person who does not take his principles upon trust from the example or authority of others, but has used to examine them himself, he will refer to the general necessity and expedience of justice, and alledge that what conduces to the general good of mankind must be good for every particular. But could it be made appear that injustice in some single instance tended to the general advantage, he would not think himself warranted to practise it, because the mischief of setting a bad example, and weakening the authority of a beneficial rule, would be greater than any present advantage that might accrue from the breach of it. And even supposing his injustice could be concealed from all the world so that it could do no hurt by example, still he would not believe it allowable for fear it should have a bad influence upon his own mind. For whoever understands human nature, knows how dangerous it is to lessen the force of those restraints that withhold us from the exhorbitances of self-interest: if we break into them in some instances where we might do it innocently, we shall run a great hazard of losing their influence at other times when it will be
absolutely

absolutely necessary for keeping us within bounds. Nor can we doubt of there being an utility in justice, when we find it acknowledged in some measure, by the unanimous consent of all mankind: it is a vulgar saying, that Honesty is the best policy, nor perhaps is there a man who, if he could accomplish his desires justly, would not choose it that way rather than by wrong. The very gangs of highwaymen and street robbers observe some fidelity, though little enough it is true, in their engagements with one another: so that even those persons who take their notions of utility and pleasure for their sole guidance, still pay some regard to justice, being led by their experience of its conducing necessarily thereto.

11. The just man, to deserve that appellation, must be so throughout, in small matters as well as great: he will regard natural justice and legal too when it is not superceded by the other: he will abstain from injuring, not only the persons, possessions, and liberties of his neighbours, but likewise their good name, reputation, and claim to the merit of their performances, neither deceiving by flattery, blackening by calumny, overbearing by haughtiness, nor overreaching by cunning: he will beware of wronging anybody, even in his own private estimation, nor give credit hastily to unfavourable reports, but judge of
persons

persons and interpret actions candidly and cautiously: he will look upon all untruth or bias to the prejudice of another as a species of injustice, and will esteem ingratitude one of the most flagrant.

12. As justice consists in a hearty desire of doing right to every one against the solicitations of other desires urging another way, and as among contending impulses the most vigorous will always prevail, therefore justice, though distinct from temperance and fortitude, cannot well subsist without them, because it is their office to reduce our other desires within a manageable compass. Ambition, covetousness, extravagant fondness for pleasure, anger, and all kinds of intemperance, hurry men on, otherwise well disposed, to unwarrantable actions. Fretfulness, sloth, over delicacy, effeminate softness, and every other branch of impatience, will not suffer them to do justly, where any pains or difficulty are requisite. These vices lay them under a necessity of transgressing: but though we have seen before that a real necessity takes away injustice from a deed, yet an unnecessary necessity, if I may be allowed the expression, that is, one brought upon us by our own folly, leaves it in full colours. Therefore, the ancients were right when they said that

whoever possessed one virtue compleatly must possess them all, because they mutually nourish and protect one another.

CHAP. XXXIV.

BENEVOLENCE.

The grand impediment against making philosophy universally understood arises from the particular style unavoidably employed therein, different from that used upon common occasions. Sometimes it is found necessary to frame technical terms unknown to the man of plain sense: at other times when words of general currency will serve, yet a peculiar idiom and structure is necessary to make them answer the purpose effectually. This is nowhere more apparent than in speaking of the virtues, which are vulgarly conceived infinitely numerous and various: but the moralist, being willing to methodize his thoughts and reduce the wilderness into a regular plan, endeavours to comprise them all under four general heads, to which he assigns names already in use, but must extend

CHAP. 34.]   *Benevolence.*   355

tend their signification beyond what custom will warrant, in order to bring them wide enough to take in all he would have them. By this means it happens that the plain man, attempting to follow his method, finds himself frequently perplexed : for after being fully satisfied that an action is right, he still remains at a loss to know what particular species of virtue it belongs to; or perhaps sometimes mistakes that to be the virtue recommended which is really no virtue at all. Thus prudence, the principal virtue comprehending all the rest, stands in vulgar acceptation for sagacity, penetration, experience, and clearness of judgment, which are not virtue but good fortune; or if attained by our own industry, still are the fruits of virtue rather than the tree itself: and as prudence is vulgarly understood of a cautious regard to interest, we find it often standing at the greatest variance with virtue. But we have seen before, that moral prudence consists in making a due use of our lights, not in the abundance or clearness of them, and vigorously adhering to the dictates of reason, against the solicitations of interest, or any other desire whatsoever. So likewise fortitude is made to include patience, because the same robustness of temper that enables the possessor to stare danger in the face, is supposed to render

A A 2   him

him invincible by pain. But to common apprehension a man may be very patient and yet very timorous: nor on the other hand, if we see him preserve an uninterrupted presence of mind in perils of all kinds, shall we think him deficient in courage, because he frets under imprisonment, or cannot bear disappointment and contradiction. In like manner temperance implies the moderation of every desire and appetite that would carry us on unadvisedly to present gratification: but in our familiar discourses, we confine it to sobriety in eating and drinking, for if we find a man abstemious in these points, we count him a model of temperance, notwithstanding he may be ambitious, or slothful, or revengeful. To come lastly to the cardinal virtue of justice, the philosopher must comprise under it benevolence and whatever we do for the benefit or pleasure of others without regard to our own: but nobody else would esteem that person a friend or good neighbour who should do no more to serve another than what the strictness of justice obliges him to.

2. For this reason I have thought convenient to make a distinct article of benevolence, which if you please may be called a fifth cardinal virtue. For though it has been hitherto reputed a branch of justice as springing from the same ground, namely, that our own

own good is contained in the good of others, yet I do not see why it may not as well be reckoned the root and justice the branch, since it bears that and many good fruits beside: for we do not use to behave dishonestly to our friends, and if we had a proper regard and concern for all mankind I do not imagine we could ever deal unjustly with any body. However this be, there is a manifest difference between them in the common conceptions of the world. Justice only restrains from doing damage or wrong: good nature does the same too, but over and above, this prompts to do all the service for which there is an opportunity. A debt and a favour seem essentially distinct, so that what is one cannot be the other; for a man is bound by obligation to render to every one his dues, but in doing a kindness he must be free from all obligation or else it is no kindness. If a man pays you what he owed, you do not thank him for it, he only escapes the censure you might have thrown upon him for failing: but if he does you a service you had no right to expect, he deserves your acknowledgments. Since then benevolence carries a different idea in common apprehension from justice, what has been offered in illustration of that subject, will not suffice for this: and if we consider how it is generally under-

understood, I think it may be called a diffused love to the whole species, in which light the same definition we gave of love will remain applicable here, to wit, the pleasure of pleasing: or if, as we distinguished the passion into love and fondness, so we should distinguish the virtue into benevolence and good nature, the one will be a pleasure of benefiting and the other that of pleasing. To render it perfectly formed, desire must connect immediately with these ends, for if there be any thought of our own interest or gratification between, what we do for others is not an act of kindness. I do not apprehend that nature gives us any such desire, but we have already shewn in several places by what steps desire becomes transferred from ourselves to other objects, and when we can perform good offices upon the sole consideration of their being such, then is the translation compleat. Whoever has this desire habitual, will feel a satisfaction in acts of kindness proportionable to the benefit of them which will urge him to perform them as a matter of entertainment, whenever they fall in his way.

4. Persons deficient in this quality endeavour to run it down, and justify their own narrow views, by alledging that it is only selfishness in a particular form: for, if the benevolent man does a good-natured thing, for his own

own satisfaction that he finds in it, there is self at bottom, for he acts to please himself, Where then, say they, is his merit? what is he better than us? he follows constantly what he likes, and so do we: the only difference between us is, that we have a different taste of pleasure from him. To take these objections in order, let us consider that form in many cases is all in all, the essence of things depending thereupon. Fruit, when come to its maturity, or during its state of sap in the tree, or of earthy particles in the ground, is the same substance all along: beef, whether raw or roasted, or putrified, is still the same beef, varying only in form: but whoever shall overlook this difference of form, will bring grievous disorders upon his stomach: so then there is no absurdity in supposing selfishness may be foul and noisome under one form, but amiable and recommendable under another. But we have no need to make this supposition, as we shall not admit that acts of kindness, how much soever we may follow our own inclination therein, carry any spice of selfishness. Men are led into this mistake by laying too much stress upon etymology, for selfishness being derived from self, they learnedly infer that whatever is done to please one's own inclination, must fall under that appellation, not considering that derivatives

tives do not always retain the full latitude of their roots. Wearing woollen cloaths, or eating mutton does not make a man sheepish, nor does employing himself now and then in reading, render him bookish: so neither is every thing selfish, that relates to oneself. If somebody should tell you, that such an one was a very selfish person, and for proof of it, give a long account of his being once catched on horseback by a shower, that he took shelter under a tree, that he alighted, put on his great coat, and was wholly busied in muffling himself up, without having a single thought all the while of his wife or children, his friends or his country: would not you take it for a banter? or would you think the person or his behaviour could be called selfish in any propriety of speech? What, if a man agreeable and obliging in company, should happen to desire another lump of sugar in his tea to please his own palate, would they pronounce him a whit the more selfish upon that account? So that selfishness is not having a regard for oneself, but having no regard for any thing else. Therefore, the moralist may exhort men to a prudent concern for their own interests, and at the same time dissuade them from selfishness, without inconsistency.

4. As for the influence of satisfaction, we have already seen how that gives life to all our motions,

CHAP. 34.]   *Benevolence.*   361

motions, so that if that rendered them selfish, there would be no use for the term, nor any distinction between selfish, and disinterested: for the wise and the foolish the good and the wicked, the thoughtful and the giddy, in business and diversion, in their deliberate and inconsiderate actions, all incessantly follow satisfaction. But we have shown that satisfaction is ever one and the same in kind, and the variety of motives arises from the difference of vehicles containing it, which vehicles are the objects of desire, for we know well enough we must have the satisfaction if we can attain the satisfactory object: wherefore desire fixes upon this as an ultimate point, and we take our measures according to what we conceive satisfactory. Nature first conveys satisfaction by the ministry of the senses, from thence it becomes transferred to the instruments or materials we have found qualified to furnish us with agreeable sensations: by degrees we come to have an intercourse with mankind, and find that they get away the materials of pleasure from one another, we then learn a desire of securing as many of them to ourselves as we can, and this I apprehend, gives rise to self-interest, which is never understood, either in common or philosophical language, of the natural propensity to pleasure, but of the pursuit of our own ends in opposition

tion to those of other persons. In process of time, wantonness, or resentment, or bad company brings some to delight in mischief, and these we term mischievous: others are led by consideration, or kind usage, or better example to take the like delight in good offices, and these become benevolent: such as have neither of those tastes, but always do either good or hurt, just as it serves their own purpose, are properly selfish. Hence the following of inclination does not constitute selfishness, for in this respect, all men are alike, but the difference results from what they severally fix their inclinations upon: for it is the object of desire, the ultimate point is prospect, that denominates an action. He that abstains from mischief, out of fear or punishment or for some private advantage, is selfish, not benevolent in the deed, and if he do it because he thinks it his duty, still he is not benevolent, though he may have some other virtue which guided him in the doing; for to entitle an action to that epithet, it must proceed from the sole motive of good-will, without thought of any thing beyond the benefit of the party who is the subject of it.

5. Nor need anybody be at a loss to form an idea of such an inclination, for I suppose the most selfish creature breathing may chance to be sometimes in good humour, and has some

some child or mistress, or boon companion, to whom he can take delight in doing a favour when he has no end of his own to serve upon them: let him only reflect upon the state of his mind in these hearty moods, and he may understand that benevolence is no more than the same disposition carried as far as human frailty can extend it. Neither need we seek for any greater refinement or purity of intention than this I have been speaking of; we may lawfully and laudably follow our pleasure, provided that be set upon such an employment. The good old rule holds in this case, of doing and standing affected to others as we would have them do and stand affected to us: now what can we desire better, than that they should take delight in pleasing us? Could your family, your friends, your neighbours, your acquaintance, come and say with truth and sincerity, Sir, please to let us know wherein we can serve you, for we shall take delight in doing it: what would you want of them more? what other disposition could you wish them to put on? Would you answer them, Look ye good folks, while you take delight in serving me, you do it to please yourselves, so I do not thank you for it: but if you would lay a real obligation upon me, you must first hate me with all your might, and then the services you shall do me will be purely disinterested. Surely

Surely he that could make this reply must have a very whimsical turn of thought, and a strong tincture of envy, since he cannot be content to receive a kindness, unless the person conferring suffers for it, by forcing himself against his inclination.

6. As commendation, and a return of good offices tend to encourage benevolence, therefore it deserves them: for we have seen in a former place, that honour and reward belong properly to where they will do most service. But the reward must not constantly follow too close upon the action, for then it will be apt to catch the eye, and become the end expected, at every performance, which will render it selfish. But when good offices meet with a return of the like only in general, or in the gross, they lie too wide to be carried always in view, and desire will fix upon the acts of kindness as upon an ultimate point: wherefore many spoil their children by hiring them perpetually with playthings to do as they would have them. As an action takes its quality not from the thing done, but from the motive operating to produce it, therefore benevolence, to be genuine, must be free and voluntary: for what we are drawn or overpersuaded to do, does not proceed from inclination, and is rather an act of impulse than choice. There is a softness and milkiness of temper

temper that cannot say nay to any thing, but he that can never refuse a favour, can hardly be said ever to grant one: for it is wrested from him, not given; he does it to rid himself of an importunity, and save the trouble of a denial, in which case it is a weakness rather than a virtue. Hence good nature is often called, and sometimes really proceeds from folly, which gets no thanks when it proves most beneficial: for men applaud themselves for having gained a compliance by wheedling or pressing, and secretly laugh at the silly thing that could be won by such artifices.

7. There is likewise a spurious benevolence which flows from vanity, it makes men helpful and obliging to show their power and importance, or gain the incense of applause, or bring others into dependance upon them. Persons actuated by this motive, may behave kindly enough to such as are submissive to them, but are generally envious of their superiors, and carry themselves haughtily to those who do not want them, and cannot endure to see any good that is not done by themselves. Wherefore how much soever they may value themselves upon their good deeds, they carry no intrinsic merit: for their desire never terminates upon the good of another, but only urges to it as a necessary means for serving their own ends. So that the

the commendation bestowed on them by such as penetrate into their motive, is not paid as a debt, but thrown out as a lure, drawing them to a continuance of the like practices, and the commerce on both sides is rather a traffic of interest, than a mutual intercourse of kindness.

8. But true benevolence, as it will not bear mingling with any other motive or passion, so neither may it become a passion itself, for it must be judicious, and then can never be such. We have laid down in the chapter of passion that the difference between that and affection lies only in the degree, and that not in the absolute strength of it neither, but in its rising so high as to become uncontrollable by reason. If this description of passion be admitted, I can readily come into the stoical doctrine concerning apathy: for the wise man will always remain master of his own actions, he will never suffer any inclination, not even the best of them, to gain an ascendant over him, he will permit them to recommend and invite, and will employ them to assist him, but never follow them implicitly, and will preserve his seat of empire over them to prevent their encroaching upon one another's rights. By this impartiality and steady tenor of conduct he will fall deficient in no one branch of benevolence, and though he will prove a tender and affectionate relation, a sincere and zealous friend,
yet

yet his attachment to particulars will not overwhelm his regard to mankind in general, but rather cherish and purify it; for by reflecting on the sincerity and heartiness wherewith he can run to oblige those who are dearest to him, he will have a pattern from his own experience, instructing him what kind of disposition to put on with respect to others. Nor will he carry himself stiffly and austerely, despising little good offices, when they do not stand in the way of more important; for though his benevolence will not degenerate into fondness, neither will it want for tenderness. He will study not only to do solid good, but to please and humour whenever it can be done without ill consequence, and will be as much though not so weakly compliant, as the good-natured man a little before spoken of, to every innocent desire and fancy: but in the manner of his compliance, will resemble the ivy which twines and conforms itself freely to all the inequalities of the substance whereto it adheres, rather than the metal that takes an impression forcibly stamped upon it, or the vapours drawn up out of their element by the insinuating action of the sun. Courteousness is the skin and outside of virtue, and though a man would wish, in the first place to enjoy vigour of limbs, and soundness of constitution, yet if he can have a good skin too, it is no
detriment

detriment to his person. Therefore this will not be neglected by the sage we have in idea, he will finish his virtue in every part, small as well as great, ornamental as well as serviceable, nor think the body of it compleat until the bones and muscles are invested with their proper covering.

9. But the having one inclination does not necessarily imply the utter banishment of all others, therefore benevolence will never make a man's regard for another destroy his proper regard for his own interests, nor supersede the obligations of justice, temperance, or other rules of action: much less will it prompt him to humonr any body to their own real detriment. If we take our idea of benevolence from the notions of it current among the polite world, it should seem to consist wholly in trifles, subscribing to a concert, making one in a party of pleasure, saying civil things, promoting any little scheme of one's acquaintance, or complying with them in all their follies and fancies. What is this but placing the essence of virtue in her outside, making her a man of straw, an empty covering containing nothing within? But the wise man, though not regardless of an agreeable complexion, will desire to have a solid substance underneath; he will aim constantly at the greater good, use his judgment to discern it, consult his moral sense

sense and discretion as the surest guides to find it, and exert his resolution to follow their directions.

10. Nevertheless, if different inclinations may reside in the same person, yet inclinations directly opposite cannot; wherefore pure and perfect benevolence can never delight in mischief, nor harbour any thought of revenge: I do not say that it will preserve the same behaviour under all kinds of usage, for this would make it a weakness instead of a virtue, but a proper notice may be taken of injuries without any sentiment of revenge. The judge is not revengeful when he pronounces sentence upon the criminal, nor the magistrate when he chastises those who contemn his authority: for they do it to preserve peace, property, and order, the greatest blessings of society. But revenge, is properly, a desire of hurting those who have offended, without any further consideration: the view terminates on that point, which it can never do in the good man, being always turned a contrary way. He may punish or censure where he has it in his power, and judges it expedient and necessary, but he always carries that necessity in view: so that his animadversions will be matter of compulsion not of choice, an undesirable means to attain a greater good. He will consider wickedness as a distemper of the mind, dangerous

to the patient, contagious and pernicious to the public, and proceed against it in the same disposition as a surgeon who performs a painful operation for the sake of a cure, or cuts off a limb that would endanger the whole body. He will take injuries patiently when he has not power to resent them, or finds the retaliation attended with more inconvenience than advantage. He will be ready to forgive whenever repentance renders punishment unnecessary, and rejoice to find it become so. Nor will he not retain a good will even towards his enemies, for enmity he will have none himself, nor any resentment against them, but will only oppose them so far as to repel their attacks, or take away their power, or restrain their inclination to do hurt: in all other matters consistent with those purposes he will be ready to do them any kindness. He will have that laudable love of pleasure as to take it in all the good he sees, and feel the prosperities even of strangers; and be so covetous of enjoyment, as to make that of other persons his own, by partaking in the satisfaction attending it.

11. This it may be said is a glorious and happy temper of mind, but possible only in speculation and unattainable by frail mortal men, who are so deeply engaged in providing for their own necessities as not to be capable

of

of opening their thoughts much beyond themselves, whose passions prove too strong for their reason to control, and whose aptness to injure would perpetually break out into act, if there were not a desire of revenge to keep it in awe. I am afraid all this is but too true, yet by contemplating the character of an ideal sage, we may learn what it is we are to aim at, and if we despair of arriving at perfection, we may endeavour to resemble it in some particulars we find feasible. For we are none of us without some seeds of good nature, which, with due cultivation may be made to produce something in the most barren ground. Our own occasions do not so perpetually engage us but that we may sometimes spare a look elsewhere, nor do any of us want our seasons of good humour, wherein we can find a sensible delight in assisting and obliging without prospect of advantage to ourselves. The business then is to encourage these favourable dispositions whenever they appear, for though we cannot raise nor change an inclination at once, yet experience testifies that like a tender twig it may be brought to grow in any shape by continual bending: so that though we must force ourselves at first, yet repeated acts will contract a habit, which we shall then follow with ease and pleasure. It will be of signal service frequently to place ourselves in the situation

situation of other persons, to adopt their desires, and imagine ourselves under their wants, at least, to paint as exact a representation as we can of their condition of mind, according to our manner of behaviour towards them: for then the force of sympathy will assist us greatly, because as a chearful countenance makes the company chearful, we shall be willing to brighten the prospect as much as we can, that it may reflect the more pleasurable ideas upon ourselves. Nor must we neglect to root up those weeds that check the growth of benevolence, an intemperance of self-interest, an averseness to trouble, a contemptuousness of pride, an inconsiderateness of vanity, but, above all, a spirit of animosity. I hope we are none of us insatiable in our resentments, and if we can set a measure to them all, what better able to assign the proper limits than reason? but this will always apportion them to the necessity of preventing some greater mischief that could not otherwise be avoided. And though passion may sometimes suspend the influence of reason, we may hinder it from enslaving her: and if we cannot help being angry, may take care that the sun shall not go down upon our wrath. As an encouragement to practise the methods above pointed out, or any others our observation may suggest, let us consider and inculcate in our memory the

the benefits naturally redounding to ourselves from a benevolent temper of mind, which I shall now endeavour to investigate.

12. I have assigned happiness, a man's own happiness, or the aggregate of his satisfactions, for the ultimate end of action: therefore it behoves me to show what reference the quality I recommend bears to that end, or else it will not appear worth the wise man's possessing. Nor does this contradict what I laid down a little while ago, that a benevolent act must carry nothing of self in view: for it has been made evident upon several occasions already, that our ultimate end is very rarely our ultimate point of view, but we have divers principles, like so many stages of our journey, which occupy our thoughts from time to time as we proceed. Thus, when the wise man meets an opportunity of doing a kind thing, he follows his disposition to embrace it without looking for any thing further, he performs the good office because he likes it, because he judges it right: but we must imagine he had taken his own heart under examination before, and determined to cherish benevolence there, because of the connection he had observed it to have with happiness, or with some other principle wherein he had formerly found the like connection. Let us then suppose him utterly divested of all his desires, except that

that of happiness, and that virtues, vices, tastes and inclinations of every fashion, were to be sold like cloaths ready made at the sale-shop: let us consider why he would choose to purchase benevolence as most convenient for his wear. In the first place, he would presently discern the benefits of society, which arise solely from the mutual help afforded by mankind to one another: and though there be other motives urging them to provide for one another's conveniences, as fear, shame, glory profit, self-interest, or custom, he would see these are only expedients to supply the want of mutual good-will, but cannot answer the purpose so compleatly nor universally. We see how, in parties of diversion or intercourses of friendship, the pleasure and interests of all are much better provided for by a willingness to promote them than they could be by any regulations that human skill can devise: and could mankind in general be inspired with the like sentiments, there would want nothing else to keep the world in order. If the desire of promoting the general good were to prevail among all individuals so strongly as to overcome their averseness to labour and trouble, I am persuaded it would bring back the golden age or paradisiacal state again without any change in the elements: and whatever advances the happiness of all, must necessarily

sarily encrease that of every particular. Nevertheless it cannot be denied that benevolence, in the midst of a selfish world, must admit a little more reserve and caution than would be needful among persons of its own character: yet still every feasible exercise of it tends something towards advancing the general good, wherein a prudent man will see his own contained.

13. Secondly, benevolence, judiciously exercised, will generally engage a return of the like, and entitle us to the assistance or comfort of others when we may stand in need of it: at least it will afford no fuel for malice, but tend to lessen animosity. A soft word, says Solomon, turneth away anger, and kind usage seems most likely to prevent it: if it meet with unsuitable returns they do not fall so heavy as suitable returns upon the malicious; for malice, disappointed or chastised, fills with a vexation that has nothing to alleviate it, but the good man repaid with ingratitude still has the consolation to reflect that he acted right, and possesses a quality that will yield him better fruits upon other occasions. One receives no pleasure unless successful: the other feels a delight in the action as well as the event, so misses a part only of his reward by failing of success. Add to this that a readiness to do good offices

begets

begets esteem even with those who want it themselves: it gives a confidence in the possessor and renders his transactions of all kinds easier to be dispatched, for nobody will scruple to trust him whom they find always wishing them well and ready to do them more than justice.

14. Thirdly, benevolence is an inclination oftener to be gratified and less liable to disappointment than malice: it is true, mischief may be done easier than good, but then mankind will quickly be aware of it and take measures to prevent it, whereas they will be ready to assist the endeavours of him that designs them well. So that though according to the principles formerly laid down, we must admit that acts of good or ill nature may give equal pleasure to those who have a taste for either, yet the one will naturally meet with opposition and the other with concurrence from the persons upon whom they are to be exercised. If I take delight in mischief there may be ways of vexing another which I do not know; these he will carefully conceal from me, and so I shall miss a pleasure that was in my power to have enjoyed: but if he knows me fond of good offices he will be ready enough of his own accord to tell me wherein I can serve him, and so furnish me with opportunities of gratifying my inclination that I might never have thought of myself.

15. Fourthly

15. Fourthly, good nature multiplies the sources of enjoyment, for as the pleasure of life consists for the most part in action, and he is the happiest man who can always find something to engage his pursuit, therefore a relish for good offices is an advantage to the owner, because it will furnish agreeable employment for many spaces of time wherein he has nothing to do for himself. Besides, it will teach him to rejoice in services wherein he had no hand, make him partake of the pleasures he sees, and even lighten his misfortunes by reflecting how many people are exempt from them. Nor let it be objected that those who sympathize with the successful will be apt to do the like with the afflicted, for the perfect wise man would feel none of the uneasiness of compassion, and though we imperfect creatures must encourage it so far as to give a spur to our industry in helping, yet we may prevent it from making us suffer much at the sight of distresses we cannot possibly relieve. So that for a few troubles of this kind the tender-hearted man meets with, he finds a multitude of enjoyments the cross-grained and selfish never taste of.

16. Fifthly, benevolence prevents groundless suspicions and jealousies, ill opinions of mankind, unfavourable construction of words and actions: for men are not wont to think ill

ill of those to whom they wish well. It will likewise make us observant of happy events befalling other people, for we naturally take notice of objects we are pleased to see: which will give us a better notion of external nature and the dispensations of fortune. For the tastes and wants of mankind varying infinitely, what suits one extremely well is wholly useless to another, wherefore those narrow souls who can see nothing good that does not relate to themselves, if their own desires happen to be disappointed, grow melancholy, discontented, and out of humour with the world. But the generous openhearted man sees a thousand bright spots in the prospect around him, not striking directly upon himself but reflected from others: when the clouds hang over his own head he can smile at the sunshine on either hand, and please himself in contemplating the uses of things that cannot do him any service. I believe it may be generally remarked that the best tempered people are the best satisfied with the persons and things about them, freest from gloominess and repinings at the condition of human life, and consequently easiest in themselves, most uninterruptedly cheerful, and best pleased with their situation.

17. By often contemplating these advantages of benevolence, a man may bring himself

self to a hearty liking of it, and then whatever opportunities of exercising it offer, he will embrace them out of inclination, not from any selfish views, but because he thinks it the best, the most becoming, and most satisfactory thing he can do. For desire being perfectly translated to the act itself, he will no more need to retain in mind the reasons first inducing him to put on that disposition, than the covetous man has to keep his eye upon the conveniences he may purchase with his money, or the mathematician to run over perpetually the whole process of demonstration by which he arrived at his theorems. For we have remarked more than once before, that it is the motive at present in view, not any inducement formerly recommending that motive, which denominates the action: therefore he who shows an habitual readiness to do good offices without further consideration than their being such, is truly benevolent, whatever prudential or other causes first gave him that relish.

18. But there is a spurious benevolence, too often mistaken for the genuine, which proceeds from violent attachments to particular persons: some will do any thing for those they fancy, but nothing for those whose faces they do not like. This stands but one little remove from selfishness, being a weakness
rather

rather than a virtue, rendering men partial to their favourites, unjust or indifferent to every body else, and therefore ought carefully to be guarded against. For the virtues do not use to destroy nor interfere with one another, nor will sterling benevolence ever make the possessor unequitable, or intemperate in his likings; it knows no bounds besides those of reason, and diffuses itself to all capable of receiving benefit by it: I do not say in equal measure, but as justice, though not requiring an equality of possessions; yet secures the rights of all alike, so will benevolence deal out to all their proper share of kindness, nor ever confine her regards so closely to one or a few objects as to have none left for any others.

CHAP. XXXV.

MORAL POLICY.

P<small>LATO</small>, in his fifth republic, introduces Socrates declaring, that the world would never go well until either philosophers were entrusted with the management of public affairs, or persons in authority became philosophers:

sophers: that is, as he explains it afterwards, until both sciences of political and moral wisdom centered in the same persons. If this assertion be taken literally, I am afraid it will not conduce much to the benefit of mankind, for each science being more than enough to employ the thoughts of any single man, were our ministers to spend their time in hunting after the abstractions of metaphysics, they must unavoidably neglect many duties of their station; and on the other hand, were the helm of government committed to persons well versed in these matters, the ship would quickly strike against the rocks for want of skilfulness in the pilots, who would be more attentive to the rectitude of their course than expert in their measures for pursuing it. This construction then savours more of philosophical vanity than sound prudence: as it arrogates to the studious a claim to power, or at least would make him of consequence with men of power, by urging them to a pursuit wherein they must resort to him for instruction. Therefore I should rather interpret Socrates's meaning to be, that either professor, without interfering in the province belonging properly to the other, should only adopt so much of each other's science as may render his own more compleat and effectual.

2. How

2. How much of philosophy may be requisite for politicians I shall not presume to determine: for as they must be possessed of great sagacity and penetration to have merited that character, they are much better qualified to judge for themselves than I can be to direct them. Yet I think I may without offence, exhort them to use their own judgment, not only in contriving methods for bringing their schemes to bear, but in discerning the propriety of the schemes they take up. What tends most effectually to encrease their power and aggrandizement, it belongs to their own science to ascertain; but I could wish they would ask themselves further why they desire power or aggrandizement at all. I do not propose this question by way of defiance, as if I thought there could no solid reason be given for entertaining such desire: but if we have ever so good reasons for our conduct, I conceive it expedient we should know them, because they may direct us how far and in what manner to pursue it. Common persons may be allowed to act implicitly upon principles instilled into them by others, for their want of capacity to strike out lights for themselves will plead their excuse: but for men of extraordinary talents to make power their ruling passion merely because they were taught to admire it in their childhood, because they

they see others aspiring eagerly after it, because it gains the applauses of the multitude, because it happens to hit their fancy, seems unbecoming their character. It may be expected from such that, instead of acting upon impulse or suffering themselves to be drawn by sympathy and example, they should trace their motives up to the first principles whereto reason can carry them, and before they begin their career of ambition, examine the grounds which may justify them for entering upon such a course. If they should find upon such enquiry that happiness or complacence of mind, from whatever object received, is the sole proper and ultimate end of action, that the good of every individual is best promoted by promoting the general good, that our passions and particular aims ought to be regarded as engines, employed by reason for spurring on our activity to work out her purposes, and that whatever desire can be no longer gratified it is most prudent to extinguish, they might then employ their power while they had it, in advancing the welfare of their country, as well by procuring it strength and security against foreign dangers, as by establishing regulations for its internal polity: and if age or infirmities, the intrigues of a cabal or popular distaste, should divest them of their authority, they might resign it quietly,
without

without reluctance, without attempting to raise disturbances, and without want of employment to solace themselves with, in a private station. I am the more emboldened to offer this exhortation, because I conceive it not disagreeable to the taste of the present times; if one almost immured within his closet may judge of the sentiments of the great by so much of their behaviour as stands exposed to public view. For our wars are made, not for ambition or conquest, for particular views or private resentments, but for the security of commerce and advancing the public interests: wholesome provisions are annually contriving for the better order, the convenience, and even pleasures of the community: when changes happen in the ministry they pass on silently without interruption to public affairs, except a little clamour and invctive while the smart of a dissappointment is fresh, which disturbs the quiet of none but such as are fond of the sport for want of something better to employ their time in: and in general I think I can discern a stronger tincture of sound philosophy and regard to the general good among our modern statesmen than I can find in the histories of our ancestors.

3. Thus much may suffice for the politicians, and more it might not have become me to urge upon men of their superior talents:

lents: but with regard to the philosophers, under which class I would beg leave upon the present occasion to comprehend all who apply any serious attention to study the measures of right and wrong, I may be more free and particular, as reckoning them to lie nearer my own level. And I cannot help remarking that their ardour for virtue sometimes outruns their discretion, and like other strong desires defeats its own purposes through too great eagerness in pursuing them. It is possible with the best intentions in the world to bring much mischief both upon ourselves and others, by following headlong a blind zeal without knowledge and without examining the expedience of our aims or fitness of the measures taken to effect them. The province of zeal lies in seasons of action, and its office is to carry us through labour, pain, difficulty, danger, to bear down the force of any passion that shall obstruct our passage; but it does not become us to act without considering why nor wherefore, and in seasons of deliberation the mind cannot be too calm and unprejudiced, nor the mental eye too disengaged from any single point, or too much at liberty to look upon every object around and discern them in their proper colours. Wherefore, I apprehended with Socrates, that the world would go on much better, if well disposed persons would not confide too implicitly in their rules, but examine them from time to time as they have leisure and opportunity, consider their tendencies, mark how they succeed, and observe whether in particular instances they lead to that ultimate end of all rules, the encrease of happiness: and further if in the prosecution of them they would mingle a little policy with their uprightness, choosing such measures, as upon every occasion will contribute most to the purpose they have in hand. Craft, cunning, and artifice, stand opposed to fair dealing, sincerity, and open-heartedness; from whence it seems to have been unwarily concluded, that to be honest a man must have thrown aside his understanding. But there are honest arts as well as deceitful tricks, and it is not the manner of proceeding, but the aim driven at, that denominates them either. The same sagacity and attention to catch opportunities, which makes craft in the selfish, becomes prudence and good policy in the benevolent: nor do I see why a man should not employ all the talents nature and education have furnished him with to good purposes, because some others have perverted them to bad ones. The covetous man, who makes money his idol, will cheat for it if he cannot procure it otherwise: what then should hinder the good man, who

takes

takes happiness for his sole aim, from cheating his neighbours into it, if he cannot get them to receive it willingly?

4. The foundation of politics I take to lie in submiting every other desire to the ruling passion: though honours be particularly alluring to the ambitious, yet if the statesman sees that he shall have greater influence by sitting among the commons, he will not accept of a title; and how strongly soever he may have established maxims with himself for encreasing his interest, if he perceives them by any circumstances rendered improper for his purpose, he will readily forego them. Now the virtuous man's principal aim is the advancement of happiness, to which every other consideration ought to give way; and though he may have contracted desires as subservient thereto, and set up marks for himself to guide him on the way, yet if by any accident his desires become incompatible therewith or his rules lead him astray, he ought to depart from them without scruple; he may cast his eye upon the marks for the direction they will afford him, but ought never to forget the main purpose for which they were set up. We have seen that satisfaction consists in perception, that action is good only as it affords satisfactory perceptions, and virtue good as it leads into a course

of such actions: so that virtue is a means only conducting to our ultimate end, and stands at least two removes from happiness. It is true we cannot expect to attain our end without using the proper means, and I know of no means so proper or effectual as a steady adherence to whatever our moral sense represents to us as right. Were our internal senses of nature's immediate donation, they would probably discern their objects as truly and distinctly as the bodily senses, but it has been shown in a former place that their judgments are of the translated kind, conveyed to us through experience, sympathy, or the instructions of others, which channels sometimes corrupt the stream: so that this guide, though the surest we have, does not always prove infallible, nor is there any thing so idle or absurd but what men have been reconciled to, under a notion of its being right. How many have been led into all the follies of fashion, drawn into mischievous compliances with the company, put upon ruinous expenses, urged to take revenge for slight affronts and supposed injuries, hurried on through all the cruelties of persecution, because they esteemed them right? Perhaps their own judgment and inclination would have carried them another way, yet they proceed, though with reluctance, because they think

think they ought? For shame, resentment, vanity, and prejudice, will sometimes assume the garb and countenance of a moral sense.

5. Nor is reason herself to be trusted too hastily, for she may find occasion to correct her own mistakes: and an obstinate adherence to her decisions once made, against further information, tends as much to produce bigotry as any deference to authority whatsoever. Persons of this tenacious turn alledge ordinarily in their defence, that we must necessarily follow our reason, because we have no higher faculty to control it: but it is no uncommon thing for the same faculty to control its own judgments. What have we to judge of visible objects beside the eye? yet this eye, upon their being brought nearer, or placed in a different light, may discover the fallaciousness of the notices itself had given before: or on perceiving a haziness in the prospect, may know its own appearances to be imperfect, and yield to the information of others who stand in a situation to discern them clearer. So reason may find causes sometimes to submit herself to authority, and trust to others in matters belonging to their several sciences, although appearing paradoxical to herself: nor can she ever be so sure of her determinations, but that evidence may
arise

arise sufficient to overthrow them. Let us then admit it possible that a man may act very unreasonably through too strong an attachment to reason; let her therefore continually watch over her own motions, as well as those of our inferior powers, for if she treads confidently and carelessly, she may be as liable to trip as appetite.

6. Besides, it has been made appear before that reason actuates very few of our motions, she acts chiefly by her inferior officers of the family of imagination: while her treasures remain in her own custody they rest in speculation alone, nor do they become practical until she has made them over in property to her partner, in which case they take the nature of appetites. For it avails nothing to know what is right, nor to resolve upon it, until we have contracted a desire and inclination strong enough to carry us through all difficulties in the pursuit of it: so that virtue itself when compleatly formed is but an appetite, acquired indeed by our own industry, but impelling to action in the same manner with the natural. Now none of our appetites, not even the best of them, can be left entirely to themselves without extreme hazard: our very hunger and thirst after righteousness, like that of meats and drinks,

drinks, if eagerly and fondly indulged, may rise to extravagant cravings, or hanker after unwholesome food.

7. But neither can the love of rectitude in general answer all the purposes of life: we must divide it into various branches, and furnish ourselves with under propensities suitable to the various occasions wherein we are to act, from whence spring those inferior virtues that help to diversify the characters of mankind. Now how much soever the main foundations of right and wrong may be laid in nature, and consequently unalterable, certain it is that the particular habits and propensities, conducting us in the several parts of our behaviour, may change their rectitude with a change of situation or circumstances; and what is virtue at one time or in one man, become vice or folly in another. What is more commendable than application in a young lad, while the spirits are brisk, and the animal circulation vigorous? but if he continues the same intenseness of application after age and infirmities have disabled him from doing any good thereby, when it takes him off from other duties whereof he may be capable, or tends to impairing his health, it becomes faulty. To the young trader beginning upon a slender stock, a habit of parsimony and attention to little matters is a necessary duty: but if any
sudden

sudden fortune should cast an estate upon him, the same disposition of mind would remain no longer proper or becoming. It is well known what strong hold our habits of all kinds take upon us, and those first recommended by reason, or taught us by persons in whose understanding we confide, are looked upon as right in themselves, taken as first principles of action, and not easily laid aside when grown unreasonable; unless we have practised that statesman's habit of casting our eye frequently upon our ultimate end, and used ourselves to try our rules of conduct by a reference to expedience.

8. The same consideration likewise may induce us to regard other things more beneficial to the world in some cases than what is ordinarily esteemed virtue. A man that wants shoes, will sooner resort to a clever workman, than one scrupulously honest, that is a bungler in his trade: and when attacked by a distemper, had rather call in a debauchee physician, skilful in his profession, than one strictly conscientious, but of dull capacity and little experience. Were all our artisans and professors to barter their knowledge and dexterity for a proportionable degree of virtue, the world would suffer greatly by the exchange: we should all be ready indeed to help one another, but could do no good for want of knowing how to go about it. Therefore there are other

other qualities, beside that of an upright disposition, worthy the attention of him that designs the general good. The want of making this reflection, seems the grand mistake of enthusiasts and rigid observers of a stoical rectitude: for by their incessant and vehement exhortations to inward righteousness they either make men selfish, so busied in improving the state of their own minds as never to do any thing for anybody else, unless to pray for them, or censure them, or give money to those who pretend to give it away again; or else take them off from the business of their callings, wherein they might do real service to their neighbours. But virtue, as has been observed before concerning reason, confers us very little benefit with her own hands, no more than by that complacence of mind we feel in the exercise of it, which we may sometimes find as well in the gratification of any other desire: the principal service she does is by keeping us diligent in acquiring all other things beneficial to us, and applying them, when acquired, to the best advantage both of ourselves and others. Wherefore he that never loses remembrance of the general good, will endeavour to procure for himself and such as lie within his influence, all useful endowments both of body and mind, as well as the disposition to use them rightly. If he should do otherwise, he

would

would be like a man who should spend his whole time in a riding school, in order to make himself a compleat horseman; but never get a horse to ride upon either on the road or field.

9. Nor must it be forgotten that our virtues do not start up in us instantaneously, but grow out of other habits and desires. Ambition, covetousness, vanity, spur us on to industry, an affectation of being thought polite, makes men obliging, fear begets caution, obstinacy produces courage, and a careful regard to our own interests generates discretion, from whence sprouts the cardinal virtue of prudence. The main turn of our future lives, is ordinarily given before we arrive at manhood: the course we are then put upon by our friends, or led into by our own particular liking taken up without judgment but by mere fancy, the tastes, inclinations, opinions, we then imbibe, lay the foundation of those virtues we afterwards acquire. Perhaps, an admiration raised at the finery of a Chancellor, or Lord Mayor's coach, may have stimulated many a young school boy or apprentice to that application which lays the groundwork of those good qualities that will make him eminent at the bar, or in commerce. Therefore a judicious lover of virtue, will study to cultivate and prepare the ground for

its

its reception, and nourish up such wild plants as may serve for stocks whereon it may be grafted most easily, and flourish most abundantly.

10. He will consider further, that the busy mind of man cannot stand a moment idle: our activity must exert itself some way or other from morning to night, and if reason has not planned out a course wherein it may expatiate, it will run after any whim or folly that shall present it with allurement. Besides, satisfaction being momentary, cannot be provided for compleatly without supplying fresh fuel every moment to keep it alive: happiness depends upon having something constantly at hand, wherein we can employ ourselves with relish. Now, the grand occasions of exercising virtue do not offer at every season, nor can the mind always find employment in her immediate service: wherefore it will be expedient to furnish ourselves with other aims and pursuits, methods of engagement or recreation, which may fill up the spaces she leaves vacant; choosing such, if possible, as may conduce remotely to her interests, or at least such as are innocent, and may protect her by preventing the growth of those evils that might blight and overshadow her.

11. It is one characteristic of policy, that it aims at things feasible rather than things desirable,

desirable, never attempts impossibilities, but applies its endeavours always to drive the nail that will go, and lays aside its most favourite schemes when the tide of popular dislike sets most strongly against them. If the nation will not have an excise, the statesman lays aside all further thoughts of it; and if they will have a militia, he concurs in planning schemes to satisfy them. In this respect, your very righteous people prove often grossly deficient: they fix their eye upon the sublimest heights of virtue, without considering whether they be attainable; they confine their exhortations to practices that would prove of excellent service, but they have no likelihood of ever being followed; and so by aiming at too much, miss of that benefit they might have done. Whereas it would become them better to study not only the abstract nature of things, but likewise the nature of men, their characters, dispositions, and capacities; accommodating their endeavours to the subjects whereon they employ them, and circumstances of the times wherein they exert them; choosing rather to sow such seeds as the soil will bear, and the season cherish, than such as would yield the most delicious grain. The interests of virtue require sometimes that we should temporize and dissemble, becoming all things

to

to all men, if by any means we may gain some, and drawing them unawares into their good, by seeming to sooth them in their favourite inclinations. He that would serve virtue effectually, must not disdain to do her small services as well as great, for occasions of the latter, as was observed in the last section, do not occur at every turn; and many times, when we cannot get her authority to prevail, we may introduce something very much resembling her, and contribute to the growth of other good qualities, that shall in some measure supply her place, by instigating to the very works she herself would recommend. Besides, when the mind has been habituated to the practice of good works, from what motive soever induced thereto, it will become more susceptible of right intentions afterwards.

12. There is a well-known maxim of politics, Divide and govern, which the moralist may turn to good account in the management of his province. The little state of man is far from being an absolute monarchy, or having any settled or well-regulated polity, the prerogative lies within a very narrow compass, but the power lodges in the rabble of appetites and passions: and any importunate fancy, that like some popular orator, the favourite of the day, can raise a mob of them

to clamour after it, bears down all opposition. Reason can do nothing to stem the torrent, unless she can stir up a party among the populace to side with her: for if they begin to quarrel among themselves, she may then cast in her weight, to turn the balance between them. Nor can she ever prevail by mere dint of resolution, to have her commands vigorously executed without aid of some passion to second her; and, as she will always find one or other of them opposing her measures, she must continually play them one against another: pleasure against indolence, selfishness against pleasure, vanity against selfishness, fear against rashness, shame against indulgence, resentment against cowardice, reputation against injustice, and particular desires against their several competitors. Wherefore she ought to bend her endeavours towards suppressing the most riotous, rather encouraging the weaker and more manageable, that she may have something ready at hand to assist in pulling down the others: but above all, she must beware of letting any one grow so powerful, as that it may wrest the staff out of her hands. If she does admit a ruling passion, let her employ it as a first minister to execute her orders, not as a favourite, to gain an ascendant over her, nor suffer it to fill the council board with a clan

of

of its own dependents. Your zealots sometimes commit this oversight; for observing that all men have a desire of excelling, they endeavour to turn this principle to the services of virtue, and herein they do well: but they go on to encourage it without measure until it begets spiritual pride, censoriousness, sourness, envy, and ill nature, possesses their whole minds, becomes the sole motive to good works, and vitiates the best of their performances.

13. The politician carefully surveys the ground before him, considers what may be done with the materials he has to work upon, does not run counter to prevailing humours nor particular fancies, but studies how to turn them to his own advantage, sets every engine at work, and neglects no trifle that may be employed any ways to advance his purposes. So let the moralist observe the disposition and qualities of his own mind, the circumstances of his situation, the temper and character of the times wherein he lives: not striving to force his way by opposition, nor vainly expecting to make every thing tally with an ideal plan, how well soever framed in his own imagination; but contriving how to draw the most good from opinions and customs already received, by grafting something beneficial upon them: not driving men violently

lently out of their accustomed courses, but turning them gently and dexterously into such track as may lead to their solid advantage. For a single person may promote the interests of virtue better by joining in with the company to encourage practices tending in any degree thereto, than he can by striking into a new road which he has nothing besides his own authority to recommend. Nor let him despise every little ceremony or vulgar notion as idle and unworthy his notice: for sometimes these small springs may be turned to good account, or made to put others in motion which may prove more efficacious.

14. It is no inconsiderable branch of the minister's art to discern the talents of men, to know what they are fit for, and employ every one in the way wherein he may be most useful. In like manner it is an essential part of the moralist's office to observe carefully with what endowments nature and education have furnished himself or any others he has to deal with, what are the duties of their respective stations, and what opportunities they have of promoting the grand design of happiness. For though it were to be wished that every virtue might be infused into every man, yet this being impracticable, it behoves each person to acquire such particular species of them as are best adapted to his use.

For different professions require different qualifications to succeed in them: courage is peculiarly necessary for some, temperance for others, impartiality of justice for others.

Wherefore let every man apply himself to the attainment of that virtue wherein he can make the greatest progress, and which will render him the most serviceable according to the situation and circumstances he stands in. Were it possible to make profound philosophers of the common artisans and mechanics, the world would be very little benefitted thereby, for it might take them from attending to the business of their occupations, and render them less useful members of the community: therefore it were better for them to cultivate the qualities of honesty and industry in their callings without aiming at much beside. Some, whose talents fit them peculiarly for the office, may do more good by improving their reason, pursuing such speculations as may produce something beneficial to others; but few of these are wanted in the world, for one man may discover what will employ thousands to use. The far greater part of mankind have little more work for their reason than to choose their guides and apply the directions received to their own particular occasions, for the service they do lies in action. The purposes of life are effected by an infinite variety of different ways, and would be better answered by every one taking the task properly belonging to him, than by all crowding in to perform a few of the most important.

15. Your statesmen are observed often to stand much upon punctilios, to contend strenously for the precedence of an ambassador, the ceremonial of an entry, or style to be used in a treaty. So the moralist, though he always prefers substantials before forms, yet where the latter affect the former he will stickle as earnestly for them: for he extends his view as far as it can reach, and regards not only the present action but the most distant consequences attending it. When he sees usages and ceremonies, however insignificant in themselves, so connected in people's minds with matters of importance as that one cannot be broken through without endangering the others, he will consider them as bulwarks protecting the essentials, and contend for them accordingly with might and main. As the inhabitants of a town exert all their efforts in defending the ramparts, though yielding neither corn nor pasture nor accommodations for their dwelling, for this obvious reason, because when those are taken the town lies at mercy. Of this kind we may reckon the rites of burial and decencies observed towards the dead,
which

which though of no real avail or intrinsic value, yet find place in all civilized countries: because they stand as barriers against that savageness which might otherwise encroach upon men's tempers and cause infinite mischiefs among the living. Nor will he consent to have his rules dispensed with whenever he sees them inexpedient for the present, if there is a hazard of their being so weakened thereby as never to recover their influence again: proceeding upon my lord Coke's maxim, that the law will rather suffer a private injury than a public inconvenience.

16. But how anxious soever the man of consummate policy may appear about niceties upon proper occason, there is nobody less hampered with scruples when he sees them standing in the way of his designs: he can throw aside animosities, put up with injuries, submit to indignities, when it serves his purpose, and join with his bitterest enemies when there chances to be a coalition of interests. Here, too, the man of judicious virtue will follow his steps, nor disdain to employ the ministry of her adversaries in promoting her designs, not scrupling to cherish any vice or folly that tends evidently to check the growth of others more enormous. It is true he can scarce ever find occasion to use his endeavours this way, for vice and folly sprout fast enough

of themselves without needing any culture, and were it possible it would be desirable totally to eradicate them all, for then we might expect to reap a more plentiful crop of happiness. But since evil dispositions will abound, since they continually oppose one another's aims, and prevent the mischievous effects that would flow therefrom, it behoves him to act circumspectly, forbearing to do good when it may occasion a greater hurt, nor attempting to reform the world in points wherein, though it may be faulty, yet a worse evil would ensue upon such reformation. Nor can it be called deserting the interests of virtue to turn our backs upon her for a while in order to serve her more effectually, for policy requires us to do the same in our other pursuits: we follow pleasure through the road of self-denial, money must be disbursed to purchase commodities that will bring in a larger return, and lowliness, says Shakespeare, is young ambition's ladder. So that virtue may well excuse us for running into the enemy's camp to turn his own cannon against him, if we have her interests at heart all the while, and a reasonable prospect of promoting her service in the long run by so doing.

17. Great pains was taken by a particular author some time ago to show that the vices

of

of men tend to the benefit of the community, and though he seems to have made good his assertion in particular instances, yet it was an unfair conclusion to infer from thence in general that private vices were public benefits: for so it might be proved that disease conduces to health, because the doctor sometimes brings on a gout in order to cure other more dangerous distempers, or wishes to raise a fever to force away obstructions causing paralytic disorders. But disease is then only salutary when necessary to remove disease, and vices then only tolerable when they put men upon actions from which their other vices would withhold them. So that the benefit of vice, when it affords any, arises from its hurtfulness: for if the vices it counteracts were not mischievous, there would be no good in that which obstructs their operation.

18. But it is the property of a politician to be close and covert and keep his motives of action to himself. This the man wisely righteous will imitate with respect to the doctrine above mentioned of conniving at particular vices occasionally, which falling into unskilful or ill-designing hands may prove of dangerous consequence, as opening a door to the most latitudinarian practices. Therefore he will lock it up among his esoterics for the use only of adepts, and think the sacred-

ness

ness of the rules of virtue cannot be too strongly inculcated upon the vulgar, who, being apt to take that for good which suits their own humours and interests, would make mad work, unless restrained by the authority of rules. For they do not stand in a situation to judge of the general expedience, but can only be led into it by the maxims of morality, and must unavoidably lose their way the moment they take off their eye from that guidance. I have said before under the article of justice, and repeat it here with regard to morality in general, that I like to see young men rather over scrupulous, nor would wish them to wear off their scruples but by degrees, as they arrive at a full discernment of their respective inconveniences: for it requires a considerable degree of skill and competent experience to prevent liberty from running into licentiousness. Our school-masters keep their lads strictly to the rules of grammar and prosody, nor until perfect therein ever suffer them to launch out into poetical licences: they would whip a boy who should write, like Milton, Adam the godliest man of men since born his sons, the fairest of her daughters Eve; or reckon only three syllables in Tiresiàs, or four in Beelzebub, or place their accent in the middle of Prosérpine. It is the master-piece of moral science to know

when

when a fundamental rule may be dispensed with, nor ought great liberties ever to be taken until we have learned by long experience how to do it safely, and have made such a proficiency in virtue, as that a single act of necessary disrespect cannot endanger the lessening our cordial regard for her.

19. There is one piece of good policy very proper for the moralist, though not at all suited to the cabinet, which is, to make others like himself, and diffuse his virtues as far and wide as he has opportunities for so doing. Considering how much of our enjoyments depends upon those we converse with, it may be made a question whether it would be more for a man's ease to be wicked himself, but surrounded with persons just, prudent, and benevolent, or to be singly good in the midst of a corrupt and perverse generation: but there is no need to canvass this point, for it must certainly make for his interest, that the morals of all with whom he has any concern should be improved, and he can take no likelier method for propagating good qualities elsewhere than by cultivating them first in himself. But then he must proceed in this culture with discretion, attending not only to the growth of his plants, but to their aptness for transplanting, taking care to make his virtues inviting as well as genuine,

genuine, to set them off with such appearance as may make them more easily catched by sympathy, to abate of such rigour and austerity as might raise a distaste against them, to forbear what is innocent when likely to give offence; remembering that things lawful may not be expedient, and to have a view in all his actions to their exemplariness, as well as their rectitude.

CHAP. XXXVI.

LIMITATION OF VIRTUE.

I HOPE what has been hitherto delivered, may be found tending to recommend virtue as the most desirable object a man can pursue, to rest it upon the solid foundation of human nature, instead of those airy notions of an essential beauty wherein some have placed it, and to purify it from those extravagances wherewith it has been loaded by the indiscretion of zealots. But to deal ingenuously and aim at truth, rather than saving the credit of our performance, let us not suppress an exception there lies against it, as limiting and confining the obligation of virtue within a certain compass

compass which ought to extend to all cases universally. For it may be urged, that if satisfaction, a man's own satisfaction, be the groundwork of all our motives; if reason can furnish no ends of her own, but serves only to discover methods of accomplishing those assigned her by sense; if she recommends virtue and benevolence solely as containing the most copious sources of gratification; then are virtue and benevolence no more than means, and deserve our regard no longer than while they conduce towards their end. So that upon an opportunity offering wherein a man may gain some pleasure or advantage slily and safely without danger of after damage to himself, though with infinite detriment to all the world beside, and in breach of every moral obligation, he will act wisely to embrace it.

2. I cannot deny that the consequence follows in speculation upon the case above supposed, but I conceive such case can never happen in fact, so long as a man has any prospect of good and evil to come. For we must take into account, not only the advantage accruing from an action, but likewise the benefits or mischiefs of the disposition of mind giving birth to it: and if this will lead us into evils overbalancing the present profit of the action, we cannot be said to do it without danger of after damage to ourselves. The virtues belong
to

to the heart rather than the head, or to speak in our own style, their residence lies in the imagination not the understanding; and to be compleat must direct our inadvertent motions as well as our deliberate, that is, must become appetites impelling to action without standing to consider their expedience. Now whoever resists their impulse soberly and premediately upon consideration of their being inconvenient to his private purposes, will thereby make such a breach upon their authority and give such a crooked turn to his mind, as must unavoidably draw him into evils greater than any immediate advantage he may gain. All vice, says Juvenal, stands upon a precipice, and if we once step over the brink, nobody can tell how far we shall go down: one of these two things must necessarily follow, either we shall continue sliding until we fall into destruction, or must put ourselves to infinite trouble in climbing the precipice, a trouble far exceeding the pleasure we may have felt at first in the ease of a downhill motion. He that cheats when he can do it safely, will want to cheat at other times, and consequently, must suffer, either by a self-denial or the mischiefs of an indulgence: so that it had been more for his benefit to have adhered inviolably to his rule of honesty. The ultimate end we have assigned for a reasonable

creature

creature to act upon was not present pleasure or profit but the aggregate of enjoyments: and we have laboured, I hope not unsuccessfully, to prove from a survey of human nature that nothing adds so largely to that aggregate as a right disposition of mind. We have indeed placed enjoyment in gratification, but then have put those who will lend us an ear, in mind, that gratification depends more upon bending desire to such a ply as that it may fasten upon things attainable and convenient, than upon procuring objects of every desire starting up in our fancy. Now the habits of moral prudence and benevolence alone can bring desire to the proper ply: but those habits cannot retain their influence with him who shall wilfully and upon principle permit his other desires to break in upon them. Therefore though the common rules of virtue may lawfully be dispensed with upon an honest regard to her interests and a judicious discernment of the greater general good, for this strengthens our attachment to those objects whereon the rules were founded: yet we may never infringe them upon any other consideration of pleasure or selfishness, for this would be introducing another principle of action inconsistent with the former. But it would be the most imprudent thing in the world for a man to allow himself in such liberties as

must

must destroy a principle of conduct that prudence and reason have recommended, so long as there remains any prospect of his receiving future benefit from its influence.

3. Nevertheless, it must be confessed that when life draws near to an end, if it should be urged upon us that then the obligations to virtue must cease, I should not know what to answer. For since they arise from expedience, they must drop of course when there is no longer a possibility of that expedience taking place. We have laid down before, that a man need never deny himself in any thing unless in order to please himself better another time; if then he shall never see that other time, there is no reason why he should deny himself at all: but he may without scruple gratify whatever desires he finds in his heart, since there is no room for any bad consequences to follow upon them; nor need he fear their subverting a principle he has found all along of excellent use to guide him in his conduct, when he has no further course to run wherein that principle may direct him. Why should he restrain his extravagance when he has enough to last him the little time he expects to live? why should he forbear intemperance when it cannot have time to fill him with diseases? why should he scruple to cheat when he shall slip out of harm's way before a discovery can

overtake

overtake him? why should he trouble himself with what becomes of the world when he is upon the point of leaving it: or do any thing for the benefit of others, when he can receive no returns from them, nor in any manner gather the fruits of his labours?

4. But notwithstanding this concession, it does not necessarily follow that a man must quit the practice of virtue when he sees his dissolution approaching: for this will depend upon the turn of mind he has already taken. If indeed he has pursued it hitherto by constraint, and still finds in himself strong propensities to gluttony, debauchery, gallantry, and other inordinate desires, I have suggested no arguments which might induce him to restrain them, nor offered advantages he can reap sufficient to compensate the trouble of a self-denial. For as physicians permit a patient whom they have absolutely given over, to eat and drink whatever he pleases, because when nothing can do him good nothing can hurt him; so the moralist will think it in vain to prescribe a regimen for diseases of the mind, when there is no time to work a cure, nor any enjoyment of health to be expected. Our motives of action are not to be changed presently, nor can we give a new turn to desire as easily as put on our cloaths, therefore, when the glass is almost run out, it is too late

to

to think of taking up a set of fresh inclinations, but every one must be left to make the most of those he already possesses. But this very consideration will engage the man who has spent his days in a virtuous course to persevere in it to the last: not indeed now from obligation or expedience, but for the ease and pleasure he finds in pursuing an habitual track. We observed just now that the virtues to be compleat must have fixed their residence in the heart, and become appetites impelling to action, without further thought than the gratification of them: so that after their expedience ceases, they still continue to operate by the desire they raise. Nor is it unusual in other cases for men to continue the courses, they have been accustomed to after the reasons upon which they began them are no more: I knew a mercer who having gotten a competency of fortune, thought to retire and enjoy himself in quiet, but finding he could not be easy without business, was forced to return to the shop and assist his former partners gratis, in the nature of a journeyman. Why then should it be thought strange that a man, long enured to the practice of moral duties, should persevere in them out of liking, when they can yield him no further advantage? To tell him that he may squander without fear of poverty, gluttonize without danger of distempers,

pers, and bring a secret mischief upon others without hazard of its ever coming round upon himself, were no temptation to him: for he has no relish to such divertisements, his appetites having been long since set upon what is just, and becoming, and beneficent. So that though prudence has no further commands, he will employ himself in the same exercises she used to enjoin, as the most agreeable way wherein he can lay out his few remaining moments.

5. Upon this occasion, I cannot avoid entering the lists once more on behalf of Epicurus, to vindicate him against a charge of inconsistency, laid by Tully in his second de Finibus, Cap. 30, 31. Epicurus it seems had written a letter, on the last day of his life, to one Hermachus, earnestly recommending his pupils, the children of his deceased friend, Metrodorus, to his tuition. And had directed by Will, that his executors should provide an entertainment, yearly, on his birth day, and on the like day of every month, for such as used to study philosophy with him, in order to preserve alive in their minds the remembrance of himself and of the said Metrodorus. Now this friendly concern for the name and family of Metrodorus, and this careful provision for keeping up the spirit of the sect, by bringing them together once a month,

month, Tully thinks acting out of character in one who referred all things to pleasure, and held that whatever happens after our decease is nothing to us. But whoever observes the motions of the human mind, may see that many things which are nothing to us when they happen, are yet a great delight to us in the prospect and contemplation. How often do people please themselves with laying schemes for raising a family, or spreading their fame to future ages, without any probable assurance that they shall enjoy the successes of their family, or have any knowledge of what the world shall say of them a hundred years hence? but the thought of what shall then happen affords them a present entertainment, and therefore they follow pleasure as much in promoting those schemes as they should do in pursuit of any favourite diversion. I would fain know how Tully would have had Epicurus dispose of his last day to have acted in character: should it have been spent in the enjoyment of nice dainties, exquisite wines, or fine women? this he might have expected had he had the same notion of Epicurus that we have of an epicure. La Fontaine's glutton having eaten up a whole salmon all but the jowl, so surfeited himself therewith, that his physicians declared him past all hopes of a recovery: well, says he, since the case is so, so then bring me the rest of my fish. Now this man we must own behaved consistently with himself throughout: but why must other people follow his example who have not the same fondness for salmon? Let us give every body their due, whether we like them or not: it appears from what accounts have been handed down to us, and which Tully was not ignorant of, that nobody was less of an epicure than Epicurus himself. He had carefully studied the sources of pleasure and found nothing more conducive thereto than temperance, patience, benevolence, and all the moral virtues; we may suppose he had so full a persuasion of this their tendency, and so enured himself to the practice of them, that he had gotten an habitual liking to them, and could not turn his hand to anything else with equal relish. Imagine then a man of this turn arrived at the last morning of his existence, and considering how to pass his only remaining day with most satisfaction to himself: how could he do it better than by continuing that course which he had constantly found most pleasurable and best suited to his taste? There is no occasion to suppose the love of probity, friendship, and public spirit, to be innate: for the perpetual experience and contemplation of their advantage-ousness is enough to make them objects of desire.

6. But though I have thus much to alledge in favour of Epicurus, towards showing that his conduct might be all of a piece when he wrote the letter and made the Will above mentioned, notwithstanding his referring all things to pleasure: yet I cannot so easily justify Regulus against all imputation of imprudence upon the like principle. For it is one thing to contrive how we shall lay out the day in a manner most agreeable to our liking, when nothing we do therein can affect us to-morrow, and quite another to take our measures wisely when it depends upon our present behaviour, whether we shall have a morrow or no. There is nothing more glaringly evident than that the end of Being must put an end to enjoyment: therefore, he that takes a course, how satisfactory soever to his own mind, which must destroy him, acts imprudently, as he consults present satisfaction rather than the aggregate of it wherein happiness properly consists. Nor am I moved with those ranting exclamations of the Stoics, that there is more joy in a day well spent than in years of sensual delights: I am sensible our pleasures are not all equal in degree, but I cannot conceive how so much enjoyment can be crowded into a small space of time as to

make

make it worth our while to neglect years to come for the sake of it; for our organs can neither bear nor contain so large a measure. Such outcries are in the style of the dissolute and inconsiderate, as encouraging the same disregard to the future with the maxim they proceed upon, a short life and a merry. But the most fatal mistake men are apt to fall into, lies in their estimating pleasures according to the degree of them: for it has been made appear under the article of pleasure, that we are much more beholden to those of the gentler kind, as adding more largely to the aggregate of satisfactions, than to the intense. Even our common diversions please more by the engagement of some pursuit they put us upon than by the joy of an acquisition. Nor shall we see cause to lay so much stress upon the raptures of virtue, when we reflect how many less worthy objects can give them as well for a time; a sudden turn of good fortune, a title of honour, a ribbon, whether blue, green, or red, the smiles of a mistress, a kind word, a delusive promise, the veriest trifle, will do it in proportion to the fondness there is for them: so that a day spent in the accomplishment of any eager desire carries as much intrinsic weight, abstracted from all considerations of the future, as a day spent in the exercise of virtue. Wherefore the preferableness of virtue does not arise so much from the transports she occasions as from the calm serenity and steady complacence of mind she ensures, the satisfactory reflections she gives scope to, the attainableness of the desires she raises, their compatibleness with one another, and their clearness from mischievous consequences: all which regard the time to come, and therefore cannot consist with whatever renders us incapable of good or evil for the future.

7. Yet neither can it be certainly concluded from men's enduring patiently for a good cause, that they feel those transports in supporting it which shall keep their minds in a state of continual enjoyment: for we may remember, that objects operate no less by the want than the desire of them; by our unwillingness to miss them than by the pleasure of moving towards them: and that there is an abhorrence of vice as well as a love of virtue. When motives act this way they fall under the class of necessity, which always throws the mind into a state of uneasiness; nor is her condition instantly bettered upon doing well while it is done out of obligation, nor until we can come to do it upon liking. If this were Regulus's case, we must certainly pronounce him to have acted imprudently, and that Epicurus could not have done the same consistently with his principles, since he gave up

all

CHAP. 36.] *Limitation of Virtue.* 421

all those enjoyments he might have expected in a longer life without receiving even present pleasure in exchange: and it had been for his benefit to have had no such strong attachment to his obligations. But not to derogate from the character of Regulus, let us suppose the utmost that can be supposed in his favour: let us allow him to have felt so great satisfaction in the nobleness of his conduct as drew out the sting of every evil that could befal him, and to have ended his days in exquisite delight amidst all the cruel torments that were inflicted upon him. Still this delight, how high soever in kind, must necessarily fall short in duration; and he had better have contented himself with smaller pleasures which might have compensated by their continuance for what they wanted in weight. Perhaps it may be said he had contracted so strong a detestation of treachery and abhorrence of infamy that he could not support himself in any quiet of mind under the reflection of them: so that being no longer capable of enjoying life with pleasure he chose to end it in a manner that might prove most satisfactory. But what brought him under this incapacity besides his own disposition of mind which could find a relish in nothing but what was just, becoming, and laudable? Another who had not the same squeamish disposition might have
found

found enjoyments enow under general censure and self-reproach to make life desirable. Nor will it suffice to alledge that he had good grounds at first for acquiring this disposition, which having once taken up it was not in his power to lay down again at pleasure: for it is not our business to find excuses for him in the weakness of human nature, which cannot suddenly change a rooted habit of acting or liking that we have long accustomed ourselves to, but to enquire whether this procedure of his were a weakness or no. And for this purpose we must imagine to ourselves a man who should have an absolute command over his inclinations to turn them this way or that as he saw proper, and consider how such an one would use his power in the situation of Regulus. We cannot well suppose otherwise than that such a person would keep his eye constantly fixed upon the original rule of rectitude which drives solely at happiness. He would establish upon that bottom certain maxims of conduct and morality as he judged them conducive thereto: but he would never suffer himself to be enslaved by the maxims himself had established, nor let any subordinate means lead him away from his ultimate end. He would know that what is good and laudable at one time, may become mischievous and blameable by a change of circumstances.

cumstances. He might encourage in himself a love of probity and honour as yielding the largest income of satisfaction, yet if matters came to that pass as to make it appear they must have a contrary tendency, he would throw aside his scruples and turn his thoughts to such enjoyments as were to be had without them.

8. Upon the whole we are forced to acknowledge that hitherto we have found no reason to imagine a wise man would ever die for his country or suffer martyrdom in the cause of virtue, how strong propensity soever he might feel in himself to maintain her interests. For he would never act upon impulse nor do any thing without knowing why: he would cultivate a disposition to justice, benevolence, and public spirit, because he would see it must lead him into actions most conducive to his happiness, and would place such confidence in his rules as to presume they carried that tendency in particular instances wherein it did not immediately appear. But it is one think not to see directly that measures have such a tendency, and another to discern clearly that they have a contrary: and when they take away all capacity of further enjoyment, this is so manifest a proof of their inexpedience as no presumption whatever can withstand. Therefore he will never let his love
of

of virtue grow to such an extravagant fondness as to overthrow the very purposes for which he entertained it.

9. I am apprehensive this conclusion will give offence to many as seeming to undo all we had done before in the service of virtue, by thus deserting her at last in time of greatest need when she is entering upon her most arduous undertakings. Yet I know not wherein we have acted unfairly either in the choice of our premisses or deduction of inferences from them. We have searched every corner of the human breast, and found that all our motives derive either immediately or remotely from our own satisfaction and complacence of mind. Nature has given us this spring as the first mover of all our actions and ultimate object of all our contrivances. We have seen that reason cannot work upon her own bottom, but must fetch materials from elswhere, for there is no reasoning unless from premisses already known before we enter upon the consultation: therefore how far soever she may investigate her principles upon one another she must at last rest in such as she finds assigned her by sense and appetite, her office being only to correct their errors in the prosecution of their aims, to take better measures than they do, and lead to the same point discreetly and effectually which they drive at
prepos-

preposterously and vainly. We have shown that the rules of morality stand on the foundation of happiness, that all notions of them which have not this basis to rest upon are fantastic and unstable: from whence it will follow that whenever, by the unlucky circustances of our situation, this support happens to be withdrawn from under them, they must necessarily fall to the ground. Thus if our premisses lead us to a conclusion we do not like, we may say with Docter Middleton, that we cannot help it: for it was not our business to hunt for arguments in support of any cause whatsoever, but to take a careful survey of nature without prejudice or prepossession, and gather such observations as should appear resulting therefrom.

10. But it will be said that we have made only a partial and imperfect survey; for if we had availed ourselves of all the light nature would have afforded, we might have discovered that the end of life is not the end of Being, that our dissolution is but a removal from this sublunary stage to act upon some other, where our good works shall follow us and yield a plentiful harvest of happiness which had not time to ripen here: therefore a man does not act imprudently who perseveres in his virtues to the very last, although, they manifestly tend to cut him off from life
with

with all its enjoyments, aud promise him nothing but pain and torment for the little time he has to continue upon earth. All this, consistently with the nature of my work, I can regard yet only as a suggestion, having found nothing in the progress of these researches to convince us of another life, or show the tendency of what we do here to affect us hereafter: yet neither have I found any thing to disprove them, so that they remain proper matter of further enquiry. And since I find them maintained by persons of the greatest learning and judgment, and almost universally received among mankind, since they are in themselves matters of the utmost importance and we see the limits of virtue cannot be ascertained without them, it would be inexcusable to pass them over unregarded, or without a thorough and careful examination; which not being easily dispatched, so as to settle those points to our satisfaction, I shall reserve them for the subject of another volume. Therefore it may be considered that I am but in the midway of my journey, and what I may learn in the succeeding stages of it is yet uncertain; nor because it is said in § 4 that I have suggested no arguments to induce a vicious man near the end of his days to restrain his desires, and in this section, that I have
found

Limitation of Virtue.

found nothing to convince us of another life, ought it to be inferred from thence that I may not in my further progress. He that has a good opinion of religion, as having a rational and solid foundation to stand upon, ought to believe that I shall find such arguments and grounds of conviction as have not hitherto occurred, when prosecuting the subject with a fair and careful examination; and may presume that what now appears the most exceptionable part of my doctrine, will then become capable of being turned to the advantage of religion, by showing its absolute necessity to make the system of morality compleat. In the mean while he cannot surely blame me for attempting to prove that the practice of virtue is the wisest course a man can follow to attain happiness even in this world; and to abate the scandal he might take at the exception made of a person in Regulus's situation, to whom a strong attachment to virtue would be a misfortune, he may please to reflect it is not unsimilar to a declaration of St. Paul's, that if in this life only we had hope we were of all men the most miserable. But one who is proceeding on a course of enquiries can take nothing for granted beforehand, he can draw his inferences only from the premisses already collected, and must shape them in such manner as

they

they shall naturally lead him. So that I must still adhere to my present conclusion, until seeing cause to alter it, for I cannot yield to any authority how great or general soever: this would be to depart from the plan I proposed at setting out, which was to try what lights I could strike out by the exercise of my reason, without calling in foreign aids; the extent of that, be it greater or be it less, is the line I am to run; and when I am come to the end of this line I must stop short, unless by another effort of reason I can chance to catch hold of another clue.

11. Nevertheless, I am very loath to leave the scrupulous reader with an ill impression of me upon him, though but for a season, and yet I do not know how to efface it myself, but must trust to his candour to do the best he can for me. Perhaps his good nature may suggest to him, that if this conclusion I pretend to abide by, were my real ultimate opinion, I should not be so inconsistent with myself as to divulge it. For the discovery that a man's own safety will supersede all obligations, is of a nature not to be communicated without lessening its value to the owner: he may believe then I should have locked it carefully up, as a precious deposit to be reserved for private use, that if ever the case should so happen as that I cannot obey the dictates of honour and

and conscience, without endangering my person, I might avail myself of this secret to slip my own neck out of the collar: but it would certainly be for my interest to persuade the world that the duties of virtue are indispensable, and they ought to sacrifice every thing for the good of the public, whereof I am a member, and must consequently share in the fat of their sacrifices. Therefore I think it is no unreasonable favour to expect, that he will suppose I have already run over in my own mind the matters I am to present him with by-and-by, and foresee something will occur among them, which will oblige me to recant the odious part of my doctrine, and come over to his sentiments. Let us then take leave in good hopes, that however we may part a little out of humour for the present, we shall grow better satisfied with one another upon our next conversation.

END OF VOL. II.

Brettell, Printer,
No. 4, Marshall Street, Carnaby Market.

BD
701
.T8
1976
v.2

BD 701 .T8 1976 v.2
Tucker, Abraham, 1705-1774.
The light of nature pursued

CANISIUS COLLEGE LIBRARY
BUFFALO, N.Y.

CANISIUS COLLEGE LIBRARY
BD701 .T8 1976 v. 2
The light of nature

3 5084 00122 0451